THE GOOD LIFE

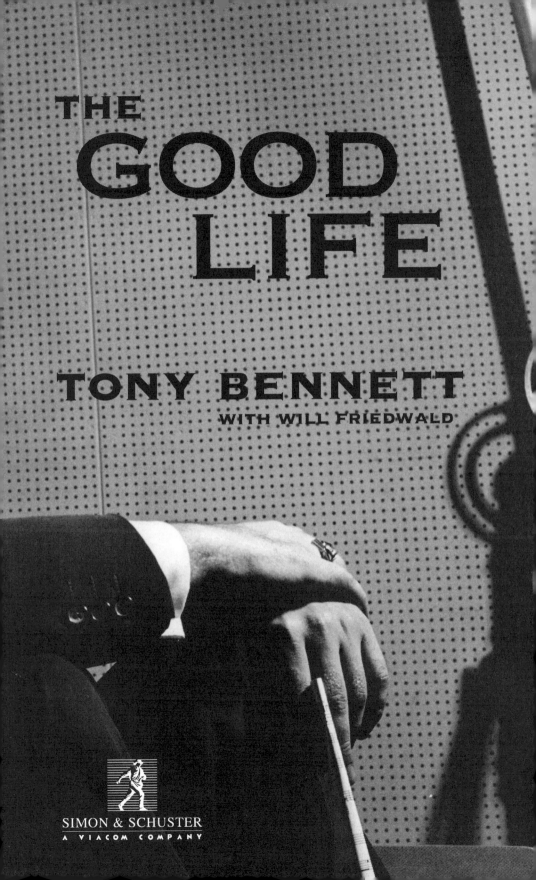

THE
GOOD
LIFE

TONY BENNETT

WITH WILL FRIEDWALD

SIMON & SCHUSTER
A VIACOM COMPANY

First published in the U.S.A. by Pocket Books, a division of
Simon & Schuster Inc.
First published in Great Britain by Simon & Schuster UK Ltd. 1998
A Viacom company

1 3 5 7 9 10 8 6 4 2

Simon & Schuster UK Ltd.
Africa House
64-78 Kingsway
London WC2B 6AH

Simon & Schuster Australia
Sydney

ISBN: 0-684-85872-X

Designed by Laura Lindgren
Photograph on pages ii–iii: © Herman Leonard

Printed in the U.S.A.

The author has made every effort to identify the source of all photos reproduced
in this book.

Dedicated to my mom

[Sincere jazz musicians] aim at excellence and apparently nothing else. They are hard to buy and if bought they either backslide into honesty or lose the respect of their peers. And this is the loss that terrifies them. In any other field of American life, great reward can be used to cover the loss of honesty, but not with jazz players—a slip is known and recognized instantly. And further, while there may be some jealousies, they do not compare with those in other professions. Let a filthy kid, unknown, unheard of and unbacked sit in—and if he can do it—he is recognized and accepted instantly. Do you know of any other field where this is true?

JOHN STEINBECK

On April 4, 1906, fifteen miles south of Naples, Italy, an ominous cloud of black smoke billowed from the mouth of Mount Vesuvius, turning day into night. The volcano erupted, releasing a torrent of boiling sulfur, massive boulders, and thick ash. The flowing, flaming lava divided into two rivers and poured down the slope of the volcano, decimating the farms, orchards, and villages unlucky enough to lie in its path.

The force of the eruption was so great that huge quantities of water were pulled away from the shore, causing the coastline to recede as far as a mile. Many ships were suddenly stranded on the sand.

Just two days before, a steamship had set sail from the port of Naples. On board were hundreds of Italian emigrants who were leaving their homeland in search of a better life in America. Among the passengers was a widow whose husband had died before the birth of his youngest child, now eleven years old and clad in a little girl's bonnet and a dress of ragged calico. They *huddled together on the deck of that ship and watched in terror as the beginnings of a huge tidal wave rolled toward them. The wave hit the ship broadside, tossing it dozens of feet into the air.*

⌐⌐⌐

Lucky for me the captain was an able seaman, who managed to gain control of his vessel, because that woman was my grandmother, and the young child she held so close was my father. In those days, families who traveled steerage class were not allowed to stay together: men were separated from their wives, boys from their mothers. Since my father and grandmother were traveling alone, she refused to let him out of her sight, so she dressed him in girl's clothing to keep him by her side. My father endured twenty-one days of seasickness before finally reaching New York harbor.

This is the story my father told to me, and it scared the hell out of me. He said that if the ship had capsized, I wouldn't be here today, because neither would he! He made light of it, but the joke only caused me, at a very young age, to contemplate the delicate balance of my own mortality.

⌐⌐⌐

I've been asked many times why I haven't written my life story before. To be quite honest, I'm not the type of person who likes to look backward. I've always felt compelled to move forward, and I've never been one to dwell in the past. All the people I've met, all the places I've been, and all the things that I've done have simply been part of who I am.

Now that I'm seventy-two years old, I find myself having a different experience. The pieces of my life have begun to fall into place like an intricate mosaic. I'm able to step outside myself and look back at all the unexpected twists and turns of fate, at my sorrows and my successes. I finally understand

the Zen teaching that the cool, flowing waters of a stream
will tame the rough edges of the hard rock lying in its path
and shape it into a beautiful form: over the seven decades of
my life, I've learned that no matter how tough the struggle of
day-to-day living, with enough dedication and patience I will
persevere and accomplish my goals, no matter how unattain-
able they may at first seem.

My most vivid memory from my childhood is of myself as a
ten-year-old boy during the Depression, sitting at my mother's
side in our modest home as she worked as a seamstress. Her
salary depended on how many dresses she could make and I
remember the constant hum of the sewing machine that
stopped only long enough for her to cook our dinner. The
more dresses she completed, the more money she made—
which even for that time wasn't much money at all. I loved
her so much, and I felt so sorry for her because she always
seemed worried, and I could sense how much she suffered to
make a meager living. To this day the most devastating
memory I have is of my mother getting her finger caught
beneath the sewing needle. It passed through her thumbnail
and into her flesh, and she screamed out in pain. I felt as if
it were happening to me. It was then that I made up my
mind to become successful enough so that my mom would
never have to work again.

But I never imagined I'd be fortunate enough to become as
successful as I have. To think of where I started and where I
landed! Benedetto means "the blessed one," and I feel that I
have truly been blessed.

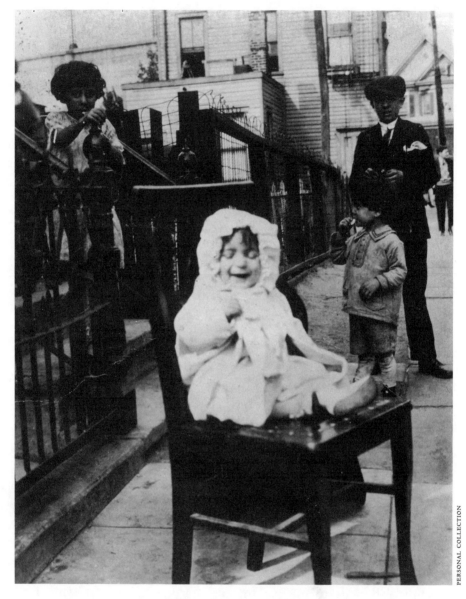

Me at about a year old

CHAPTER ONE

———————

*M*y paternal grandfather, Giovanni Benedetto, who died before my father was born, grew up in the small, isolated village of Podargoni in Calabria, Italy.

Because the Benedetto family originally came from the north of Italy, they were fair-skinned and fair-haired, like northern Europeans, and quite unlike their fellow dark-haired, dark-skinned Calabrese. My father's mother, Maria, was so fair that she was known as "La Germanesa," the German woman. The Benedettos were essentially poor farmers, producing olive oil, figs, and wine grapes. My mother's side of the family was named Suraci, and they also made their living farming in Calabria. Like everyone else in the region, they were unable to read and write.

My paternal grandmother and my maternal grandmother were sisters. Maria Suraci married Giovanni Benedetto, and they became my father's parents, and Vincenza Suraci married Antonio Suraci (who by coincidence had the same last name), and they became my mother's parents.

My father, Giovanni (John) Benedetto, was born in 1895. The youngest of five children, he was named after my grandfather. When my grandmother was pregnant with my father, she dreamt that her late husband came to her from the "other side" and told her to name the boy "Giovanni," after him.

Italians at that time were very superstitious. My father was very sickly as a child, and although they didn't know it then, we later found out that he had suffered from rheumatic fever. But as family lore has it, everyone attributed his aches and pains to the fact that my grandmother grieved for her dead husband while she was pregnant, and her grieving had made my father a sickly child. The older people in the village served as the only available "doctors," and they made their diagnoses based more on old-fashioned superstition than on medicine. Nobody went to the hospital—there weren't any—and the only remedies were home remedies.

Despite the problems with his health, my father was essentially a joyful child. My Aunt Frances used to tell me that she often looked after my father while she and Grandma would be out working the land. They'd set my father down to play in the shade of the nearest tree. He'd smile happily and watch the blue sky above, and she'd never hear a peep out of him. From the beginning, I've been told, he loved music and song, and as a boy he had a wonderful singing voice. He would often climb to the top of the mountains in Calabria and sing out to the whole valley below. Singing is a part of my heritage. I'm convinced it's in my blood, and that's why I'm a singer today.

By the 1890s a widespread blight had forced thousands of farmers, including the Benedettos and Suracis, to leave their beloved homeland, and my mother's parents, Antonio and

Vincenza Suraci, were the first of my relatives to make the trip to America.

The emigration of an entire family was a gradual process in those days. When they left Italy in late January 1899 with their two children, my Uncle Frank and my Aunt Mary, my grandmother was one month pregnant with my mother. When they arrived in New York, they had no relatives to greet them or show them the ropes. But some friends from their village had made the journey a few years earlier, and had written to tell them that they would have a place to live when they came over.

I consider my grandparents, as well as the many immigrants before and after them, to be the most courageous of people. It astounds me even to contemplate what it meant for them to leave behind everything they knew. They journeyed across the ocean without any idea of what they'd find on the other side, and none of them had ever ventured more than a few miles from the spot where they were born. It must have been terrifying, knowing that they would never see their childhood homes, or their own parents, again.

My grandparents packed up their essential belongings and took the train north to Naples. At the Naples Emigrant Aid Society they went through some minor processing and were then ferried out in a small boat to the middle of Naples Bay, where they boarded the huge steamship that would take them to America.

After three weeks crossing the Atlantic, the ship finally entered New York harbor and my grandparents put on their best clothes and stepped onto Ellis Island. There they were subjected to a series of humiliating and frightening questions put to them by the immigration inspectors. After they passed their physical examinations they were led into the great hall, where they waited for their names to be called.

Because of the high rate of illiteracy, many new immigrants arrived without the right documents. The derogatory term "wop," an acronym for "With Out Papers," would be stamped on the forms of these unfortunates and officials would call out, "We have another 'wop.' Send him home." I can only imagine how my grandparents felt, not knowing whether they might at any moment be rejected and sent back to Italy.

But fortunately my grandparents at last heard their names called, had their entry papers stamped, and were loaded onto another small boat that took them to the southernmost tip of Manhattan Island at Battery Park. They made their way along the crowded streets to the address they had been given by their friends, a five-story tenement building at 139 Mulberry Street, and their first home in America. The following September, my mother, Anna Suraci, was born. She was the first of our family to be born in the United States.

Gradually my grandparents helped the rest of the family make it over. Once they found work, they sent money home to the family in Calabria to sponsor the rest of the family's passage. When the new arrivals got here, my grandparents took them into their home and helped them find jobs and a place to live.

At about the same time, my grandmother Maria Benedetto, now without a husband, began to contemplate joining her sister Vincenza in America. Most of the Benedetto family, including my Uncle Dominick, arrived in the early 1900s. Finally, in 1906, they sent for my grandmother and my father.

When the Benedettos arrived in New York, most of them settled, as had the Suracis, in Little Italy. Tenement buildings lined the narrow dirt streets and pushcarts crowded the sidewalks. The streets were packed shoulder to shoulder with crowds of people: men with big mustaches, wearing bowlers or Italian straw hats; women with their hair pulled back in a bun, wearing long dresses and brightly colored striped shawls and clutching woven baskets as they tested the street vendors' fruit and vegetables for that day's meal. Children were everywhere, playing in the muddy streets among the pushcarts, vendors, and the horses and carriages. This neighborhood was a far cry from the lush open fields of Calabria my family had left behind.

Grandpa Antonio Suraci really lived the "American dream," and took full advantage of the opportunities offered to him in his new country. He moved the family to a quieter neighborhood on Twelfth Street on the East Side between First and Second Avenues. It was here that my grandfather started a wholesale fruit-and-vegetable business catering to the pushcart owners. Every morning they congregated at his basement warehouse before sunrise to pick up the produce they'd sell all across downtown New York. My grandfather got up early in the morning every day and worked until the sun went down. He wasn't much at numbers, so he let my grandmother handle all the money. At the end of the day he gave her whatever he'd earned, and she paid all the bills and stashed whatever was left over in an old trunk she kept hidden under their bed. They had a big family at this time. Although my Uncle Frank and Aunt Mary were out on their own, my grandparents still had five children living at home.

My mother, like my father, had also been a sickly child, and I guess because he thought her prospects for marriage were slim, my Uncle Frank decided that she should study to become a schoolteacher so she could support herself. Uncle Frank was the oldest brother, and traditionally the oldest brother had as much to say as the parents in family matters. Frank decided it was time for him to take charge and start planning my mother's future.

Education had been nonexistent in Calabria. Children worked the fields from a very early age, and people felt that reading and writing were not as important as learning the skills necessary to survive. The idea of taking a child out of its mother's care was seen as an absolute threat to the Italian family and was vehemently resisted. But this was America, and against the family's protests Uncle Frank arranged for my mom to attend school.

But as it happened, he was courting a young Austrian woman named Emma. Even though she was a Catholic, my grandparents were against Uncle Frank's involvement with somebody who wasn't Italian. They threatened that if he married this woman they'd take my mother out of school. In spite of the threat, Frank married Emma, whom he loved very much (more than tradition, I guess), and so my mother never had a chance to finish her education.

The Benedetto family was also busy establishing themselves in New York. My grandmother Maria continued to live in Little Italy, but my father's sister Antoinette and her husband Demetri moved to midtown in 1918. They opened a grocery store on the corner of Sixth Avenue and Fifty-second Street and lived in an apartment above. My dad went to work for them and moved into a spare room.

This part of town was remote; most everything was downtown, and it was years before the growth of modern-day midtown. Ironically, this grocery store was on the very same spot that, years later, my recording label, CBS, would build their headquarters, informally known as "Black Rock," which is descriptive of the color and style of this massive structure. I was told by one of the presidents of the company that sales of my records subsidized at least ten floors of that building!

When my father was twenty-four years old, with a steady job, his thoughts naturally turned toward marriage and raising a family of his own. Now, in those days, tradition dictated that marriages be arranged, and family discussions began in earnest about the possible pairing of young John Benedetto to his attractive and amiable cousin Anna Suraci. By contemporary standards these arrangements must seem quite unusual: my parents were betrothed to each other by their parents, and they were first cousins. But both of these practices were common among immigrants who came from small villages. So on November 30, 1919, my mother and my father were married in lower Manhattan.

My father kept his job at the grocery store, and they lived at my uncle's on Fifty-second Street until my sister, Mary, was born in October 1920. By then the apartment was overcrowded, so my father's brother Dominick, who owned a general store in upstate New York, suggested that my father come to work for him. My parents moved with their new daughter to Pyrites.

Everything went well for a while. When my mother became pregnant again, my father asked Dominick for a raise, and my uncle turned him down flat. Hurt and upset, my parents packed up and moved back to Fifty-second Street, and that's where my older brother, John Benedetto, Jr., was born in 1923.

My grandfather and grandmother Suraci decided they had also had enough of city life. One night my grandfather told my grandmother of his dream of buying a house for just the two of them, a place with a garden. She looked at my grandfather and then she said very casually, "Oh, we have money to buy a house." All those years, Grandpa Antonio had just assumed that everything he made got spent on raising his seven children. But then Grandma went into the bedroom, reached under the bed, and pulled out that old trunk. Inside was ten thousand dollars in cash, a fortune at that time! My grandfather had never suspected that she'd managed money so well.

So Grandpa and Grandma were able to make another dream come true. They moved to a suburban part of New York known as Astoria, Queens, and they bought a two-family house at 23-81 Thirty-second Street. Astoria was rural by today's standards, and compared to Manhattan, it was the country! With their ten thousand dollars my grandparents were able to buy their new house and the undeveloped lot right next door. I remember my grandmother had a goat and some chickens wandering around on the property, and a huge garden. Sooner or later, the rest of the Suracis and Benedettos moved to Astoria, and that house on Thirty-second Street became the heart of our family life for decades to come.

A few years earlier my parents had followed my grandparents to Astoria and had opened up a grocery store of their own. They and my brother and sister lived in the apartment upstairs.

In 1924, soon after my brother John was born, my father got sick. My parents were running the store and taking care of the kids—the whole thing was a family affair—but it was too much for my ailing father and my mother, so by the time my mother became pregnant with me, they were already thinking about selling the store. Despite these problems, my mother told me they were thrilled to be having another child, and they eagerly awaited my birth.

Mary, John, and me

CHAPTER TWO

I was born on August 3, 1926, at St. John's Hospital in Long Island City. I was the first person in my family to be born in a hospital.

By 1927, my father's health had deteriorated to the point where it was impossible for him to do any physical labor whatsoever. Because my family wasn't quick to visit doctors, no one knew what he was actually suffering from. They simply assumed that the rheumatic fever he had as a child had resurfaced and was causing his present condition. My parents sold the store and looked for an affordable place to live in the neighborhood. They found an apartment in a four-story apartment house on Van Alst Avenue and Clark Street. It was a typical four-room railroad flat: the rooms were lined up in a straight row, like train cars, and you had to go through one room to get to the next. We were on the second floor of the building, above a candy store.

We had a kitchen, two bedrooms, and a living room that was all the way in the back. The front door opened directly into a kitchen approximately fifteen feet square—which was pretty large for those days. The first thing you'd see when you came in was a big, black, ornate coal-burning stove. It dominated the whole room. In addition to being used for cooking, that stove was the only source of heat for the whole apartment, since there was no such thing as central heating in those days. When we first moved in, we didn't even have hot water. The kitchen was the main hub of activity, and the kitchen table, to the left of the stove, was where the family ate meals, played their favorite card games, and socialized.

Right off the kitchen there was an anteroom that had a small tub where we bathed and also did the dishes. The toilet was in a little room to the left with its own separate door, and this was the only private room in that small apartment.

From the kitchen you walked directly into my mom and dad's bedroom, then into my sister's bedroom, which she would eventually share with my grandmother Maria, and in the very back of the apartment was the small living room, where for most of our early childhood my brother and I slept on a pull-out couch. There were also a couple of sofa chairs and an antique buffet that held all our dishes. On very rare occasions my parents would set up a table in the living room, where we kids ate when guests came for dinner. Even though the kitchen stove was large, it never adequately heated the very last rooms. I remember so clearly many a cold winter night trying to get to sleep in that chilly living room. Eventually my dad was able to put a potbelly stove in the living room for extra heat and my brother and I were thrilled: warmth is a wonderful thing.

It became harder and harder for my dad to leave the apartment. My mother had to find work in order to support the family. She eventually found a job as a seamstress in the garment district. The El train took her from Ditmars Boulevard into downtown Manhattan, where she worked all day long and then came home at night to take care of us. But her work was never done. In those days seamstresses brought piecework home from the factory to earn extra money. Mom brought dresses home every night, and for as long as my father was able to lift a finger, he helped her do the alterations on a sewing machine they had set up in a corner of the kitchen. In the morning she took the finished work back to the factory. This routine was repeated every day of my early childhood.

⁜

My father was a very poetic, sensitive man, full of love and warmth, and I vividly remember being cradled in his giant arms until I fell asleep. Even to this day, when I think of my father, I see the "huge" man of my earliest memories. His arms were strong and his hands were big and his eyes were deep, dark, and soulful. When I looked into those eyes, I felt there wasn't a problem in the world that he couldn't solve.

My father inspired my love for music. He derived tremendous pleasure from singing to anyone who would listen, just like he did when he was a child. He had a beautiful voice. He used to sit on the front stoop of our house and sing *a cappella* to my brother and me, in the gentle, sensitive voice I can still hear. He loved Italian folk songs and he used to sing one song written in the twenties called "My Mom," which has always had a very special meaning for my brother and me.

My father was fascinated by the whole idea of show business, and when I was three years old, he took us to see one of the first talking pictures, *The Singing Fool*, in which the vaudeville star Al Jolson sang "Sonny Boy." In a way, you could say that Jolson was my earliest influence as a singer. I was so excited by what I saw that I spent hours listening to Jolson

and Eddie Cantor on the radio. In fact, I staged my first public performance shortly after seeing that movie. At one of our
family gatherings, I went into my aunt's bedroom and got her
makeup. I covered my face with some white powder in an
earnest attempt to imitate Jolson. Of course, Jolson covered
himself in blackface, but, hey, I was only three, and I was making the best of what I had to work with. Then I leaped into
the living room and announced to the adults, who were staring at me in amazement, "Me Sonny Boy!" The whole family
roared with laughter. I loved that attention, and I guess that's
when I was bitten by the showbiz bug.

My father also loved art and literature. When we were old
enough, he'd read to us from great classics, like *Of Human
Bondage* by Somerset Maugham. The characters in these
books helped us develop an appreciation for all the different
kinds of people around us. My father was a real humanist.
Astoria had quite a diverse population, and we learned at an
early age to respect people for who they are, and not to judge
them by the color of their skin or the way they looked. He had
great regard for courageous individuals like Mahatma Gandhi
and Paul Robeson, and he passed this on to his children.

He also loved to watch the sky. He told me that there
were a lot of lessons to be learned by studying nature. I
remember one starry night, when we were outside looking up
into the vast darkness, he pointed to a star that seemed to me
to be incredibly close to the moon. I was afraid that the star
would crash into the man in the moon. My father explained
to me that the moon and the stars were millions of miles
apart. He pointed out that things aren't always what they seem
and that I should always learn the facts before jumping to con-
clusions. I've never forgotten that bit of advice.

One summer night my father took me by the hand and we
walked along the East River. We looked into the northern sky.

All of a sudden it lit up like a Christmas tree. There was an eerie glow, a multitude of pastel colors and designs. He told me that I was seeing a natural light show called *aurora borealis,* but I couldn't believe my eyes. He knew that there were certain times when, if the weather conditions were just right, you could actually see the northern lights right there in Astoria, Queens. Of course, today the city is so lit up by electricity that you can barely see the stars.

That moment made such an impression on me that shortly afterward I had a dream that I was walking through glorious mountains hand in hand with my father. The valley was ablaze with all those different colors. I was mesmerized. I couldn't believe the size of the mountains and the peaceful beauty of it all. I'm convinced that dream inspired me to become a painter. It still inspires me today.

My father also had deep compassion for human suffering, which he instilled in his children. His sensitivity made his shoulder a very popular one to cry on, and he eventually became, in a sense, a psychologist for the whole family. Everybody came to him with their problems, and he'd try his best to come up with solutions. He sat my relatives down and gave them practical advice, and everyone respected him for that. Friends and relatives also knew that they could count on him for a helping hand when they were down on their luck. He always brought people into our house who needed a place to stay and he never expected anything in return.

My mom once told me about the time someone broke into our grocery store. The guy was drunk, and in his clumsy attempt to rob the store he made such a racket that my dad went downstairs to see what was going on. When he turned on the lights, he found the guy out cold, sprawled over some egg crates. He called the police, but when they arrived, they told my father that if he pressed charges they'd have to lock the guy up. My father looked the would-be thief straight in the eyes and said, "Do you have a job?" And the guy said, "No." My father replied, "Well, you have one now if you want it. How would you like to work for me?" He gave him a job right on the spot. You can't beat that kind of thoughtfulness. It wasn't charity; it was an example of the kind of human spirit that kept people going. After all, we were all in the same boat.

Italian tradition dictates that family is the most important thing in life and that Sunday is the most important day of the week, so every Sunday our entire family gathered at my grandparents' house. They cooked all morning, and as soon as we arrived at noon, we'd sit down at the dinner table. There were so many different courses: antipasto, soup, and spaghetti—*al dente,* of course—with tomato sauce. Then we had meat or fish with vegetables, and to top it all off, desserts that seemed to go on forever. Sometimes we had picnics in Astoria Park. All the relatives were there, and after dinner the uncles took out their guitars and mandolins. The grown-ups made a circle around us and played their instruments while Mary emceed, Johnny sang, and I rounded out the entertainment by being a comedian. We had so much fun, I couldn't wait for the next Sunday get-together.

By the time the Great Depression started at the end of 1929, my father's health had gone from bad to worse. He had developed some sort of phobia that was never really properly diagnosed. One Easter Sunday at a very crowded Mass, Dad passed out. After that episode his condition became severe. It got to the point where he couldn't ride the subway or go anywhere where there was going to be a crowd. He just couldn't handle it. On top of all this, the stress of his inability to support the family, and of having to sit home and watch how hard my mom had to work to make ends meet, affected him badly. He started having trouble with his heart, which was already severely weakened by his childhood rheumatic fever. The doctors told him that it wasn't safe for him even to climb three steps. Eventually he couldn't even leave the house. He hated being confined, and that made his mental condition and his heart condition even worse.

My father's mother, Maria Benedetto, came to live with us so she could take care of us kids while my mom was at work. She was a wonderful lady and loved her grandchildren dearly. She was very religious and was never without her rosary beads, and her ever-present crucifix hung on the wall above her bed. I remember her praying to her favorite saint every morning. Since she couldn't speak any English, she prayed in Italian, and this ritual was very mysterious to me; I used to love to watch her and try to figure out just what she was praying about. My mother later told me that she had been asking for a quick and painless death when her time came. And wouldn't you know it, she fell ill on a Friday afternoon and that Sunday she died quietly in her sleep, just as she had prayed for.

I was only five years old when she died, but I clearly remember my feelings. Like most people in those days, my family never talked about things like death and dying, so it was left to my childish imagination to try and work it out. I was very confused. On more than one occasion, late at night when I was half-sleep, I stared into the darkness and saw an image of a person approaching my bed. As the figure got closer I made out my grandmother's features. She gently approached me, then sat calmly on the edge of my bed. With her warm, delicate hand, she stroked my forehead and reassured me that everything would be all right with my life. This really scared the hell out of me every time it happened. I'd jump out of bed and run screaming to my mom and dad, convinced that I'd been visited by my grandmother's ghost. My mother had to get up very early in the morning and go to work, so she'd explain to me that I was dreaming, then shuffle me back to bed. I still get chills thinking about these "visits," and with my family's superstitious heritage running through my veins, I'm not totally convinced I was dreaming.

My other grandmother, Vincenza Suraci, became ill around the time her sister passed away. At that point, Uncle Frank and Aunt Emma were living downstairs from Grandma and Grandpa. Emma, despite the family's initial resistance, had become an all-around favorite. She taught herself Italian so that nobody could talk behind her back or plot against her. She learned to cook just like an "Italian wife," treated us like angels, and pretty soon nobody, not even Grandma, could find a bad thing to say about her. Grandpa used to like Italian card games, and Emma learned them so she and her father-in-law could play together. They played for hours on end.

When Grandma was ill, even though Grandpa had a nurse for her, the daughters and daughters-in-law each took turns keeping her company every day. Even my mother, who had a sick husband, took a day every weekend and did her part.

Vincenza was a very hot-tempered, determined lady. She was always starting some kind of disagreement with somebody in the family, and when she got sick, she wasn't about to leave this earth without a fight! She was ill for about two years and then she had a stroke and was in a coma for months. She never regained consciousness and died in 1933.

Fortunately, Grandpa Antonio Suraci lived another ten years. He was very funny and a lot of fun to be with. He was a real guru, a gentle giant with big red cheeks and a white beard. All the kids in the neighborhood thought he was Santa Claus. He sat on the stoop smoking his pipe all day long, and

I sat with him. He couldn't speak English very well; in fact, he was a quiet man who hardly ever said a word, even in Italian. He always seemed deep in thought.

He smoked a pipe that he filled with Ivanhoe tobacco, and when he ran out, he'd send me to the candy store for more. Because of his accent he pronounced the name "Ivan-a-hoe." "Nino," he'd say, "I need some more Ivan-a-hoe." So when I went to the store, that's exactly what I asked for: I'd say, "My grandfather needs some more Ivan-a-hoe tobacco, please," and all the old men would break up laughing.

My grandfather made a smart move bringing the family to Astoria. It was a perfect place to grow up. Instead of being surrounded only by Italian Americans, as we might have been if we'd stayed in the city, the neighborhood was ethnically diverse. There were Irish, Polish, Greek, Italian, and Jewish families living side by side. I remember the Irish families were especially fond of the Mills Brothers, and Irish quartets hung out on street corners and sang traditional rhythm and blues songs like "Paper Doll." It was kind of surreal.

My young life in Astoria reminds me of *Dead End*, the classic Humphrey Bogart movie that introduced the Dead End Kids. When we were children, we hung out just like those kids you'd see in the movie and we got into just as much mischief. Once I nearly burned down the whole house! I found some matches lying around and I didn't know what they were, so I started playing with them. Next thing you know, the living room curtains were ablaze!

Luckily, somebody on the street saw the flames in the window and ran up and started pounding on our door. My grandmother was in the kitchen and quickly came to the rescue, so nothing was damaged except the curtains. I still remember the screaming and the blare of the fire trucks. Boy, did I learn my lesson! I got a whipping I'll never forget.

I was quite a handful and used to scare the devil out of my mom. I had this habit of walking backward down the street; don't ask me why. Somehow it fascinated me to look at things as I was moving away from them. One day I was walking along backward and BAM! I got hit by a car. I was knocked out, and when I woke up at home, I had a huge bump on my head.

As it turned out, the car was driven by the New York commissioner of highways. Now, if a city official hit a child today, the parents would probably sue for millions of dollars. But my mom and dad didn't see it that way. I wasn't really hurt, and anyway it was my own fault. They said, "Why should we get somebody in trouble? Our son shouldn't have been out in the street like that. He should have been looking where he was going." They didn't press charges or try to collect any money, even though they were very poor and this was during the Depression. They took the responsibility for me and I loved them for that. Unfortunately, this wasn't the last time such a thing would happen. I was hit two other times—once by an ambulance. How I survived I'll never know!

My brother, Johnny, and I were very close, so close in fact, that he and I were convinced we had ESP. We used to have fun playing these little mind games. We'd go into different rooms, concentrate on something, and then write down what we were thinking, and most of the time, we'd have written the exact same thing. It was really strange, and kind of scary, but it was a lot of fun.

John insists that I have the power to will things to happen. He remembers one particular Thanksgiving. We were preparing the holiday dinner, but we didn't have money for a turkey. Mom was crying because she felt she'd let us down. I was overwhelmed with emotion; I simply couldn't stand to see her suffer that way another minute, so I told her the local movie theater was raffling off turkeys, and somehow I convinced her that if she gave me a dime to go to the movies, I would win that turkey.

I ran down to the box office with that dime and bought my ticket, which had a raffle number printed on the back. I took my seat, but I didn't even watch the movie. I just sat there clutching that ticket stub. The number on my ticket— I remember it so clearly—was four. I visualized that number over and over again in my head. I'm not really superstitious, but I kept saying, "It's going to win, it's going to win. It's *got* to win." The movie ended, and an elderly gentleman told everybody to get their ticket stubs ready. All the tickets were in one of those big bingo tumblers. The man spun it around, reached in, and sure enough, he called out in a loud voice, "Number four." Next thing you know, I was dragging this turkey down the street to my front door, just like a scene out of a Dickens novel. When I showed up at home, the whole family looked at me like I was a magician. John just shook his head in disbelief.

John and I both loved music from the time we were little boys. In fact, for a long time it looked like John was going to be the star singer of the family. His voice was so pure and angelic that my parents thought he might have a future as a singer, so they scraped together the money to give him formal singing lessons. When his teachers heard the quality of his voice, they decided that he should study *bel canto* singing, a style of singing developed by the nineteenth-century Italian composer Vincenzo Bellini. *Bel canto,* which literally means "beautiful singing," treats the human voice like a musical instrument. This style emphasizes purity of tone and ease of projection, rather than the melodramatic, emotional performances that were popular in opera at the time. Johnny was so good that he was chosen to perform in the children's choir of the Metropolitan Opera, and was even given solo spots. You can imagine how proud my father was.

Our Uncle Frank was very involved in the local Republican party. In the mayoral election of 1934, Frank helped deliver the Astoria vote to Fiorello La Guardia. Later, Frank became commissioner of libraries for all of Queens and ran for the state senate. On many occasions, he arranged for Johnny to sing arias at various political functions. Johnny became known as "The Little Caruso."

I was aware of all the attention Johnny was getting, and I asked my folks if I could take lessons too, but this was during the Depression and they couldn't afford it. But I was determined. I listened to the radio and emulated the singers I heard. I loved opera and the way my brother sang, but pop songs really made me happy. For me it's still the best music in the world: of the moment and full of life. When I was around six or seven years old, the local Catholic church staged a show with all the neighborhood kids. I did my impression of Eddie Leonard, a famous comedian and singer who went back even farther than Jolson, and sang his version of "Ida (Sweet As Apple Cider)." I was getting my taste of performing too.

Unfortunately for Johnny, by the time he was thirteen or so, his voice started to change. Some people in the neighborhood were jealous of his success, and this gave them the opportunity to say things like, "Poor Johnny, his voice isn't the same." I think this psyched him out. Instead of riding out the change in his vocal range, he just gave up singing altogether.

But nothing could discourage me. In grammar school I had a teacher who divided the class into "golden birds," the kids she felt could sing, and "black crows," those she felt couldn't. When she heard me sing, she said, "You're definitely a black crow," and I thought to myself, "What is she talking about?" When somebody tells me I can't do something that I believe I can, that's when I rise to the occasion. Besides, my whole family encouraged me to sing, even if they couldn't pay for lessons.

I never really enjoyed school much when I was a kid, but I did like playing the prince in my first grade's production of *Snow White*. There was one teacher who really loved me. She thought I was a cute kid, especially when I showed up in my little prince outfit. I don't remember her name, but she treated me like I really was a little prince, and it made me believe that I was special. Her acts of kindness will never be forgotten. It's funny how one positive person like that can mold your whole attitude and change your life.

A couple of years later I had another teacher who really believed in me. Her name was Mrs. McQuade and she helped me get what may have been my first public performance. She arranged for me to sing at the local Democratic club. That undoubtedly annoyed my Uncle Frank, who eventually ran for state senate on the Republican ticket, but I was unconcerned with politics: this was my first gig! Since I was only nine years old, my older sister Mary had to come with me because I was too young to walk home alone.

Mrs. McQuade later helped me when I got to sing side by side with Mayor Fiorello La Guardia at the opening of the Triborough Bridge in 1936.

Construction of the bridge that would link Queens to Manhattan and the Bronx had begun on October 25, 1929— the second day of the stock market crash that set off the Great Depression. Over the next several years construction was repeatedly stopped and started. By 1932 it still hadn't been completed, and the people of New York City were tired of the inefficient and corrupt administration of Mayor James

Walker. It was time for a change, and the civic-minded Italian-American Fiorello La Guardia appealed to the voters.

Mayor La Guardia was an extremely popular man and he endeared himself to New Yorkers by always being sensitive to common people's day-to-day concerns. I remember once during a newspaper strike, my brother and I listened to La Guardia do a dramatic reading of our beloved *Dick Tracy* comic strip on the radio. He said that no one should be deprived of their favorite Sunday comic just because the newspaper men couldn't work things out.

La Guardia fought against racism and economic inequality. He ran for mayor in 1933, and during his campaign he promised that if elected he'd complete the construction of the Triborough Bridge. He won the election and kept his promise: the bridge opened on July 11, 1936. A grand celebration was planned. Mayor La Guardia would officially open the bridge to traffic and invite everyone to walk across with him in a show of unity and progress. I don't know how she did it, but Mrs. McQuade arranged for me to sing at the opening ceremony. There I was in a white silk suit, standing next to Mayor La Guardia when he cut the ribbon! After his speech I led a throng of hopeful people across the brand-new bridge, singing the song "Marching Along Together." Everybody sang along— even the mayor.

I was ten years old when I marched across the Triborough Bridge. My dad wasn't there; he was too ill. He had finally been diagnosed with an "enlarged heart." Today doctors could treat his illness, but in 1936 they were at a loss. Dad just got weaker and weaker. He still tried his best to help Mom with her piecework, and he looked after us when she went off to her job in the city. I remember him being at home with us all day long, which was quite a role reversal for that time. He even taught my sister how to cook.

⌗

My father's body ached so badly at night that he could hardly bear to have the bedsheets touch his limbs. He spent a lot of time in and out of the hospital on Governors Island; sometimes he'd have to be rushed there in the middle of the night. For some reason his heart would swell up and push against his lungs, which would fill up with fluid, making it almost impossible for him to breathe. I was always so confused and frightened when this happened. Every time he had an attack the house would be in chaos, but one night I woke up to find everyone in a complete uproar. Somehow, this time it was different; I could feel my mom's panic. I remember shouting over and over, "Oh, my God, Ma, what's happening?" But no one answered me. It was very late at night, everyone was running around like crazy, and once again they rushed my father to the hospital. This time he was diagnosed with congestive heart failure, and he contracted pneumonia. He soon lapsed into a semiconscious state.

I went to the hospital every day to visit him. The shades in his room were drawn, and there was a simple lamp by his bed. I sat next to him in the dim light just holding his hand and hoping more than anything that he would get better. After an agonizing three days he regained consciousness and seemed so alert that the doctors told us he had pulled through and would be able to come home. The next morning we readied his bedroom and marched down to the hospital. But when we arrived, the doctor came out to the waiting area and gathered us together. He told us that my father had suffered another bout of congestive heart failure and had died in the night. We were devastated. My father was only forty-one years old. I couldn't believe that this wonderful, beautiful man was really out of my life and that I would never see him again. I was heartbroken. My eyes welled up with tears and I wept.

The news hit us all like a ton of bricks, and I wasn't sure my mom was going to get through this tragedy. That night the family gathered at the house, and there was complete pandemonium. My aunt Millie, in her grief, came up to my brother and me and shouted, "You killed him; you two killed my brother!" I was stunned. I had just lost my dad, and now, of all things, I was being blamed for his death. My mom was too distraught to reassure me that this was not the case, so I was left with the horrible impression that I had killed my father, and I suffered with this for a very long time.

The whole situation was so painful that this entire period of my life is a bit out of focus. I barely remember my dad's funeral. To top it all off, after the funeral my father's brother, Dominick, decided that now that my mom was a widow at thirty-six, with three kids to take care of, it would be better for her if I came to live with him upstate in Pyrites. That way, he said, she would have one less kid to worry about. I looked around in amazement as my uncle spoke, waiting for someone to veto this ridiculous proposition, but everyone thought it was a good idea. Everyone, that is, except me. Even my mom consented, and off to Pyrites I was sent.

Pyrites was a small, working-class mill town in 1936, about fifteen miles from the Canadian border. My Uncle Dominick and his wife Dominica owned the general store and farmed, and since it was summer, I helped out with the chores. Uncle Dominick never had kids, and he didn't know the first thing about how to treat a child. He wasn't a bad guy, but he wasn't particularly sensitive, either. One afternoon I was hanging out with my aunt in the kitchen while she was ironing, and she asked me to sing to her. So there I was, leaning against a chair, singing, when in came my uncle. He started yelling at me, "Why don't you do some work around here? Why don't you milk a cow or something!" And with that he kicked the chair out from under me. He yelled at me all the time and he made me sleep on the floor. This kind of treatment certainly wasn't what I was used to, and I missed my family desperately.

Fortunately, we had other relatives up in Pyrites. Our cousins the Futias lived next door. They had some wonderful kids my own age, including my favorite cousin, Mary Lou. I spent as much time with the Futias as I could. I hated going back "home" to my uncle's house.

That fall I went to school with Mary Lou and her brothers and sisters. I didn't like it much better than I had in Astoria, but I got to do some fun things. One time the whole school put on a play, and all the kids dressed in costumes representing the different nations of the world. Mary Lou and I were made up like we were from Japan. We were supposed to sing a song together called "Sing-A-Lee, Sing a Low-Down Tune," but the teacher was so taken with my singing that I did most of the song by myself. After the show, all the parents gathered around me and asked me to sing. They thought I was "sophisticated," since I had just come from New York, and they wanted me to do all the latest songs, like "Pennies from Heaven." They dug into their pockets and gave me dimes and quarters to sing for them, which was extraordinary, since this was during the Depression.

Having lived in the city my whole life, my time in Pyrites was my first real exposure to nature. I'd never seen so much open space, so many trees and flowers, lakes and rivers, and just because it was so different from Astoria, I instantly liked it. I experienced a sense of freedom unlike anything I'd ever felt before. One of my favorite things to do was ice-skate on the beautiful St. Lawrence River. It was so peaceful there. I'd go for miles and miles. The river froze solid—people drove big trucks right over the ice, that's how thick it was.

After about nine months—a whole school year—my mom decided she missed me so much she wanted to have me back, so plans were made for my return.

I found out later that not long after my father's funeral my Uncle Frank had decided my mother needed a vacation, and he took her and my Aunt Emma to the country for a week. He also decided that my family should move to a smaller and more affordable apartment. Although Mary was only sixteen at the time, it was left to her to make all the arrangements for the move, and have everything ready when my mom returned. So all by herself Mary found us a new apartment right across the street from Grandpa's house on Thirty-second Street. Frank and Emma lived downstairs from my grandparents, so the family was now very close. Mary decided that she would share a room with my mother, and John and I would once again share a pull-out couch in the living room. I don't know how she was able to handle so much responsibility at sixteen, but the move went smoothly. Mary has always been an amazing person.

When I returned from Pyrites, my family was already moved into the new apartment. It was one more shock in a very traumatic year, but I think I understood why we needed to make the move. With my father gone and my mother working all day, Mary was left to watch after John and me, and it was much easier on her for us to be in a smaller apartment, right across the street from my grandparents. My sister is a beautiful, wonderful woman whose whole life has been devoted to family. She was a surrogate parent to John and me, and she's always been my main source of emotional support.

My mom kept working all day at the factory, and as before, she did piecework all evening. We'd meet her every night at the subway station so that she wouldn't have to carry that big bundle of dresses by herself, and in the morning we'd do the same thing in reverse. Even though she got paid by the dress, she'd sometimes pick one out and throw it aside. When I asked her why she did that, she told me, "I only work on quality dresses." She wasn't intentionally teaching me a lesson about integrity, but many years later, when producers and record companies tried to tell me what type of songs to record, in the back of my mind I could see my mother tossing those dresses over her shoulder. This has always been my inspiration for insisting on singing nothing but great songs.

My brother John at eighteen, and me at fifteen

My uncle Dick, one of my mother's younger brothers, had been a "hoofer," a dancer-for-hire on the vaudeville circuit. He performed under the name "Dick Gordon," and was quite well-known. At the height of his career he even played the New York Palace, a huge theater in Manhattan and about as big a venue as one could play in those days. In the early 1900s vaudeville was the most popular form of entertainment. This was before the advent of movies and radio. For the price of one ticket you saw a multitude of different acts: singers, dancers, jugglers, acrobats, comics, everything you could think of. But by the late thirties, vaudeville's popularity had declined, and it became harder and harder for Uncle Dick to find work.

Eventually, because of his show business connections, he got a job at the box office of the Broadway Theatre on Broadway, between Fifty-second and Fifty-third Streets, a landmark theater that is still around today. It was a beautiful place and Uncle Dick was proud to work in such a distinguished theater.

Uncle Dick filled my head with all sorts of fascinating stories about show business. He told me all about the ins and outs of being a successful entertainer and warned me of the dangers of the road and what to watch out for. He taught me that talent isn't everything; it's really those entertainers who have empathy with their audience who are the most successful. He told me that nothing is ever really new: when people are raving about some new trend, chances are it's been done before.

I loved to visit Uncle Dick at the theater. Once when the legendary French crooner Maurice Chevalier was playing there he got me in so I could watch both the rehearsals and Chevalier's shows, the whole thing. It was wonderful. I got to know Chevalier later in my life, and he gave me some advice that I still use to this day. He told me to introduce the musicians to the audience. He said, "Show the people that there are artists on the stage other than yourself." Not only does this give the audience a rest during the show—they're not just watching a singer with a microphone in his face the whole time—but it also acknowledges the many people on the stage and behind the scenes who are responsible for a great show. I've always believed in giving credit to those who work so hard to make it all happen.

I have a favorite Maurice Chevalier story. There was a musicians' strike once when Chevalier was working at the Waldorf-Astoria Hotel. Instead of canceling his performance, Chevalier came out and sang the whole show *a cappella*. And he got five standing ovations. Now that's showmanship! In fact, I've used that very same technique during my own performances. I'll turn off all the microphones and perform for the audience with only the pure acoustics of the hall to amplify my voice. Chevalier performed the whole show without any microphones *or* musicians! I can't think of a better illustration of the old adage, "The show must go on."

Uncle Dick also taught me that there are many rules to be followed in show business, but that sometimes breaking those rules is just as important as keeping them to become a classic performer. For every golden rule there is one waiting to be broken.

One day he sat me down and said in a very serious voice, "There is one singer who has changed the face of this business, and you must watch everything he does. His name is Bing Crosby, and he's the boss." From that day on I studied Bing. I learned a lot watching him grow as a performer. He's the one who showed all of us how to do it. Bing's early movies were overly dramatic; he was almost too hot for the screen, but with experience, he started relaxing. He'd just sit there on a stool and tell everybody to take it easy, why not just go out fishing! He developed this real relaxed attitude that appealed to everybody.

Bing was one of the first performers to effectively use the microphone. Before the microphone, a singer had to sing very loudly in order for his voice to hit the back of the hall or, as Rudy Vallee is classically known for, he would use a cardboard megaphone to amplify the sound. Because of the microphone, Bing was able to relax his voice. There was no longer any need for operatics, and he was able to pioneer the art of intimate singing, which we call crooning. He developed a psychological style that got right under your skin. This was a revelation for singers, and Bing was the most popular singer of all time, bigger than Elvis and the Beatles combined.

It was now 1939, I was a teenager, and my mind was set on becoming a singer. Although I was passionate about music, painting and drawing had always been just as important to me. I amused myself during school by drawing caricatures of my teachers and classmates. Although this didn't go over too well with the teachers, it made me quite popular with the kids. After school I spent hours drawing in the street with a piece of chalk, creating little masterpieces that got washed away with the next rainstorm or by someone's garden hose.

My first art teacher, James MacWhinney, encouraged me to study painting. When I was twelve years old, a few days before Thanksgiving, I was outside creating another one of my "murals" with colored chalk, a big picture on the sidewalk of the Pilgrims and Indians. I saw a shadow fall slowly across the sidewalk. I looked up, and there was this big, handsome Irish guy standing above me, watching me draw.

He asked me what school I attended, and I told him P.S. 141. He said he was Mr. MacWhinney, the art teacher at my school, and told me he thought I was doing great work. As it turned out, he lived in my building, but I had never run into him before. Then he told me that he went out watercoloring every Saturday, and said if it was all right with my family, he would love to take me along and show me how it's done. I couldn't believe that someone was giving me so much encouragement! So I ran home right away and told my mom what had happened, and she gave me permission to go.

I loved our weekly outings. For me these afternoon sessions were pure magic, transporting me to another place. Each week we went someplace different, and we'd work side by side. During the week I would finish the painting I'd started on the weekend, and he'd critique my work the next time we met.

James MacWhinney has been a huge influence on everything I've done. His wife, Julie, is a beautiful, intelligent lady. She taught English at our high school, and together the two of them directed my cultural education. They took me on day trips into Manhattan, where I went to the opera, visited museums, and saw my first Broadway musical, *Carmen Jones*. It was all so new and fascinating to me, a tremendous revelation. Later, I was able to join his class in school, and I was so enthusiastic about it all that I actually helped him clean up afterward! All the other kids ran out the door when they heard the bell, but I hung around and washed brushes and cleaned up everyone else's mess. I'd do anything I could just for the opportunity to soak up more training.

Even today, when I put brush to paper to do a watercolor, I think of those glorious days. It was the first time I learned how important it is to be honest with yourself in order to do good work. I believe that one must always step back from one's work, try to be as objective as possible, and be willing to do the work needed to make it better. It's a great lesson to learn. In fact, years later I was fortunate enough to become friends with the great Fred Astaire, and he had the same philosophy. He told me that when he worked on a show and felt that it was perfect, that's when he'd pull out fifteen minutes. Now that's perfectionism!

James and I still keep in touch. The last time I saw him he compared the two of us to the Renaissance painter Cimabue and his pupil Giotto, who eventually outshone his master. One day Cimabue discovered Giotto drawing on the sidewalk, and asked him to make a circle. Giotto drew it perfectly, freehand, without the use of a compass. Cimabue was amazed and immediately took him on as a student.

I'm still flattered by the comparison today.

So at thirteen years old I was actively pursuing painting and performing, and getting advice about both from some very experienced professionals, but boy, was I an amateur! Early on I made so many mistakes that sometimes I can't believe I've come as far as I have. Years later George Burns reinforced

something I'd always known. He said that it was very important for there to be little clubs where performers could have
"the opportunity to get lousy before they get better," that it
takes at least ten years to learn one's craft. The truth is, it
took me much longer than that. In fact, even now at the age
of seventy-two, I'm still learning.

When you're first starting out, you do a lot of things
wrong, but that's how you learn. If you want to succeed, you'll
need a lot of courage and a lot of faith, but eventually it will
happen. You need to meet opportunity with preparedness.
Many, many people told me that I'd never make it. And there
certainly were lots of auditions where I didn't get the job. This
happens to all performers. Young people just starting out have
to work long and hard and have the faith that eventually
they'll master their craft.

Above all else, they must never lose heart.

⚓

By the end of the thirties I got a chance to get a little theatri-
cal training. There was an academy in Astoria run by a British
woman named Mae Homer. Several well-known performers
came out of that school—the movie star Nancy Kelly and the
movie comic Eddie Bracken. It was primarily a dance school,
but she taught all the rudiments of show business. I studied
with her for a while, and I learned all the basics of performing
in front of an audience, including how to tap dance while
singing! I really loved her.

Mae helped me get a singing gig that I'll never forget. It
was September, 1939. There was a special club for British officers in New York, basically their equivalent of the USO, and
Mae Homer had some kind of connection to the club and
arranged for me to perform there. I sang "There'll Always Be
an England." It was a new song then, written at the start of the

war by Ross Parker and Hughie Charles. I got up on stage, and all these British officers were knocked out that this little Italian-American kid knew that song. It went over great— they even gave me an ovation.

When I was fourteen, the time came for me to go to high school. I'd decided to pursue painting as a career, although I never retired my dream of becoming a singer. I just wanted to focus seriously on painting for a while and get some good solid training. The public school system in New York offered, and still does, the opportunity for students to go to special- ized schools rather than the regular-curriculum, regionalized schools one would normally attend. I tried to get into the High School for the Performing Arts, the school made famous years later by the hit movie *Fame*. But the requirements were stringent, and I couldn't get in. I was at a loss as to what to do next when my boyhood buddy Rudy DeHarak suggested I try to get into the High School of Industrial Arts (now known as Art and Design), which was on Seventy-ninth Street near the Metropolitan Museum. This was a new school, where the emphasis was on commercial art, and Rudy had been in one of the very first graduating classes.

I met Rudy around 1938. My family had moved once again to what I always refer to as "the projects," but what was actu- ally a complex called the Metropolitan Apartments, residential developments created by The Metropolitan Life Insurance Company as a side investment. We were able to move into a four-room apartment at a very affordable rent. The buildings were modern and spacious for the time, and each had a court- yard with landscaped gardens. It was quite a change from what we were used to. Rudy came from California originally and had moved to New York with his sisters, who were dancers on Broadway. We lived on the second floor and they lived on the ground floor.

Rudy was a great kid and encouraged me in my love of both art and music. He became a dear friend of my family's, and even came to think of my mom as his "other mother." We both went to P.S. 141, although Rudy was a few grades ahead of me. But we hung out together because of our mutual love of jazz and drawing. In fact, Rudy took up the saxophone as a kid. I remember it well because in the summertime, when everybody had their windows wide open, the whole building could hear Rudy blowing away, learning his scales. Eventually, he became quite a proficient sax player.

Rudy's career became sort of the mirror image of mine: he had great success as a graphic artist and loves to make music on the side. His graphic design has been exhibited internationally and is in the collection of New York's Museum of Modern Art. Rudy lives way up in Maine now, but he and I still get together from time to time. He's the oldest friend I have—he's been a part of the family for sixty years, and whenever we get in touch, we just naturally pick up where we left off.

Taking Rudy's advice, I applied to the High School of Industrial Arts, and I got in. I traveled into the city every day to my new school, and the experience was a real eye-opener for me. I really enjoyed the school, but I always had this little pang of regret that I didn't get into Performing Arts until fifty years later when I met Everett Raymond Kinstler, one of America's most renowned portrait artists. I was in my sixties at the time, and he came up to me at a dinner we were both attending and said, "Your name is Anthony Benedetto, you went to the Industrial Arts school, you're sixty-three years old, and your birthday is August third, 1926." I was a bit startled by this, but it turns out that we attended Industrial Arts at the same time. The evening that we met he told me that he had been given a scholarship at Performing Arts. On his first day of class the instructor had told him, "I want you to paint what you feel." He told the teacher, "I'm only fourteen years old; I don't have a clue what I'm supposed be feeling. What I need is technique." So he closed his book, walked out of that school forever, and switched to the High School of Industrial Arts, where he received the technical art education he was looking for. We have since become the best of friends. In fact, he has become a mentor and has opened up a whole new world of painting for me.

Everett really turned my head around and made me appreciate the education I received. Industrial Arts gave kids the chance to develop all sorts of skills so that they would be suited for a wide variety of careers. They taught everything: oils, watercolors, silk screen, photography, advertising, sketching, sculpting, painting—even how to make stained-glass windows.

Whenever I have a creative dilemma, I always refer back to what I was taught at Industrial Arts. All art requires technique. The great drummer Louis Bellson taught me, "If you want to understand free form, you must first learn form before you can be truly free to experiment. You can't successfully break the rules until you learn what rules you're breaking."

Sometimes I can be working on a painting or drawing for hours and I think I'm not accomplishing anything at all. Other times I get so focused that I can nail it instantly. I remember when I started at Industrial Arts I did a sketch of my grandfather sleeping. It was perfect! I doubt that even sixty years later with all my training I could do it any better. That proves to me there's always a push and pull with the creative process. That's why I learned never to give up, even if it feels as if it's not happening the first time around. Keep going, keep plowing through it. It's all a matter of skill.

As I've said, although I was studying commercial art in school, I was still determined to pursue music. I had a wonderful teacher named Mr. Sondberg, who told me he liked the way I sang and encouraged me to sing as much as possible. Eventually, three friends from school and I put together our own vocal quartet, which included my good friend Frank Smith. Frank and I practiced singing all the time. He kept time by pounding on his desk, and he got so into it that his fingers would bleed from pounding so hard—that's how much he loved to make music.

Another great thing about Industrial Arts was that it gave me the opportunity to come into Manhattan every day. It was a very liberal school, and sometimes the teacher would give me four days' worth of work and tell me, "We don't have to see you for the rest of the week, but you must come back with four days' worth of paintings." So, as long as I did my work, I had the freedom to catch all the big band shows I could.

It was at one of these shows that I discovered Frank Sinatra, my favorite singer. I first heard him at the Paramount Theater, down in Times Square, where all the biggest shows were put on; every major star who came to New York played there. I was one of the original Sinatra groupies. Frank had just left Harry James's band to sing with Tommy Dorsey. He was big in Dorsey's band, and then, of course, he just broke out. I used to stay for seven shows a day, just to watch him and the band over and over again. Just imagine: in those days you had Tommy Dorsey's band with Jo Stafford, the Pied Pipers, Buddy Rich, Ziggy Elman, plus a dance team and a great juggler or a comic. All that plus Frank Sinatra and a movie for seventy-five cents! (To force a bit of a turnover, the management would sometimes make us kids check our lunchbags, knowing we couldn't hold out hungry!)

The whole Sinatra saga really took off from there. Even in the Dorsey days, there was the most incredible furor over

Frank. The band's press agent, for instance, would spread the word around that Sinatra was going to be in the Gaiety Record Shop on Broadway with Buddy Rich at such and such a time, and he would also arrange for news photographers to be there. The place could hold only about seventy-five people, but thousands of kids would try to cram themselves into that little store! Broadway looked like it does on New Year's Eve. No one had ever seen anything like that before, and it was certain to get Frank and the band a two-page spread in the *Daily News*.

I feel Sinatra exemplifies the best music that ever came out of the United States. Not only was he a great interpreter, but he had a magic voice. I've mentioned that Bing Crosby had really invented intimate singing, but Sinatra took it a step further, in a way that no one could have imagined. He communicated precisely what he was feeling at any moment. He knocked down the wall between performer and audience, inviting listeners inside his mind. Before Sinatra, no one had ever told such vivid and beautiful stories through song.

I encountered another amazing musician during my Industrial Arts years. A girl I went to school with was really sweet on me and her dad had some kind of connection to the legendary Copacabana nightclub in Manhattan. One day she got me in to hear Jimmy Durante. Now, that was an unbelievable act—Clayton, Jackson, and Durante. They never stopped moving, jumping, and running around. It was part of Durante's shtick to yell out "Stop the music! Stop the music!" every once in a while, but the tempo never slowed and the music never stopped. After the show, we went backstage and saw the famous "schnozzola" himself, standing in the doorway in such a way that we could only see his nose. It cracked us up. Then he walked in and entertained us with his charm and wit.

Many years later I got to know Jimmy and even shared a
bill with him. I'll never forget the things he told me. He said
that back when he was first starting out, all the Broadway theaters were really on the Great White Way, Broadway itself,
and the stars—Will Rogers, Fanny Brice, Al Jolson—and the
shows themselves—*The Ziegfeld Follies* and *Earl Carroll's
Vanities,* those big, gaudy musicals of the golden era—were
always upbeat. But later, the "legit" theaters moved to the side
streets, and, Jimmy said, "That's when everything went psychological!" referring to dark, brooding dramas à la Eugene
O'Neill and Tennessee Williams. Jimmy also used to brag
about how all the great songwriting teams had composed
music for him: "Rodgers and Hart, George and Ira Gershwin,
Cole Porter and Cole Porter." He then explained that he
dropped Cole Porter's name twice because "he wrote both the
words and the music."

I loved Jimmy. He was another reason why I wanted to go
into show business—I wanted to entertain people the way he
did. Nothing could be better than that. My three favorite performers to this day are Frank Sinatra, Jimmy Durante, and
Louis Armstrong. They always gave a hundred percent of
themselves.

<hr />

Unfortunately, I didn't stay at Industrial Arts long enough to
graduate. We moved again in the early forties to a larger and
more affordable apartment that was on the first floor of the
house that my grandparents originally bought when they first
arrived in Astoria. What goes around, comes around, as they
say. It was a five-room apartment. My sister shared a room
with my mom, and my brother and I had our own bedroom.
In addition we had a kitchen, dining room, and a living room.
We lived in that house for the rest of the time we were in

Astoria. My grandfather lived upstairs with my aunts, but he died not long after we moved in at the age of seventy-two. My mom was working harder than ever to make ends meet, and I felt I just had to find a job to help out. I was forced to drop out of school, one of the biggest regrets of my life.

So at sixteen I hit the pavement looking for employment. Not surprisingly, because of my intensive art studies, I didn't have the practical skills I needed to make a living. I once worked as an elevator operator, but I couldn't figure out how to get the elevator to stop at the right place. People ended up having to crawl out between floors. Of course, I got fired the first day. I lasted a few days longer working for a laundry that did uniforms for the navy, but eventually I couldn't take it. I did manage to hold down a job as a copy boy for the Associated Press. All day long I ran around with papers. But my bosses complained that I wasn't moving fast enough. Since I studied drawing, what I really wanted was to get a look at the art department and see the cartoonists at work. But my bosses refused to let me; it was as if they were imitating the way movies depicted hard-boiled journalists and showing a kid any sort of kindness like that would have blown their image.

I started doing what they used to call "amateur shows" in clubs all over Brooklyn, Queens, and the Bronx. Anyone could get up and perform, and at the end of the night, the audience chose the act they liked best. The winner got paid a percentage of the box office and it was a good way to earn money as a teenager. I'd enter as many of these shows as I could, and I was lucky enough to win many of them. They were fun. There was one contestant who wore a sailor's uniform, although he wasn't a sailor, and he had a phony cast on his leg. He'd come out on stage and make everyone think he was an injured serviceman. To top it all off, he'd sing "My Mother's Eyes." When he was through, there wasn't a dry eye in the house. Whenever he showed up, I knew I didn't have a chance. I'd see him and think, "God, there goes my week's salary." He'd win every time. It really broke me up.

I decided that I would do everything I could to earn a living performing music. I became a singing waiter for a while at Ricardo's Restaurant in Astoria. We'd get a request from a customer and then I'd run back into the kitchen to work out the arrangements. There was a wonderful staff of Irish waiters there who taught me all the great standards right on the spot. I really cut my teeth as a performer at that job.

One night I ran into this wonderful old-time booking agent, a Danny Rose kind of a character. He was a chubby little guy. He invited me down to his office every once in a while, and when I arrived, the first thing I saw was the back of his fedora. He'd have one phone on each ear, and he'd be saying to one guy, "Kid, will you take fifteen dollars?" and then he'd say to the club owner on the other phone, "The kid says he'll do it for fifteen dollars." He got me a spot in a Paramus, New Jersey, club called the Piccadilly. This was the first time I used the stage name "Joe Bari."

I had taken a stage name because in those days performers believed that it was important to have a snappy, "eight-by-ten glossy" kind of a name that was easy to remember. I had been told that Anthony Dominick Benedetto, or even just Anthony Benedetto, was too long and sounded too ethnic. I had come up with the last name "Bari" because it was short and it was the name of both a province and city in Italy, as well as an anagram of the last part of my grandparents' birthplace, Calabria. And to my ears "Joe" sounded pretty American.

Earle Warren, the bandleader at the Piccadilly, had been with Count Basie for many years, playing alto saxophone and singing in a sweet tenor voice. Since this was one of my first jobs, I was extremely nervous, but Earle calmed me down. He said, "You're going to be all right, kid." And I was. The whole experience was a big adventure for me, and with Earle's help, I got an early taste of the fabulous things that were in store for me in the future.

In 1939 Germany invaded Poland. In the years that followed, while I was busy going to school and setting my artistic career in motion, the newspapers and radio were filled with talk of Nazis, separationists, Lend-Lease, preparedness, and Hitler: words that were ever-present but had not fully permeated our consciousness. The war in Europe was escalating, but its consequences were not fully understood. We were just getting used to the idea of "The New Deal," and President Roosevelt was leading our country out of the depths of the Depression. Then one day, while my family was returning home from one of our traditional Sunday family get-togethers, we heard the newsboys in the street shouting, "Extra! Extra!" The big news was that some place we'd never heard of—Pearl Harbor— had been attacked by the Japanese. The next day we all sat around the radio along with millions of other Americans and listened intently while our president passionately declared December 7, 1941 "…a date which will live in infamy."

One minute it was a peaceful Sunday afternoon, and the next we were at war.

In Germany in 1945

CHAPTER FOUR

I was fifteen years old in 1941, and war was about the last thing on my mind. Like most kids, I was interested in my own world: music, drawing, baseball, roller-skating, and hockey. The war seemed very far away. But once Pearl Harbor was attacked, it wasn't long before I saw my friends and relatives being drafted and sent away.

My brother John, who was three years older than me, was drafted into the air force in 1942 and stationed in Blackpool, England. Of course, we were all worried about him and anxiously awaited his letters and any news we could get about what was happening over there. Fortunately, he was never wounded. But soon it was 1944 and the war was still going strong. Things in Europe had reached a crisis point. We all realized that Hitler had to be stopped and that every available man was needed. I turned eighteen that August, and on November second, I received my draft notice. Soon both my mother's boys would see combat.

I went down to the induction center and stood in line with a bunch of other eighteen-year-olds, wondering what was going to happen to me. When my name was called, I went up to the desk, and the induction officer asked me if I preferred the army or the navy. I said, "Navy," and the guy stamped "Army." I thought, "Oh, boy, so that's the way it's going to be." Little did I know what I was in for.

Basic training was our first stop before being shipped over to Europe and into battle. I was sent to Fort Dix, New Jersey, and from there to Little Rock, Arkansas, for a six-week stint at Fort Robinson. Everything you've ever heard about boot camp is true, only worse. I was in training to be an infantry rifleman and, man, was it tough. They'd send us out on bivouacs, mock-battle training missions that consisted of endless marches through wild terrain and muddy trails. These exercises were supposed to break us in for the rigors of battle. They called it "good training," but from what I could tell it was really an opportunity for officers to brutal-ize us and break our spirit. They treated us like animals. I began to have a really hard time with the whole military phi-losophy. From top to bottom, it went against every single thing I believed in.

The biggest shock was the level of bigotry I encountered as soon as I arrived. Unfortunately that never changed much while I was in the army, but I certainly wasn't prepared for it to begin in boot camp. Our sergeant was an old-fashioned southern bigot, and he had it in for me right from the start because I was an Italian from New York City. I wasn't the only one who experienced prejudice—it was just as bad for other ethnic groups, especially the Blacks and Jews. I had a good friend from back home, Chet Amsterdam, a fine bass player and a wonderful guy. But because he was Jewish those bigots constantly gave him a hard time. I like to think they were particularly jealous because he was so good-looking—a dead ringer for Marlon Brando—and that was just too much for those guys to take. They'd pick fights with him on the smallest pretense. But he wouldn't let them get away with it, and he always defended himself. Sadly, I saw many such incidents repeated throughout my time in the war.

I stuck up for myself too, although maybe it wasn't always in my best interest. Our sergeant was always on my case. He'd scream at me, "Benedetto! You're always late!" and accuse me of not being able to keep time while I was marching. Once during a bivouac mission he grabbed his crop and started hitting the top of my helmet with it and screaming at me. Well, that was it for me. I took my knapsack off and threw it into the nearby field and walked the seven miles back to camp alone. For that little rebellion I was put on KP (kitchen police) duty for a solid month (an awful job for even a *day*), in addition to being assigned the job of cleaning the company's Browning automatic rifles (BARs), which were extremely difficult to clean. Each rifle carried thirty-five bullets, and when they were fired, the gunpowder soiled the hammer, a small piece of metal about the size of a dime. It took forty-five minutes to clean just one hammer, and the sergeant gave me fifteen at a time. Everybody else got to go into town on the weekends for R and R, but I was virtually imprisoned in the barracks. Between KP duty, BAR-cleaning duty, and regular basic training, there was little time left to me for rest and relaxation.

When I was finally given permission to go on leave, I went home to Astoria, and by the time I got to my house I was so exhausted I fell onto the floor in a dead faint when my mother opened the door. The combination of the abuse I'd taken at boot camp and the intense emotions I felt upon seeing my family were just too much for me. My mother revived me, but I really gave everybody quite a scare. Needless to say no one was excited about my going back to boot camp, least of all me, but of course I had no choice, and two days later I went back. Everybody got a furlough after six weeks of basic training, so when my training was over, I went home again and waited to be called up. I was to be sent with a group of other replacement troops to Germany.

The fighting in Europe had been fierce for months. When the German and British armies suffered severe losses in battle, they withdrew entire divisions of soldiers, but the Americans replaced individual soldiers in order to continuously replenish the unit. The U.S. Army felt that the replacements could simply join the veterans on the field and be taught firsthand the rules of combat and the tricks of survival. It was an unrealistic assumption, since in the heat of battle there was rarely time to teach the replacements anything. Many of the replacement troops had inadequate training, no combat experience, and—unbelievably—some had never even fired a gun. It was a disastrous situation, but those were desperate times, and I guess the U.S. Army felt they had no choice. The majority of the men in the campaigns of 1944–45 were, like myself, individual replacement troops.

Most replacement troops were sent to the port city of Le Havre, France, ultimately to be deployed to other destinations in Europe. That's where I was shipped off to after basic training, and that's where I had my next shocking experience. When I arrived in Le Havre, I was sent, along with my fellow replacement soldiers, straight to a replacement depot, unaffectionately referred to by the troops as the "repple depple," essentially a holding area for the newly arrived. We were all total strangers. None of us had trained together, since we had all been pulled from different divisions, and there was no time to get to know anybody in the few days before they herded us up and shipped us out. We arrived alone, we were trained—if at all—alone, and soon, as groups of strangers, we would be shipped together to the front.

I hated the repple depple system. We all did. It was demoralizing, impersonal, and terribly lonely—although fast friendships and a keen sense of camaraderie would soon develop. Here we were, all these eighteen- to twenty-year-old kids who had just recently been at home with our families, suddenly thrust into a completely alien and terrifying environment with not even a friend to commiserate with.

⚜

Of course, what happened to me was typical of what happened to most replacement troops in the final year of the war. The American army had suffered so many casualties it simply became a matter of maintaining a flow of warm bodies through the system to repopulate the depleted divisions, no matter how ill-equipped we were for combat. More than half of the replacement soldiers became casualties within the first three days on the front line. Unfamiliar with combat, and unable to be broken in by exhausted veterans, many replacements had no idea what to do, so they stuck together and died together. Anybody who thinks that war is romantic obviously hasn't gone through one. Actually, the war comedies like M*A*S*H and Catch-22 are probably a more accurate depiction of war than the "guts and glory" films, because they show how pathetic the whole enterprise is.

I was assigned to the Seventh Army, 63rd Infantry Division of the 255th Regiment, G Company. We were loaded into army trucks and made our way east across France during the harsh winter months of January and February 1945. By March, we had entered Germany. We all went straight to the front line. It became evident upon our arrival that our basic training was just that; nothing could have prepared us for what was in store.

The Battle of the Bulge had just taken place in France over the fall and winter of 1944. The Germans had been retreating since the invasion of Normandy in June, and by all accounts it seemed as if Hitler were on the verge of surrendering. But Hitler refused to listen to the advice of his generals and sent all of his resources to the front line in the Ardennes in a last-ditch effort to prevent the Americans from crossing the Rhine River and occupying Germany. Fierce battles broke out along the front line. Hitler sacrificed everything in this final push, but the Americans refused to give in. The Allies eventually broke through the lines and crossed the Rhine, the Germans once again retreated, and the Battle of the Bulge came to an end. We then replaced the exhausted and battered American troops.

It was such a horror to see the veteran soldiers returning from the front mourning the friends they'd left behind on the battlefield, victorious in battle yet defeated in spirit. I immediately felt the weight of their sorrow. They seemed to me to suffer from what we now call survivor's guilt. I remember there was this one kid named J.R. who'd been killed before I arrived, and all the older troops kept talking about him. He must have been very special. Everybody seemed affected by his death. It's as if he represented the entire tragic reality of war. They just kept asking, "How the hell could he have died? How could a kid like that just disappear?" They couldn't get over it. They acted as if they would rather have died instead.

The winter months were rough. Snow covered the ground, and the front was a front-row seat in hell. It was an absolutely terrifying spectacle: air battles raging above me, with the roar of the airplane engines and the swirling sound of bombs; and artillery battles all around me, with shells bursting everywhere. I watched as my buddies died right before my eyes. All

Grandpa Suraci, my brother, John, and me

My mother, Anna Benedetto

My parents, aunts, uncles, and me in Pyrites, N.Y.

Uncle Dick and Aunt Millie

My two grandmothers, sisters Maria
Benedetto and Vincenza Suraci,
with my father

The sketch of my grandfather
Antonio Suraci, made when
I was about fifteen

At my confirmation

At age ten

Hanging out with friends

My father, John Benedetto,
Mary, me, and John

John, Mary, and me

With John

Me, on the right,
at five years old,
in Pyrites, N.Y., with
my aunts; uncles;
parents; brother, John,
and sister, Mary

Sketch from a rooftop in France, 1945

With brothers Freddy and Stan Katz in the army

Entertaining the troops

My mother and me

With an army quartet

With some of the guys from the 255th Regiment Band

With Mary

Patricia, my first wife

With my sons, Danny and Dae

Playing with Dae at
our Englewood home

Las Vegas Hilton marquee

With some fans, 1957

With Dee Anthony
in 1957

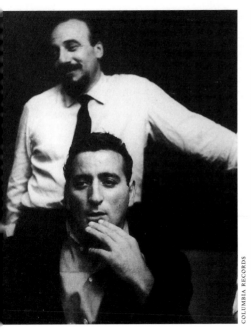

With Mitch Miller, 1955

With my friend and accompanist
Ralph Sharon in the early days

With Goddard
Lieberson, 1963

With Ray Muscarella in the fifties

At the Copacabana in New York

Recording "Yesterday I Heard the Rain" at Columbia's East 30th St. Studio, 1968

I could think of was, "When am I gonna get it?" No less than
General Patton once woke us up at four AM and gave us a
speech, saying: "Now listen up! Forget your mothers and
everything else you've ever known! You're going up to the
line." That was because we were all just teenagers, kids really.
Can you imagine saying that—"Forget your mothers!"—to a
bunch of terrified kids?

What we were most afraid of were the eighty-eight-millimeter
cannons that the Germans used. Those eighty-eights would
come whistling right down on us. What a nightmare. Shrapnel
flew and hot metal strafed anyone in its path. The only pro-
tection we had on the front line was the foxhole. Every soldier
had to dig himself a hole before he could go to sleep at night.
Sometimes it took hours to dig through the frozen ground,
and by the time you were done, you'd have only a few hours
of sleep before you'd have to get up again. Once the holes
were dug, we had to secure the surrounding area with booby
traps and set up communications lines back to the command
post. We ate cold or frozen food before going to bed. And all
this after a full day of marching or fighting. My first night on
the line I had a terrifying experience. I finished digging my
foxhole, but I was so exhausted I just passed out on the
ground before I could even get into the hole. When I woke
up, my face and body were completely covered with snow. I
was really disoriented, and once I realized what had happened, I started to look around. Directly behind me was a
tree, and embedded in the trunk was a huge piece of shrapnel, right above where I'd been sleeping. If I'd been just a few
inches higher off the ground, I would have been killed that
first night.

Nighttime was the worst. We couldn't light any fires to
keep warm; we couldn't even light a cigarette, because the
glow would be detected by the Germans and give away our

position. The winter nights were brutally cold, and sometimes they would last sixteen hours—sixteen hours of lying underground in a foxhole, alone, watching and listening for the enemy. I learned the rules of the front line pretty quickly: don't move. Someone is watching. Stay in your hole whenever you can. It was just awful. The whole thing was a big, tragic joke: the Germans were hiding from us, and we were hiding from them. Sometimes we were close enough to hear the Germans talking to each other. They must have been able to hear us too, but neither of us wanted to make a move unless we had to. Nobody wanted to get hurt. Everybody just wanted to stay alive.

Incredibly, there were some guys who actually enjoyed the war. There was one private who couldn't wait to kill Germans. He just lived to fight and kill. The rest of us would be completely exhausted from fighting all day, and he'd say, "I want this war to end sooner than later, so you guys stay here, I'm going out!" It was really spooky. We'd all look at one another and think, "What's with this guy?" He used to take his BAR and go out looking for soldiers in the trees. We all tried to stay away from him as much as possible.

Most nights we'd be awakened by the bombs that were going off around us. On the front line we'd see dead soldiers, dead horses, and big holes in the ground where bombs had exploded. To me, it's a joke that they make "horror" movies about things like Dracula and Godzilla and they make "adventure" movies about war. War is far more horrifying than anything anyone could ever dream up.

We'd crossed the Rhine at the end of March, successfully occupying Germany and driving back the German army, but there were still German soldiers who were holding out until the absolute bitter end, defending the small towns and outposts along our path. Our job was to flush out the Germans, either fighting house to house against the remaining Germans or by taking them prisoner. We did this in town after town. We checked each house from top to bottom, and once we were sure the house was clean and abandoned, we'd bunk for the night in the cellar, first checking around for any traps the enemy might have left for us. One particularly terrifying incident happened to me shortly before the fighting stopped. We were moving through a small German town. On our first day checking out a house I was standing in front of a window when one of the older soldiers tackled me. I had no idea why, until he told me that to even walk in front of a window could mean instant death; there might be a German sniper watching, waiting to pick you off.

G Company's numbers had been severely depleted, and there were only myself and a few other men left when we were passing through a town on our way to meet up with the rest of the 63rd Division. One of the remaining men was Herbert Black, a fellow I'd met when I joined G Company and with whom I became fast friends. Suddenly a German tank came out of nowhere, and we were under attack. "Blackie," as we called him, was the only man among us with any sort of usable ammunition left. He was in charge of the bazooka, and as he was getting ready to fire it, he yelled, "You'd better get down, Tony, because I'm going to let this thing fly, and it's gonna be either us or them!" With that he fired the missile, scoring a direct hit and disabling the German tank and saving our lives. It all happened in an instant. Blackie was awarded the Silver Star for his quick thinking and bravery, and I'll forever be in his debt for saving my life.

I'd have to say that only one good thing happened while I was at the front. I was pulled off the line, along with thousands of other GIs, to see Bob Hope give his show. He was there with Jane Russell and Jerry Colonna and Les Brown's band. I was in the stands enthralled. It was the greatest thing that ever happened to me. Bob was just fantastic, and all the GIs loved him so much for boosting our dismally low morale. He became a big part of the reason that I went into show business, because at that moment he made me realize that the greatest gift you can give anybody is a laugh or a song. Ask any of the legions of servicemen who saw him at that time and they'll tell you it felt like he had saved their lives. And it wouldn't be the last time I felt like Bob saved mine.

⁂

After we got back to the front, we continued to push east until we reached the Kocher River. We established a bridgehead at Weissbach by the first week of April, and by the end of the month we had reached the Danube River. We captured a bunch of SS troopers. One guy was really stubborn, and he kept screaming at us, "You aren't better soldiers than us; you just had more equipment than we had!" That really made me mad. I demanded their wallets. I decided I was going to show them that since they had lost the war, their money was worthless. I took their marks to the top of a hill, threw them into the wind, and watched them float down to the town below. So much for German superiority, I thought. My buddy took me aside and said, "You idiot! Don't you realize what you just did? You could have taken those marks to Berlin and cashed them in for American dollars!" I was floored. I had thrown away a fortune! Shades of *Sierra Madre.*

It was gratifying that the last official mission of the 255th Regiment was the liberation of the concentration camp in the town of Landsberg. It was thirty miles south of the notorious Dachau camp, on the opposite bank of the Lech River, which we were approaching. The river was treacherous and difficult to cross because there were still German soldiers protecting it, but we wouldn't let anything stop us from freeing those prisoners. Many writers have recorded what it was like in the concentration camps much more eloquently than I ever could, so I won't even try to describe it. Just let me say I'll never forget the desperate faces and empty stares of the prisoners as they wandered aimlessly around the campgrounds. Once we took possession of the camp, we immediately got food and water to the survivors, but they had been brutalized for so long that at first they couldn't believe that we were there to help them and not to kill them. Many of the survivors were barely able to stand. To our horror we discovered that all of the women and children had been killed long before our arrival and that just the day before, half the remaining survivors had been shot. We were relieved to find that many of the soldiers from the 63rd Division who were taken prisoner had been sent to Landsberg, and so we were able to liberate them as well. The whole thing was beyond comprehension. After seeing such horrors with my very eyes, it angers me that some people insist there were no concentration camps.

Hitler committed suicide on April 30. Berlin fell to the Russians on May 2, and the rest of Germany surrendered on May 7, 1945.

The main thing I got out of my military experience was the realization that I am completely opposed to war. Every war is insane, no matter where it is or what it's about. Fighting is the lowest form of human behavior. It's amazing to me that with all the great teachers of literature and art, and all the contributions that have been made on this very precious planet, we still haven't evolved a more humane approach to the way we work out our conflicts. Although I understand the reasons why this war was fought, it was a terrifying, demoralizing experience for me. I saw things no human being should ever have to see. I know I'm speaking for others as well when I say that life can never be the same once you've been through combat. I don't care what anybody says: no human being should have to go to war, especially an eighteen-year-old boy.

After Germany surrendered to the Allies, the fighting continued in the Pacific, and the men there wouldn't be able to come home until Japan surrendered and World War II ended. But Washington immediately started working out a plan to bring home the troops from Europe. They came up with a point system: soldiers were given a certain number of points for how many months or years they were in the service, a certain number of points for combat versus other types of service, a certain number of points for going overseas versus staying stateside. The guys who had the most points, like my brother Johnny, were able to come home right away.

Because I had only served four months, I had to stay behind in Germany as part of the Occupying American Army. Fortunately, I managed to get myself assigned to Special Services, the division of the military that had the task of entertaining the occupying troops. The immediate goal of Special Services was to provide as much distraction as possible, to help the troops keep their minds off the fact that they weren't going home yet. Of course, this was made even more difficult because there was a regulation that the GIs were not allowed to fraternize with German women. That lasted about a week and a half—who else were we going to fraternize with? Even the officers "fraternized" like crazy, if you know what I mean. Before the actual surrender there had been a general call put out that anyone who could entertain—guys who sang, danced, played instruments, did imitations or comedy, anything—

should report to Special Services. The way I found out about it was pretty funny: I was singing in the shower, and a passing officer heard me. He said to me, "You know, you've got a great voice. You should get into this band they're forming." That was the 255th Regiment band.

The band had originally been organized about a year and a half earlier, in 1943, back at Camp Van Dorn in Centreville, Mississippi. Marlin Merrill, who had been a music teacher back in civilian life, started it. He was something of a misfit in the army—in fact, we all were, and proud of it—and when they first drafted him, he was assigned to drive jeeps. Eventually, whoever was in charge had the good sense to ask him to put together a drum and bugle corps. He found a few guys who could play saxophone and gradually shaped them into a swing band. He eventually gathered up enough musicians to form two full bands. They played dances, USO shows, and other military social functions throughout Mississippi and Louisiana.

Most of the guys at Camp Van Dorn were given extensive training in jungle warfare and therefore assumed that they'd be shipped to the South Pacific. So they were surprised when they wound up being sent to Germany to fight the Battle of the Bulge.

The 255th Regiment had been taken out of combat by the middle of May and stationed in the town of Mosbach. To keep the morale of the troops up, the officers in charge began distributing sports equipment and musical instruments. Marlin was given permission to reassemble his band, and he started by trying to find as many men as he could from the original Camp Van Dorn unit. He managed to round up eight of them.

I was there on the second day of the band's re-formation. I found out where the band was staying, and I approached one of the musicians and told him that I wanted to try out for the singing job. It turned out I couldn't have picked a worse guy to ask, since he happened to be the band's vocalist, George Duley. Half jokingly he answered, "Nobody gets my job, son." But he helped me get an audition, and when they liked what they heard, George and Marlin went to the colonel and arranged for me to be transferred to the band. George quickly put together three background singers, and together we formed the band's vocal quartet.

Marlin Merrill was a remarkable guy. He was never officially made an officer, even though he was in charge of all of us and even though there was at least one corporal in the band. He couldn't have been more than thirty years old, but he seemed ancient to the rest of us. We were only eighteen or nineteen, so we affectionately called him Pops. Marlin conducted the band and wrote all the arrangements. He would get what we called hit kits, a collection of lead sheets or piano lines to the latest songs from back home, and he'd score them himself. He had such a great ear that he didn't even need a piano. He'd work out all the difficult transitions and create a chart, which consisted of writing out the individual musical parts for every instrument in the orchestra, in an hour. The band always sounded great.

We'd go to a different location in Mosbach every day and entertain the soldiers. I remember how glad I was to get rid of the steel helmet and the rifle that I'd been carrying around all those months. We were "billeted," as they called it, in a fabulous house in Mosbach, one of many houses that the invading army had taken over from the conquered Germans. The place was a three-story mansion that had been owned by a local beer baron—it was right behind his brewery—and he was so rich he had a piano on every floor. We weren't exactly the gracious uninvited guests, to tell the truth: we really messed the place up.

Not long after V-E Day the band was moved about twenty kilometers east to a town called Kunzelsau. We set up shop in what they called "the castle," a beautiful old structure that looked like a schoolhouse. I shared a room with Manning Hamilton, one of the band's trumpeters, who also sang in the quartet. The house in Kunzelsau had been owned by an elderly banker, and though he didn't have a brewery in his front yard, he had something even better: a small farm.

We'd been living on C rations for so long that we'd almost forgotten what real food tasted like. You can't imagine how good fresh fruit and vegetables taste after months of army food. The old banker also had a few chickens, and he came around and begged us not to kill them. We promised we wouldn't, for a very practical reason: we'd rather have the eggs for breakfast every morning than a single chicken dinner. Each morning we waited for the hens to lay an egg or two and there was always a race to snatch them. I'll never forget how wonderful genuine eggs tasted after eating the army's powdered ones for so many months. It was grand!

We were having a high old time in Kunzelsau. The army had hastily put up signs all over the area directing other groups of soldiers to this battalion or that headquarters. We took all the direction signs for the 255th Regiment band and stuck them every which way so that no one could find us. We were like phantoms: the only guy who knew where we were or where we would turn up next was the officer who handed Marlin our daily assignments. Once a week we'd go down to headquarters and pick up essentials like underwear and food, and then we'd hurry back to our house. We were free to jam all day long. It was a glorious time.

We didn't even mind that the paymasters couldn't find us. In fact, when George was about to be shipped home, he received a check for $875, a fortune for a soldier back then.

He got his entire year's salary all at once because no one had known where to find him. Money wasn't important because there wasn't much to buy anyway.

What was important to us was getting down to the PX to pick up our allocation of cigarettes. It wasn't only that we smoked a lot, which we did; cigarettes were the "legal tender" of the time. You could get anything you wanted with cigarettes. Anything. Jack Elliott, the pianist with my second army band, traded twelve cartons of smokes for a really fine camera, a prewar Leica. Red Mitchell, who played in the band, found an old German violin maker who agreed to make him a bass fiddle in exchange for fifteen cartons. That deal worked out spectacularly for both of them—the violin maker gradually bartered the cigarettes into a fully outfitted machine shop, and Red Mitchell became one of the great bassists in jazz history.

We moved again sometime in June, this time to Seckonheim, a small town between Heidelberg and Mannheim. The band kept growing as we found more and more good musicians who wanted to join up with us. The most special to me was Freddy Katz, who played the piano. He would have a very meaningful impact on my life. By now we were a full-fledged "big band" and had worked out a regular routine. Late in the afternoon, just when it was getting to be quitting time for the troops, a big army truck showed up at our house to pick us up. The driver knew where we were supposed to be playing that day and we'd all pile into the truck with our gear and drive off, usually singing the dirtiest limericks you've ever heard in your life. The truck had a piano on it, and a little PA system. When we got to the site where the GIs were working, which was often out in the middle of a field somewhere, we got out our instruments and started playing and singing and the soldiers would gather around and listen.

At that time I was singing a lot of blues, things like "How Long Blues," "Don't Cry Baby," "Blues in the Night," and Louis Jordan's "I'm Gonna Move to the Outskirts of Town." I also sang a blues tune that reflected the place and time we were stuck in called "The Non-Fraternization Blues." We always went over great with the men; they were thrilled that we took the trouble to come out to entertain them. We'd play until it got dark. We never had any lights, so when we couldn't read the music anymore, we'd pack up and drive off. Sometimes we'd play dances at an officers' club, like the Starlite Club in Heidelberg, which General Dwight D. Eisenhower had recently dedicated, but most of our gigs were right in the trenches—literally.

Because of the stress we'd been under in combat for all those months, the comic relief provided by being in the freewheeling regiment band was a welcome change, but we knew it couldn't last. I was taken out of the band by midsummer. I was still an infantryman and had never been officially assigned as an entertainer. At the time, we all thought we'd be shipped to the South Pacific to participate in the impending invasion of Japan. But, as anyone reading this knows, we never did invade Japan. It turned out that the soldiers assigned to the planned Pacific invasion force wound up going home long before the rest of us, since Japan surrendered before ground combat began. So I was assigned elsewhere in Special Services.

Up until 1945, the Special Services guys who put on shows for the servicemen were well-known performers who'd been drafted, guys like Mickey Rooney, the well-regarded screenwriter Alan Campbell (who was author Dorothy Parker's husband), and Joshua Logan, the famous Broadway producer and director. But they'd all been at it long enough to qualify to go back home as soon as the fighting ended. So once again, I was a replacement, only this time for the musicians who were sent home. Many of the guys in Special Services had been up-and-coming performers before the war started and were able to get a little more experience while they were over in Germany. It was in the Special Services unit that I met remarkable people like Arthur Penn, who would later go on to direct such great films as *The Miracle Worker, Little Big Man,* and *Bonnie and Clyde.*

Arthur first got involved with the Soldiers' Show unit of Special Services in Paris. When he got to Germany, Arthur became stage manager of a production of Clifford Odets's play *Golden Boy,* which toured liberated Europe. Then in August, the *Enola Gay* dropped the atomic bomb on Hiroshima, and the Japanese surrendered. Now that the war was over in the Pacific as well, even more guys were shipped home from Europe and Arthur was promoted. Arthur himself was very new to show business then. He was just a few years older than me, and even though he hadn't had much experience, he found that he knew more than anybody else over there, so he was officially mustered out of the service and put in charge of the whole Soldiers' Show project as a civilian government employee. In order to really occupy the minds of the troops, Arthur arranged for the army to ship over one hundred American actresses to take part in these productions.

The new unit was started in Wiesbaden, and that's where I met Arthur. I was basically just hanging around the set sharpening pencils or doing any other little job I could until I got a chance to sing for him. Arthur told me that I bowled them over, and he immediately invited me to perform in a musical production he was mounting.

Arthur had heard that there was a big hit on Broadway called *On the Town* about three sailors on leave in New York. He thought the plot was perfect for his group to perform, but he had no script and no score so he cobbled together his own version, writing an original script and using whatever new hit songs and show tunes he could find. We didn't even have sheet music for the songs—we'd simply pick up records or V-discs (records produced especially for American soldiers) and the piano player would learn them by ear. Arthur made the leads soldiers instead of sailors, but nobody knew the real story line anyway, so it hardly made any difference. I played one of the three leads in our very eccentric version of *On the Town*.

Everything about the show was like one of those Mickey Rooney/Judy Garland "Let's-put-on-a-show-in-the-barn" movies. Most of the cast couldn't sing, I didn't have any acting experience, and Arthur, who couldn't dance two steps, was choreographing the dance numbers. We staged it in the magnificent Wiesbaden opera house, which had miraculously been untouched by the bombing that had destroyed much of the city. The show ran there for several months.

I spent Thanksgiving of 1945 in Mannheim. The town was completely flattened. You could see clear to the other end of the city from any point. It was totally leveled except for the Ford Motor plant. It was really strange. I was out walking around Thanksgiving afternoon and I ran into my old friend Frank Smith, who had sung with me in our quartet back at the High School of Industrial Arts. I couldn't believe it. Frank Smith, in Mannheim, Germany! I was thrilled to see a familiar face from back home after being surrounded by strangers for so many months. He took me with him to a holiday service at a Baptist church he'd found. We wanted to spend the whole day together—it just felt so good to be with a friend—and since I was allowed one guest at Thanksgiving dinner, I asked him to come along. We were going to get a real home-cooked meal and not the dreaded C rations.

We got as far as the lobby of the building when some bigoted officer came up to me and screamed, "Get your gear, you're pulling out of here!" For a moment I didn't know what he was talking about. Even though Frank was in the army too, he was Black, and therefore he wasn't permitted into the white servicemen's mess hall. It's a sad fact that segregation was official U.S. Army policy during World War II, and obviously this officer was determined to pull rank on me. At some point during my career in Special Services I had made corporal, but that didn't last long. This officer took out a razor blade and cut my corporal stripes off my uniform right then and there. He spit on them and threw them on the floor, and said, "Get your ass out of here! You're no longer a corporal; you're a private again!"

This was another unbelievable example of the degree of prejudice that was so widespread in the army during World War II. Black Americans have fought in all of America's wars, yet they have seldom been given credit for their contribution, and segregation and discrimination in civilian life and in the armed forces has been a sad fact of life. The War Department believed that Black soldiers had to be separated from whites or all sorts of problems would arise. The type of "problems" they cited were standard-issue racial prejudices, and I don't even like thinking about it after all these years. Blacks had their own units, their own mess halls, barracks, and bars. It was actually more acceptable to fraternize with the German troops than it was to be friendly with a fellow Black American soldier! I just hadn't been brought up to think this way about people, and neither had Frank. Needless to say it was a terrible shock when this officer treated us both with such contempt. And this institutional racism continued until Harry Truman officially integrated the military after the war ended. In the meantime we all suffered because of it.

As a result of my inviting Frank to eat with me, we were denied Thanksgiving dinner and I was immediately reassigned to Graves Registration, which was just as horrible as it sounds. During the heavy battles that had been fought earlier in the war, there often hadn't been time for the soldiers to properly bury the men who died on the battlefield. The surviving soldiers often had to wrap the bodies in the dead soldiers' own mattress bags and bury them in common graves. Men like myself in Graves Registration came along later to retrieve them. I'd spend all day digging up dead bodies and reburying them in individual graves. They fed us horrible, starchy foods like rice and potatoes to dull our senses.

For a while the whole affair soured me on the human race. Frank was one of the sweetest guys I ever met. I couldn't get over the fact that they condemned us for just being friends, and especially while we served our country in wartime. I've thought back to that incident so many times. There we were, just two kids happy to see each other, trying to forget for a moment the horror of the war, but for the brass it just boiled down to the color of our skin.

Luckily a certain Major Letkoff found out that I'd been assigned to Graves Registration and was able to pull some strings. Through the efforts of this man I was assigned to the American forces radio network in Wiesbaden, and that led to one of the great experiences of my life.

The 314th Army Special Services Band of the European Theater was the brainchild of Warrant Officer Harold Lindsay "Lin" Arison. Lin was the only one in either of my army bands who was a "lifer," that is, someone who spent his whole career in the military and government services. He'd begun organizing army bands as early as 1941 and had been greatly influ-

enced by the most celebrated of all military orchestras, Glenn
Miller's Army Air Force Band. Miller's AAF Band was a mile-
stone in both military and musical history and had a huge
impact on us all. Miller was in active service when his plane
disappeared over the Atlantic in December of 1944, and it
was a huge loss to the entire country. It was devastating. His
band valiantly continued to perform without him for about a
year.

After the AAF Band was sent back to the States the chief
of Special Services of the European Theater asked Lin to put
together another band to take its place, and that's when the
314th was formed. It had been Lin's dream to put together a
new band with new music that was on par with what was happening back in the States, a first-class American pop-jazz
orchestra, and he got the go-ahead.

It was crucial that the new band's home base be in occu-
pied Germany. It was obvious that the German people felt ani-
mosity toward the occupying army, and we saw the new band
as an opportunity for us to raise morale and serve as unofficial
goodwill ambassadors. So in late 1945, Lin set up shop at the
Herzog Hotel in Bad Schwalbach and announced that he was
holding auditions for first-rate musicians. He immediately
landed some great players, many of whom went on to successful civilian careers in music after the war, among them sax
player Dick Stott and trombonist George Masso. In addition
to being a tremendous trombonist, George is one of the great
orchestrators of all time. Whenever we played one of his
arrangements, the whole orchestra applauded. His pieces were
simple to play, and it just felt great to perform them.

I was originally appointed as the band's official librarian,
but when Lin heard me sing, he said, "For Chrissake, take care
of the library, but I want you to sing a couple of songs a week
with the band!"

Our duty was to do a weekly broadcast of a show called *It's All Yours* over the Armed Forces Network, the title being our gift to American GIs stationed in Germany and to our former enemies as well. We broadcast from the Wiesbaden opera house every Sunday, and our theme song was a number I later recorded, "Penthouse Serenade." Wiesbaden was one of the few German towns that was left comparatively untouched by the Allied bombing raids. The British and Americans had agreed not to drop any bombs on the town, since they wanted to use it as headquarters once Germany was taken. Unfortunately a British plane had once messed up a raid and dropped its payload over Wiesbaden, but by and large the town was still standing, which was more than you could say for most of the rest of Germany. The opera house was acoustically perfect, and sometimes we'd cram in as many as two thousand GIs. Once we even performed a special show that was transmitted back home to the United States via shortwave radio.

The band was the whole focus of the *It's All Yours* show, much as the Glenn Miller band had been spotlighted on the *I Sustain the Wings* transmissions. As an added attraction, the USO usually sent over a guest star, like Paulette Goddard or Bob Hope, to do a sketch or a monologue. The band was extremely versatile. On one hand we were a swing band, like Benny Goodman's or Count Basie's, and could play the dance music and current hits of the day. On the other hand, we could play light classical numbers by composers like David Rose or André Kostelanetz. At its peak, the orchestra included fifty-five musicians, including a fully symphonized string section.

We got another shot in the arm and an influx of new sounds with the arrival of Jack Elliott in 1946. Our first piano player, Bob Jacobs, was leaving, and we were so glad to get a new guy that Lin assigned a master sergeant to pick him up and carry his bags. Needless to say, that didn't happen very often to a private, particularly one who'd spent most of his enlistment thus far doing guard duty. When Jack began to play for us, we heard a new kind of music we'd never been exposed to before. He explained that it was called bebop, and that it was the latest thing to hit jazz back home. We loved it. The first time I'd ever heard of Dizzy Gillespie was through Jack Elliott.

It was to the credit of Lin Arison that he was able to incorporate new sounds into the band so successfully. He was a remarkable guy who was able to inspire us all and draw out our best performances. Even though he was regular army, he wasn't strictly by the book. Sometimes he'd come out and conduct a rehearsal wearing an outrageous pair of fuzzy green bear slippers—not exactly standard issue duds. Eventually Lin's wife, Janie, came in from the States, and the two of them took care of us all.

I was one of four vocalists in the band, and I usually got to do one or two numbers per show. There were two "boy singers," Bob Lawrence, who did the straight romantic ballads, and myself. At that time I was still using the name "Joe Bari." (To this day Arthur Penn and Freddy Katz think of me as "Joe.") I usually did the rhythm tunes, the blues numbers, and the novelties. The "girl singers" were similarly divided: Judy Brines handled the love songs and Janie Thompson was the army's answer to Betty Hutton. On numbers like "Doctor, Lawyer, Indian Chief" Janie was loaded with energy and excitement, and she really thrilled the crowd when she launched into a boogie-woogie number and accompanied herself on the piano. That's one thing we had that the Glenn Miller AAF Band never had: female singers.

While we were staying at the Herzog Hotel, the first thing we did was find the wine cellar. The Germans were crazy about wine and champagne, possibly even more than the French. The cellar was behind a heavy, locked gate, but we figured out a way around that. Pretty soon we were sneaking our way in there every night. We stashed champagne everywhere. Since we didn't have any refrigerators, the only way to keep the bottles cool was to run cold water over them, so of course every sink in that hotel was full of cold water and had a bottle of champagne in it. This being the army, we weren't supposed to be drinking at all, but Lin made a rule that you were allowed to bring alcohol into the hotel, so long as it was only one drink. Pretty soon the guys were carrying in bowls and buckets full of hooch and counting that as a single drink. We even made contact with a couple of guys from the air force who were flying in marijuana from Algiers. This was the first time I ever smoked pot. But after what we'd been through, we felt that anything that would help us forget was worth looking into.

There was a USO office across the street from our hotel, and soon some of the guys worked out a scheme to attract the attention of the ladies who worked there. Irv Luden, who played baritone saxophone in the band, would go over to the USO lobby with Jack Elliott. Jack would start playing piano in this melodramatic, hearts-and-flowers fashion, while Irv would recite poetry. Gradually, the ladies noticed these two guys doing their act, and they'd wander over to listen. It was only when they got closer that they discovered that Jack wasn't reading poetry at all. He was reading aloud from the works of one of the leading writers of Victorian erotic fiction, Frank Harris. Jack was actually describing sex acts disguised in florid prose. Usually the serenade continued in private up in the ladies' rooms.

During this period in the army I enjoyed the most musical freedom I've ever had in my life. I could sing whatever I wanted, and there was no one around to tell me any different. I remember I heard an Armed Forces Radio Service broadcast of Frank Sinatra doing Johnny Mercer's "Candy," and I felt like I just had to do that song. So I did. It was as simple as that. I heard all the latest songs on V-discs, which was an amazing collection of music. The first time I ever heard the voice and piano of Nat Cole was on a V-disc, and I fell in love with his sound right then and there. Postwar Germany was a hell of a place to discover an American institution like Nat.

I sang a lot of numbers in Germany that I did later on in my career, like "Body and Soul" and "On the Sunny Side of the Street," which I did as a duet with Janie Thompson. But my big number was "St. James Infirmary." I must have done that every other week, and I never stopped getting requests for it. Some of the shows were preserved on sixteen-inch radio transcriptions, the medium that most studios used to document live shows before tape was invented, and as far as I know, that's the only vocal of mine with this band that still survives.

The whole band felt the same musical freedom. Whatever I wanted to sing, I sang; whatever the musicians wanted to play, they played. We couldn't get enough music. When we weren't playing or rehearsing, we were having jam sessions in the basement of the hotel. Lin gave us complete freedom to come up with the best and most interesting music. It was like a musical workshop, particularly for the arrangers, since it was free from all commercial constraints. What's more, everything they wrote went over big. The GIs were the greatest audience in the world. They were never critical or judgmental, and they loved everything we did. Some of the pieces that George and Dick Dorsheck wrote were highly experimental. In many ways, they presaged some of the things that Stan Kenton did years later with his Innovations and Neophonic Orchestras. They were very "progressive" or even "avant-garde," but the guys loved it. That's really proof to me that the public is much more aware than they're given credit for. I learned a big lesson with that group: an artist should never underestimate the public's taste.

So many of my army buddies did well in the music world after the war. George Duley went into Les Brown's band; George Masso began his postwar career playing trombone for Jimmy Dorsey and later became a composer; Dick Dorsheck became the principal composer for the BBC Radio and Television Orchestra; Red Mitchell was for many years the leading bass player on the West Coast jazz scene; Janie Thompson, a devout Mormon, has devoted her life to music education at Brigham Young University; and Jack Elliott became a major composer of movie and television soundtracks.

By August 1946, I had finally accumulated enough points to come home and I sailed home on the SS *Washington*. While on board I ran into my old friend Charlie Russo. I'd met him in Mannheim, where he was leading a quartet at the Truman Hotel and also putting on jam sessions in the basement. He was organizing a big band concert featuring all the musicians who were traveling home on the ship and invited me to sing "St. James Infirmary." One of the soldiers on board had a portable disc-recording machine. He cut a disc of me singing "St. James," and I played it for my family back in Astoria, but I don't know what ever happened to that record. Chuck Russo later became a great classical clarinet player, one of the best in the world.

On August 15, I was officially honorably discharged as a private first class. I still remember coming into New York harbor a few weeks later. My mother and my aunt were waiting on the dock, and when they saw me holding a cigarette, they started crying. I had never smoked before I went to Europe. They couldn't believe it, and neither could I. I was all grown up, and I was home.

At the Triborough Bridge

*A*fter I was discharged I moved back in with my family. Everything was different than it had been before. "The Good War," as Studs Terkel calls it, had changed everything in ways I couldn't explain. All I knew was that I wanted to get my life started again as soon as possible.

One of the first things I did when I got home was get in touch with Freddy Katz. We had grown so close during the war that I couldn't wait to see him again. He lived in New York City too, so it was easy to get together, and soon we were hanging out all the time. I got to know his whole family, and I became buddies not only with Freddy, but with his brothers, Stan and Abe, and their father, a learned man who taught me many things. They became my second family.

They were a very close family who all had a deep respect for music, art, and literature. I swear I received the equivalent of a university education from hanging around the Katz family. Mr. Katz, a dentist, was a Russian-Jewish intellectual who could talk about any subject. Listening to him was like going to hear a great lecturer. We sat around and discussed music and philosophy over coffee: Marx, Plato, Spinoza, music theory, all the great subjects. All three brothers were terrific musicians—Abe was first trumpet player in the Metropolitan Opera Orchestra. He taught me how to breathe correctly when I was singing.

The Katzes hosted an informal "musicale" every Friday night, and great musicians around the city dropped by to jam. We went into the library and somebody would pull the music for, say, a string quartet off the shelf, deliberately one they'd never played, and those guys would sight-read (that is, read the music and play it straight off the page without ever having heard the piece before) it right on the spot. It was amazing. One Friday night there was a terrible blizzard that virtually shut down the city and Freddy figured that nobody was going to come. I was already there, of course—no snow storm was going to keep me away from my beloved Friday night ritual—and I guess everybody else felt the same way too, because by eight-thirty there were about thirty people in the house. Those Friday evenings were incredibly inspiring. By the end of the night I was so elated when I walked out of their house I felt like I was three feet off the ground. Sometimes I didn't leave at all; I slept over so I could do it all again in the morning.

I was now determined to do whatever I had to do to become a professional singer. This meant pounding the proverbial pavement of New York City and knocking on the door of every booking agent, club, and promoter in town. Believe me, I got a lot of rejections, which was a bit of a shock after all the success I'd enjoyed in Germany, but I didn't let it get me down. I just kept at it. I went on so many auditions, but for years I couldn't get work as a singer. I even tried out for the chorus of a Broadway show, but with no luck. I kept singing wherever I could—not for money mind you, because at that time there was none to be made—for the experience and the chance to work with some

great talents. As an unknown singer I was amazed at the caliber
of the jazz musicians I was able to perform with and learn from
as a result of my persistently hanging around the good clubs.

The first time I sang in a nightclub was at the Shangri-La.
It was right under the El train in Astoria and was a very fancy,
hip place in 1946. The great trombonist Tyree Glenn—who
earlier in his career had played with Louis Armstrong, Ethel
Waters, Benny Carter, and Cab Calloway—was leading the
band. I sang informally at the bar, and when Tyree saw how
much I loved his band, he said to me, "Come on up and sing
with us." What a thrill! After he heard me and saw the audience's reaction, he gave me a job. It didn't last long, though,
because a few months later Tyree joined Duke Ellington's
orchestra, and after that became one of Louis Armstrong's
All-Stars. But those were very successful moments for me, and
they encouraged me to keep going. I knew if I just had the
chance to get up in front of an audience, I'd win them over.

I "worked" all kinds of clubs in Queens and Manhattan. I
sang once or twice at the old Venice Gardens in Astoria,
although mainly I used to go there to dance and look for girls.
For a while I was once again a singing waiter, this time at the
Pheasant Tavern and the Red Door in Astoria. Occasionally I
sat in at the Yukon Bar on Fiftieth Street in New York, and for a
while I performed at the Bal Tabarin on Broadway around Forty-
fifth Street. That was the biggest job I'd had yet, and when I got
it I said to myself, "I've hit the big time, I'm right on Broadway!"

The Nestle Inn in Astoria was fairly typical of the kinds of
gigs I was getting. It was a tiny club "nestled," as it were, under
the Hell Gate Bridge. Stan Weiss had a nice little jazz thing
going there as the leader of a quartet. He'd just come off the road
with Tony Pastor's Orchestra, where he got to play with Rosemary Clooney, so he was doing great. When I heard he was playing the Nestle Inn, I went over and asked him if I could sit in.

Stan apparently liked what I did, because he told me I could sing with his band whenever I wanted. As usual there was never any talk of paying me anything, but like I said, it was all about the experience of working with Stan and his pianist, a wonderful guy named Bobby Pratt. Bobby knew millions of songs, and he turned me on to a lot of them. He gave me a song called "While the Music Plays On," a great tune which I later recorded on my first jazz album for Columbia.

Stan's friends, like Zoot Sims and Al Cohn, two of the most swinging tenor saxophonists in the entire history of jazz, would often drop in to jam. That was the first time I heard them, and from that moment on I became a fan for life. When I met them I didn't realize how famous they were— they had both been featured in Woody Herman's Second Herd, probably the greatest big band of those years. Like the great sax player Stan Getz, who was also in Woody's band, they were heavily influenced by the legendary Lester "Prez" Young of Count Basie fame, who created the light and swinging style of tenor saxophone that was a jazz revelation. Zoot and Al became like brothers to me, and when I started recording regularly many years later, I was thrilled to have them play with me. Back in 1947, all three of us were sitting in with Stan Weiss's group at the Nestle Inn for the fun of it.

I was showing up at the Nestle Inn whenever Stan was playing there, and we got to be great pals. Between sets I'd show him all the cool places to eat in Astoria—it was my neighborhood, after all—and once we double-dated with a couple of nice local girls. A few months later Stan got an offer to go back on the road with Elliot Lawrence's band. I was sorry to see him go, but happy for him, because Elliot had a fine band.

I met quite a few lifelong friends in those years after the war. There were a lot of showbiz bars around midtown and Greenwich Village where I'd hang out and socialize with the guys. Right near the Winter Garden Theater, on Seventh Avenue between Forty-ninth and Fiftieth, there was a place called B-G Bottomless Coffee, where I spent many happy hours. Right next door was Hanson's, where all the comics hung out, and across the street were Hector's and Charlie's Tavern. It was an all-star line-up of hangout joints all along Seventh Avenue between Fifty-first and the legendary Fifty-second Street. I met John Cholakis at one of these clubs. He was a struggling bass player and I was a struggling singer, so we hit it off right away. John had inherited a resort hotel in Far Rockaway Beach, all the way at the end of Queens, practically in Long Island, and in the summer we opened up the place and got it ready for the guests. We fixed up any broken-down furniture, aired out mattresses, did any odd job that needed doing, and in exchange I got to stay at the hotel all summer. It could have been a Neil Simon play, two kids spending the summer on the beach, dreaming of stardom.

John and I used to go to Fifty-second Street to hear great jazz: swing, bop, and Dixieland, in one little funky club after another. It was incredible. John had a friend named Billy Verlin who played trumpet and ran a rehearsal studio. All the musicians hung out and jammed there, but Billy was in no better shape than the rest of us, so he asked each of the guys to cough up a dollar to help with the rent. It worked out great for everybody. Marlon Brando, who was then on Broadway in *A Streetcar Named Desire*, often came down and hung around with the musicians at Verlin's studio on his matinee days. This was long before the general public knew who he was. Billy didn't recognize him and was about to tell him to split until one of the guys said that he was an actor. That was okay with Billy. Brando always had a pretty girl on his arm and strolled into the studio wearing his trademark T-shirt.

John later made it himself, not as a bassist but as a television director, and his wife, Betty Frasier, a wonderful woman, is one of the country's leading illustrators of children's books.

I was living on a dime a day, literally. I'd get up and go into the city every morning and start my door-to-door rounds. My mom always left me a dollar's worth of change on the table before she went to work, but I never took more than ten cents. She was still working as a seamstress and I couldn't bear to take her money. I still dreamed about being a successful singer so that she wouldn't have to work anymore, and in the meantime I wasn't going to take more than I had to.

What really struck me as strange was the fact that, after all the positive stories about show business my uncle Dick had told me, he now gave me a hard time about pursuing my dream of getting into the business instead of getting a "steady job" to help support my family. I guess he felt it was his duty to read me the riot act. He'd say things like, "You're just a bum! You're not going to make it, so you might as well just get a regular job. Help your mother out! Don't be a gigolo!" He was really rough on me, and he made me feel like I was talentless. But at the time Uncle Dick's ridicule only made me more determined to succeed. I know now that he was just telling me what he thought I should hear, what the upstanding Italian uncle should say to the son of a widow, because years later I found out from Gary Stevens, a famous press agent, that Uncle Dick used to talk me up all over town. He was still working at the Broadway Theatre then, and he'd tell anyone who would listen: "I've got this nephew who can really sing! He's going to be a big star. He's really gonna make it. You gotta go out and see him!"

The best thing that happened to me after the war was the opportunity to study at the American Theater Wing on Forty-

fourth Street. The government set up a program called the GI
Bill that provided benefits for returning soldiers. It paid the
tuition for college or trade schools, and provided other important services—anything to help the vets get back on their
feet. It gave a lot of guys like myself the opportunity to continue the education that was interrupted by the war or to go
to a school that we otherwise would never have been able to
afford. In fact, in 1954 I was presented with a special citation
that singled me out as "the ex-soldier who'd accomplished the
most with his GI Bill of Rights training" by President Eisenhower. I am particularly proud of this award.

The American Theater Wing (which later became The
Actors' Studio) was one of the greatest schools in New York
City. I had amazing teachers, most notably a Russian professor
named Zhilinski who had performed with the world-renowned
Konstantin Stanislavsky at the Moscow Art Theatre. Stanislavsky was the founder of what became known as Method acting, a discipline that has been made famous by actors like
Marlon Brando and Dustin Hoffman. To this day I've never
seen performances on Broadway or anywhere else that were
better than the ones Zhilinski gave us. In one class, he demonstrated fifteen different ways to play a drunk and fifteen different ways to cry.

I've since applied the techniques I learned there to my
singing. When I sing a song, I think autobiographically, as
though the lyrics are about something I've experienced. I look
for songs that lend themselves to that type of expression,
songs that are full of powerful emotions, so that the public can
"dream along with me," as Perry Como used to say. That's
what I look for in a singer too. Nat "King" Cole, for example,
just hypnotized me when he sang a song like "I Realize Now,"
because he revealed himself so honestly. That's the idea: to let
the audience know how you feel.

At the same time that I was learning how to tell a story at the American Theater Wing, I was also studying vocal technique. Pietro D'Andrea taught me *bel canto* singing, the same method my brother had studied when he was a kid. These techniques and exercises have really saved my voice. There's nothing like knowing the basics. I also studied with Helen Hobbs Jordan for a while. She taught me sight reading, which was quite a challenge, and gave me a whole new appreciation for what I was trying to do.

Another tremendous coach of mine was Mimi Speer. She had a studio right on Fifty-second Street, across from all my favorite haunts. We'd look out her window down at the marquees across the street: Art Tatum, Erroll Garner, Stan Getz, George Shearing, Lester Young, Count Basie, and Billie Holiday, all lined up in a row. It was enough to make your head spin. She'd tell me, "Do not imitate another singer, because you'll end up sounding just like they do, and you won't develop an original sound. Instead, find a musician you really like and study their phrasing. That way you'll create a sound all your own." It was a great tip. I paid particular attention to sax players Stan Getz and Lester Young. Art Tatum was the greatest piano player of all time and was particularly instructive to listen to because he did unexpected stuff, all those jumps in and out of the melody.

I was particularly taken with Charlie Parker and the early beboppers. I knew a lot of soldiers who came back after the war and felt alienated by what had happened to jazz, but I was crazy about it. I remember the first time I heard Parker. It was at the legendary Birdland, and I didn't even know who he was at the time. I was so intensely overcome with emotion at what I heard that I actually went into the alley behind the club and threw up.

By studying the great artists over the years, I've learned ways to keep the public's interest. I spent a lot of time with Count Basie, and his music was all about dynamics and nuances, first soft and then BOOM! There would be unexpected little body blows and then knockout punches, BOOM, BOOM, BAM! I try to do the unexpected so that the audience doesn't know what's going to happen next.

I was fortunate to catch the tail end of an era when performers helped each other out. There was camaraderie then. Established stars helped young performers coming up. If you got a hit song, the veterans took you along with them on the road and helped you break in. And the public was so encouraging. They rooted for you if they saw that you were nervous and you were trying, and they kept plugging for you. Showbiz today seems much more cutthroat. I think young performers should be encouraged and nurtured much more carefully, and be given a chance to grow.

I never did actually get a paying gig on Fifty-second Street, although I basically lived there for a few years. I did perform once at Leon and Eddie's, thanks to Milton Berle and Jan Murray, who had heard me sing and arranged for me to perform at the club on a Sunday night so agents could come in and see me.

The wonderful entertainer Barbara Carroll invited me to sing with her at a club called La Cava on Fifty-second Street, and that was a terrific break. She said, "Come in and just sing, and maybe someone will hear you." I did that for a while, still making no money, but I did get free drinks and experience. One night someone came up to me and said, "There's a big songwriter in the audience, Rube Bloom. Sing for him." He had written "Don't Worry 'Bout Me," and many other standards. I started singing for Mr. Bloom, looking right at him, but instead of being flattered by the attention, he was annoyed that I was trying to catch his ear. When he discovered I wasn't going to let him enjoy his drink in anonymity, he got angry and abruptly turned his back on me. I was singing "Blue Moon," and when I got to the second chorus, I sang, "Rube Bloom, you saw me standing alone." He got up, threw his money down on the table, and stormed out of the place. Timing is everything.

My closest friend in these early years was Jack Wilson. We'd been friends since 1939; his family lived next door to us in the Metropolitan Apartments. When we were kids, he, my brother, and I hung out together all the time. He was a few years older than me, but that didn't make any difference because we liked to do the same things. Jack and I discovered that we both wanted to make it in the music business. Most kids would get together and talk about girls or sports, but not us. All we thought about was music. I had my heart set on singing, but Jack was an aspiring songwriter. We listened to the latest big band records and got to know them so well that we could stand on the corner and scat-sing all the solos. We sang for dimes on the streets of Astoria. It was a great friendship.

I taught Jack about drawing and painting, and he taught me about poetry, but not from a book. Jack had the mind and soul of a poet, and I was very much inspired by his point of view. Before the war he used to talk about the three bridges that connected Astoria to the rest of the world. The Queensboro Bridge went straight into midtown Manhattan. We played hooky (same as I did with my friend Rudy DeHarak), and we'd catch all the big band shows—Glenn Miller, Tommy Dorsey, and Frank Sinatra—and the comics, like Bob Hope and Red Skelton. The Triborough Bridge took us uptown to Harlem and the world of jazz: the Apollo Theater and the Savoy, Count Basie and Billie Holiday, soul food and church choirs. Then there was the Hell Gate Bridge, the bridge that really set us dreaming. We saw these long freight trains coming in from all over the country, one boxcar after another. We'd try to count them, but we'd always lose track. Jack and I would imagine where they'd come from, where they were going. Some nights we'd go watch the barges and ships in the river, and it was the same kind of feeling. Those trains and boats really fed our wanderlust and made us dream about all the wonderful places we hoped our music would take us.

During our wanderings around town, Jack introduced me to Abby Mann, an aspiring screenwriter and director who was struggling just like the rest of us. At the time Jack and Abby were throwing ideas together for a musical comedy, and the three of us met on Central Park South. We'd been hanging around for a while, looking at the grand apartments lining the street, and I remember that we said to each other how glorious it would be to live in one of those fancy places along the park. I can't help feeling it was some kind of omen or something, because that's exactly where I live today. Abby and I have been friends ever since. His writing career was a big success, and he eventually went on to win an Oscar for his screenplay of *Judgment at Nuremberg.*

I introduced Jack to Freddy Katz, and from that point on the three of us were together almost constantly. Jack and Freddy became a great writing team. Jack wrote the words, Freddy wrote the music, and then the three of us went around town to different record companies to "demonstrate" the finished compositions by performing them live. Today musicians use what they call demo tapes that are mailed out to record companies or music publishers in hopes of selling their work. In those days we sold our work live. One day we decided to try our luck at the Paramount Theater. Frankie Laine was on the bill with Stan Kenton and his Orchestra, and June Christy was his vocalist. We got backstage and demonstrated the song for them. They all liked it, and Frankie Laine said to me, "Why are you demonstrating songs? You should be the one making records and singing here on this stage!" I was floored.

Freddy was working primarily as a pianist and accompanist for different singers then, but the bandleader Skitch Henderson knew what a great cellist he was and hired him to play in the orchestra at the Capitol Theater. He played for the entire show, including for the headliner, Lena Horne. One of Lena's arrangers, Phil Moore, had written a very fancy orchestration of "Frankie and Johnnie" for her, with a really difficult cello part, and Freddy carried it off with characteristic aplomb. After the run was over, they had a big cast party, and Freddy got a chance to impress everybody with his piano playing. Lena liked it so much that a few weeks later he got a call from her manager offering him the job as her accompanist. Needless to say, he took it.

Freddy also played piano for a while for the up-and-coming Vic Damone. Vic was being managed by a man named Ray Muscarella. He ran a few businesses in Brooklyn, his family owned a winery down in Little Italy, he managed prizefighters, and he dabbled in show business. In those days, there wasn't a business or industry that wasn't connected one way or another with the underworld and nightclubs were run by unsavory characters. It was understood by everyone in the business that if you wanted to play the big clubs, if you really wanted to make it, sooner or later you'd run into one of these guys. There was nothing you could do to avoid it. The underworld also ran the jukebox operations across the country, and it's no secret that they built Las Vegas.

Freddy was always talking me up to Ray, so sometime around late 1948 he agreed to give me an audition. We got together in the basement of Freddy's house, and he played the piano and I sang. Ray Muscarella loved it.

So Ray became my manager. When Jack Wilson found out, he pulled me aside. "You realize, don't you," he said, "what we're talking about here?" He wanted to make sure I knew what I was getting into. But I felt that I couldn't pass up the chance to get the good gigs I was sure Ray could get me.

Jack was completely opposed to my getting involved with Ray. He said, "You're making the wrong move." I told him that I'd been scuffling long enough, living on ten cents a day all these years, and I just couldn't turn down any kind of help. Ray was going to give me financial backing, and I was sure he was gonna make something happen. But Jack was adamant. He felt so strongly about it that he really let me have it: he took his best shot and slapped me hard right in the face. I knew he had my best interest at heart, though, and we worked things out between us. When I started touring, Jack even became my road manager for a while.

⬩⬩⬩

With Ray as my manager, I felt for the first time that somebody professional really believed in me, somebody who could actually do something for me. He started in right away by getting me a good gig at the Shangri-La in Astoria, where I had sat in with Tyree Glenn. That first night I was wearing a new suit and the club hung out an enormous picture of me. I was so excited about my first real publicity shot that I not only saved the picture, I made a special frame for it.

Ray was convinced I could make it, but he thought I needed some polishing first, and I agreed. He hired coaches and arrangers for me, starting with a guy named Nat Debin. Nat was a nice guy, but he wasn't the right teacher for me. His teaching technique was just too stiff. I've learned that just as important as practicing the proper technique is knowing how to relax. You can't be concerned about technique every minute or you'll never get the emotion across. The trick, really, is to learn all the rules and then throw it all away and be yourself.

Ray got me a spot on the *Arthur Godfrey's Talent Scouts* program, which was in the tradition of the famous radio program, *Major Bowes Original Amateur Hour* and its TV successor, the *Ted Mack Amateur Hour*. Godfrey was a giant on radio and early television, the Jack Paar of his day. The Godfrey show differed from the Bowes and Mack shows in that the focus wasn't on pure amateurs but on "rising" young talents who hadn't made it yet. I appeared on the show with another unknown singer by the name of Rosemary Clooney. Freddy Katz wrote out a special arrangement for me, and it went over well, but I lost to Rosie, who by that time was already touring with Tony Pastor and his Orchestra. It's funny: I remember she sang a song called "Golden Earrings," but I can't recall what number I performed.

Rosie has always been good, a natural singer, and she was the first big star to do a whole album with Duke Ellington. We worked together a lot over the next few years. She jokes that I more than got even with her for beating me on that show: for most of the last decade we've been competing in the same category at the Grammy® Awards, and she likes to kid about losing to me every year. She says, "Maybe I'm in the wrong category. I should be in the category for women over sixty who were born in the Ohio Valley." Around the time of the 1998 Grammy Awards, Rosie was very sick. She ran a temperature of 107 degrees, and the doctors didn't think she was going to make it. She later told me that when she was unconscious she had fever dreams, and in one dream she was surrounded by fifteen Tony Bennetts, all walking up to her and handing her the Grammy! What a great person she is, my buddy. I'll always love her.

I appeared on the Arthur Godfrey show right around the time Pearl Bailey came to Greenwich Village to check out the Village Inn. The club owner would let me come down, hang out, and perform whenever they had an open spot. I was sitting at the bar one night and I overheard him say to the bartender that he was planning to turn the club into a more legitimate showroom and that he was trying to persuade the legendary performer Pearl Bailey to headline the room. After the show, the club owner came up to me and, much to my astonishment, said, "Miss Bailey agreed to play the room on the condition that you, 'that Joe Bari guy,' stay on the bill." I couldn't believe it! "Can you beat that?" he said. "If you don't stay, she ain't gonna play the room. And I was gonna tell ya' to take a hike."

That was, as they say, my first big break. It was also the beginning of a long and wonderful friendship between Pearl and myself, a relationship that grew even closer when she married my dear friend, the wonderful drummer Louis Bellson, in 1952. Pearl wanted me to know just how much hard work lay ahead of me. She said to me, "I can start you out, kid, but it's going to take you ten years to learn how to walk on the stage." It was great advice, but she probably underestimated how long it actually takes to get everything right. I think all performers starting out today should be given the same advice, so that a little bit of success early on doesn't go to their heads and screw up their future careers.

I learned a lot from Pearl, especially how not to take any nonsense from anybody. There was a girl in the chorus line at the Village Inn who was very jealous of Pearl's success and had it in for her. One night when Pearl was dancing, this girl got behind her and started mimicking her dancing, trying to make a fool of her. So Pearl, without missing a beat, just turned around and knocked her out! Then she turned to the audience and said, "That's the end of the show, folks. I can't top that!" Classic Pearl Bailey.

She always took great care of me and had me work with her whenever she could. She once hosted her own TV special for PBS and brought in Sarah Vaughan and myself as her guests. She had a fifteen-week series on ABC and she invited me to come on. It was really special, since Louis Bellson was playing and conducting the orchestra; it was so comfortable I felt like I was hanging out with friends and jamming. Pearl was a great lady who treated me very kindly. She gave me a copy of her autobiography that was inscribed: "To my son Antonio—Mama Pearl." What an honor.

In the spring of 1949, Ray arranged for my first record date for a small label called Leslie Records, owned by Sy Leslie. Their claim to fame was that they had made a couple of successful records featuring famous baseball players.

I was thrilled to find out that George Simon would be producing my recording session. George, the head writer for *Metronome*, the greatest music magazine of all time, was already a legend in the business. He always knew who the best bands and singers were. It was thrilling to be in a full-fledged recording studio for the first time, and I was grateful for the opportunity to work with George. He knew more about music and had a bigger record collection than anybody I ever met. Spending an evening with him at his place in the West Fifties was like taking a course in the history of jazz.

The recording from this session was a two-sided 78 RPM disc, as all records were then. One side was an original composition by George, an Italian-style novelty called "Vieni Qui." The other side was the Gershwin standard "Fascinating Rhythm." I'm proud that I sang a Gershwin song at the very start of my recording career—for me, that really was beginning at the top! We did it at the New York Decca studios on Fifty-seventh Street, the same historic place where Bing Crosby, Louis Armstrong, Woody Herman, Count Basie, and so many others made so many classic recordings.

There was a vocal group backing me up who had recently worked with Bing Crosby on his recording of "Jamboree Jones," a Johnny Mercer song. The group had earlier been known as the Skyriders but had, by this time, changed their name to the Tattlers.

"Vieni Qui" and "Fascinating Rhythm" by "Joe Bari" went absolutely nowhere, but it was still a kick for me to have a record of my own. My friend John Cholakis had a cousin who owned a bar called the Rainbow Bar and Grill out in Far Rockaway. As soon as we got a copy of the disc, John and I hopped on the Long Island Railroad and went straight to the bar and put the record on the jukebox. That was a thrill too. It's been almost fifty years since I made that record and I can't say I remember what it sounds like. The one copy I had literally crumbled in my hands in the 1960s.

There's another record I made a few months after the Leslie record that's been completely lost. This was a "demonstration disc" of two old songs I loved—another rhythm song, "Crazy Rhythm," and a great old standard I remembered from the early thirties, "The Boulevard of Broken Dreams."

Ray was trying everything he could to get some attention for me. He used every contact he had in the music business, one of whom happened to be a very smart show-business lawyer named Jack Spencer. Spencer had a number of famous clients, the biggest of whom was Cole Porter. Mr. Spencer was friendly with Hugh Martin, the composer who had written the great score to *Meet Me in St. Louis* for Judy Garland (which included one number I later recorded, "The Trolley Song"). So they sent me over to Hugh Martin's apartment with my demo disc of "Boulevard of Broken Dreams" and told me "When he plays the record, have him call us and tell us what he thinks."

Mr. Martin called and said, "This kid is another Martha Raye!" Now, lately people think of Martha Raye strictly as a comedienne, and of course she was one of the best. Charlie Chaplin, in his whole career, hardly ever hired another comic to work opposite him—Jack Oakie in *The Great Dictator* and Buster Keaton in *Limelight* were practically the only ones, and Martha Raye in *Monsieur Verdoux*. She was also a truly great vocalist. So I was very flattered by Mr. Martin's comparison. That comment also confirmed for Ray that he had made the right decision in taking me on.

Through Ray, I eventually found a vocal coach who was just right for me, and he was about the most spontaneous guy I ever met. A tremendous musician and a great person, his full name was Tony Tamburello, but he sometimes worked under the name "Tony Burrell," and usually everybody just called him Tony T. When I first met Ray, he had me and two other singers audition for Tony T., who immediately pointed to me and said, "This guy is the one you want." I was always grateful for that.

Tony T. was one of the first to teach me one of the big lessons of my life: he told me never to compromise and to stay with good music; a sentiment that Frank Sinatra would reaffirm years later. Tony T. was a terrific coach. We just rolled up our sleeves and got to work, full of ambition to make something happen. We spent hours working on a song or an arrangement, never thinking about the time.

Tony T. could play every great song ever written, and his playing was as smooth as silk, just brilliant. He was like a character in a Fellini movie, way ahead of his time. As an example of his sense of humor, he started his own label, which he called "Horrible Records," and the company's slogan was "If it's a horrible record, it's bound to be a hit!" He also started a company called "MOB Records," which featured a singer named "Al Dente." The discs were pressed at "45 Caliber Speed." He rented space in the famous Brill Building, but when the rents got too expensive for him, he got one of those huge old dry-cleaning trucks and put a little spinet piano in the back. He rigged up a staircase so people could get in and out, and he gave vocal lessons in the truck! Students would call to make an appointment, and he'd say, "Meet me at the corner of Seventh and Forty-ninth at three o'clock." That was the address of the Brill Building, and when his students got there, they were surprised to find they'd be having their lesson *outside* the building. He even had someone paint "Fresh Fish and Music" on the side of the truck.

For years Tony T. was practically my musical conscience. When songwriters came around with something they wanted me to hear, Tony T. acted as a buffer, helping me find the good songs, which I sang and recorded. I like to think that after fifty years of singing professionally I know what I'm doing, but I still wish I had Tony T. with me.

⚓

Ray had one other connection that was to prove important to me: a man named Charlie Cooley, who worked for Bob Hope. At the beginning of Hope's career, Bob had a vaudeville act opening for Charlie, who had given him one of his first breaks. Bob had been a tough kid; he came right from the streets and had done time in reform school, so for Charlie to give him a break meant a lot to him, and he never forgot it. Bob's a wonderful man. Anybody who ever did Bob Hope a favor of any kind has had it repaid tenfold. Anybody who helped him, any of the girls who went on the USO tours—he always made sure to use them in one of his movies or on one of his NBC-TV specials. Charlie stayed on Bob's payroll for the rest of his life.

Ray waited until Bob Hope was in town playing the New York Paramount, then he called Charlie and got him to come down to the Village Inn and catch the show with Pearl and myself. Charlie liked what he heard well enough to bring Bob back with him. So the same week Pearl Bailey saw me at the

Village Inn, Bob Hope came down to check out my act. He liked my singing so much that after the show he came back to see me in my dressing room and said, "Come on, kid, you're going to come to the Paramount and sing with me." The Paramount! Talk about the big time! Bob Hope and Pearl Bailey, all in the same week! But first he told me he didn't care for my stage name and asked me what my real name was. I told him, "My name is Anthony Dominick Benedetto."

"Oh, no, too long for the marquee," he said. (Little did he know that someday there'd be a performer named Engelbert Humperdinck.) He thought for a moment, then he said, "We'll call you Tony Bennett."

And that's how it happened. A new Americanized name, the start of a wonderful career and a glorious adventure that has continued for fifty years.

It was an honor to be part of Bob Hope's troupe. I could hardly believe it: here I was performing with the man I felt had saved my sanity during the war and who had inspired me to go into show business. It was a dream come true.

He had a great bunch of people working with him: Jane Russell, the great tap dancer Steve Condos, and Les Brown and his wonderful Band of Renown. They were all very supportive. I was young and didn't know what to do with myself while I was singing. Between Bob Hope and Pearl Bailey, what an amazing education I had! They showed me the value of being positive: when you walk out on a stage, the audience has to know that you want to be there, that you want to entertain them. I'm still using what they taught me fifty years later.

When I finished my number, Bob said to the audience, "Well, I was getting tired of Crosby anyhow!" It was a great line and helped me win over the audience at the Paramount.

It was also a thrill working with Les Brown. His was the first major band I ever sang with. I remember being so excited about that gig that I ran out and bought myself a brand new zoot suit for the occasion. Working with great musicians like the kind Les had in his Band of Renown really rubbed off on me. I sang a couple of songs a night, mainly tunes from the early recordings I had done—"Crazy Rhythm," "Fascinating Rhythm," and "Boulevard of Broken Dreams." But I kept working hard to become a better singer.

When the gig at the Paramount ended, Bob took me and the rest of the troupe on a brief six-city tour. Everywhere Bob Hope went, people went crazy; in each town the local sheriff and the entire police force escorted us to the theater. Every night was an event.

That tour was the first time I ever flew. Bob did everything first class. He was one of the first entertainers to fly from city to city, which I guess he got a taste for in the war. The tour ended when we reached the West Coast. I didn't do Bob's radio show at that time, but I got to attend a broadcast, and meet Margaret Whiting, one of my favorite singers, who was a regular on Bob's show at that time. At one point I sang for her, and her reaction was one of warm approval. Bob also introduced me to Bing Crosby when he dropped by the show one day, and that was one of the greatest thrills of my life.

It wasn't long after I got back from the coast that I had another happy surprise coming to me. Ray had been sending out copies of my demo disc to anybody he thought would listen. As it turned out, the "Boulevard of Broken Dreams" disc had attracted the attention of a gentleman named Mitch Miller, who had just taken over as head of the "pop singles" division of Columbia Records. I didn't know exactly what was in store for me, but I did know that getting a recording contract was the next big step.

In the Columbia Records studio in the early 1950s

By the time I arrived in 1950, Columbia Records was the oldest record company in business. William S. Paley, who owned CBS radio, bought Columbia Records in the late thirties and quickly established it as a major label by releasing recordings by some of my favorite acts: Count Basie, Kay Kyser, Mildred Bailey, Gene Krupa, and Benny Goodman. He even signed Harry James's "boy singer" Frank Sinatra.

The label grew throughout the big band era, then signed the pop singers who succeeded those bands in the late forties. Mannie Sachs headed "artists and repertoire" (A&R), the department responsible for discovering and developing new talent for the label. He launched the careers of Sinatra, Dinah Shore, and Buddy Clark, acts that ended up selling more records for Columbia than any other artists before. At the end of the forties, Mannie was offered a better deal at RCA Records, and he took it. Columbia went into a panic.

Paley decided to restructure the company and brought two men into the picture who would have a tremendous impact on my recording career: British-born Goddard Lieber-son, a composer who went into the business side of music, and producer Mitch Miller.

Goddard Lieberson had a reputation for fighting hard to ensure that the business side of music never overwhelmed his artists. He was appointed Columbia's executive vice president, and started recording cast albums from original Broadway shows. He was the first to realize that the original cast package was perfect for the new medium known as the LP, or long-playing record, which Columbia had recently introduced. *South Pacific* became their biggest album, selling over a million and a quarter copies, unheard of sales at that time.

Mitch Miller had recently headed A&R at Mercury Records, where he'd been responsible for making that company a major force in the industry. Lieberson persuaded the top management at Columbia that Mitch was the guy to replace Mannie Sachs. Mitch had started out as a classical oboe player and gradually reinvented himself as perhaps the single most influential producer in the history of recording.

Not long after Mitch took over as head of A&R, he heard my demo discs of "Boulevard of Broken Dreams" and "Fascinating Rhythm." This was around the same time that he had his now-infamous feud with Frank Sinatra. They constantly fought over what songs Frank should record. The industry was beginning to give Mitch a lot of flack for that, and I always suspected he signed me partially to show people that he wasn't prejudiced against Italian singers! He had never heard of me, but he was so impressed by the way I sang "Boulevard of Broken Dreams" that he signed me to the label sight unseen, and selected "Boulevard" as my first single for Columbia. As it turned out, it would be one of the few times that Mitch and I saw eye to eye on the subject of repertoire.

Mitch was very supportive of me. He believed in my talent, and he wanted to make my career happen. He tended to like novelty songs, so everybody associates him with the "square" side of the pop scene, but that's not really fair. Mitch innovated the "Sing Along with Mitch" records that became so popular that the concept was turned into a television show, making "Mitch Miller" a household name. His trademark was his goatee and his cigar, and pretty soon other producers were growing goatees and smoking cigars. Everybody was imitating Mitch, so obviously they felt he had something cool going on.

The modern incarnation of Columbia Records had only been around for eleven years, so these were still the early days of the record business. I loved those days, when things were much looser and less bogged down by big business. I was still a star-struck kid back then.

We cut everything on these big old wax discs; even a major record company like Columbia hadn't begun using tape yet. Recording artists had to do four songs in a three-hour session, and we had to come into the studio with all of our songs memorized, and if you went over the three hours, Columbia would have to pay overtime to all the musicians in the studio orchestra. Sometimes it was crazy, but usually we got the job done without going into overtime.

On my first recording date with Columbia, April 17, 1950, I was so nervous I couldn't get through all four tunes like I was supposed to. I had to do two that first day, and the other two three days later. My engineer on that first date was the great Frank Laico, and he remained my engineer for the entire time I was at Columbia. We made all my records together in a magnificent old church on East Thirtieth Street that Columbia had bought and had converted into a recording studio. It was a beautiful building—the best recording studio on the planet.

Many Columbia artists, including Igor Stravinsky, Frank Sinatra, Count Basie, Dave Brubeck, Leonard Bernstein, Duke
Ellington, and Bill Evans recorded there until Columbia sold
it in the late sixties. What a shame that was.

Right from the start Frank knew how to get just the sound
I was going for, and though I've worked with other engineers
over the years, he's always been my favorite. He was able to
get inside my brain and capture the essence of my performance on record. Mitch also paired me with the great
arranger Marty Manning. Some musicians didn't think his
writing was "hip," but all I can say is that every time I made a
record with Marty, it was a hit, from "Boulevard of Broken
Dreams" to "I Left My Heart in San Francisco."

When "Boulevard of Broken Dreams" was released on
June 12, 1950, it wasn't a smash, but it was a huge local hit
and was well received by the critics. On the twenty-eighth of
that month the single earned me my first notice in Walter
Winchell's popular entertainment column. It simply said,
"Orchids, Tony, orchids." I was working in Dallas at this time
and I ran into the wonderful drummer Mickey Scrima, who
for many years had played with Harry James. He pulled me
aside and said, "Do you know what Sinatra says about you?" I
said, "Does Sinatra even know who I am?" It turned out that
Frank had said, "That kid's got four sets of balls." It was a little
raw, but it was one of the nicest things anybody ever said
about me. I was knocked out. With the attention I received in
New York, and with Frank Sinatra bantering my name around
music circles, I felt like I'd really hit the big time, and I
decided to celebrate by taking my first-ever vacation. I went to
Miami, hung around on the beach, and basked in my first real
success.

I began getting some good work on radio and TV. A producer named Irving Mansfield, who was married to Jacqueline

Susann (she was around the early TV scene before she became an author), came up with a concept for a summer replacement show called *Songs for Sale,* basically a talent contest for aspiring songwriters. Each week two popular male and female singers sang the songs of that week's contestants, and then a panel of experts judged the songs they'd just heard. I was chosen as the male singer, and my great friend Rosemary Clooney was chosen as the female vocalist. Jan Murray was the host. The show started on CBS radio on June 30, and beginning on July 7, it was simulcast on CBS-TV.

Gary Stevens was one of the producers of *Songs for Sale.* It was Gary's job to put together the panel of judges for each week's show. He always made a point of having a well-known songwriter and at least one radio deejay in addition to "a regular guy" who would represent the opinion of the man in the street. Gary had several reasons for bringing in the deejays. For one thing, they knew as much about songs as anybody. For another, Gary knew that if they were going on a TV show on Friday night, they'd spend the preceding week promoting the show in their local markets. It was free advertising. A lot of famous jocks got their first TV exposure on *Songs for Sale.*

Gary did a great job assembling the panel of judges, but unfortunately the same thing can't be said for whoever it was who picked the contestants. They were never selected on the basis of their songwriting ability. The producers made a point of picking the wackiest, weirdest people in the world for the show, and then considered it entertaining when these people made fools of themselves on national TV. I thought it was cruel.

Needless to say, the songs these characters came up with were consistently mediocre but we had to sing them. We didn't have time to actually memorize the songs, since they were different every week and eminently forgettable, so we had to rely on cue cards. This was before there were professional cue card holders, and the producers made the mistake of using the stagehands to hold the cards up. It was clear they'd rather be drinking or playing poker, and that they hated actually working, so they'd intentionally hold the cue cards sideways or upside down. Anything to make it more difficult for us, and these songs were already tough enough to sing! We were in a panic every week because we often had to make up our own lyrics, live on the air. It was a disaster.

I managed to slip in a good song once without the producers realizing I'd done it: the tune "Kiss You," with words by my old friend Jack Wilson. Jack was a professional songwriter by this time, but we were able to get his song onto the show on the grounds that Jack's collaborators, Georgie Brown and Alex Fogarty, were unknowns.

Only one song a week could win, and the losing songwriters inevitably blamed Rosie and me. They would corner us somewhere and harass us to no end. In order to avoid their attentions we were experts at finding sneaky exits out of the studio, taking our leave through basements and down fire escapes. All that for a hundred dollars a week!

But what was nice was, the three of us—Rosemary, Jan, and myself—got our picture in the *New York Times* as a result of being on that program. It was the first time the *Times* ever covered me, and I can still remember what a thrill it was. We also did a brief tour of the local movie theaters, the first time I worked that circuit since I was with Bob Hope's show.

Around the same time, Hubbell Robinson, a top booking agent at MCA, called Mitch to see if he had any ideas for a radio series that could serve as a summer replacement for Bob Crosby's daily variety show. Mitch said, "I've got two fabulous young people here, Tony Bennett and Rosemary Clooney." So on Mitch's suggestion CBS put together a show called *Steppin' Out*. It aired every weeknight from 7:45 to 8:00 PM, beginning on July 3, 1950. We did *Steppin' Out* five nights a week, then on Friday night we'd stick around and go directly into the simulcast of *Songs for Sale*.

I guess Hubbell Robinson didn't like how we handled the show, because after one week he called Mitch and tried to fire us. Mitch told him that we were the best young talents he knew, and that he was getting us for nothing, so the least he could do was to keep up his end of the bargain. Mitch talked to Goddard Lieberson, who then talked to William S. Paley. We were able to continue on the show, and as a last bit of advice Mitch told Robinson, "Enjoy them while you can. Next year, you won't be able to afford either one of them."

We were glad to do that show because the songs were first class, but it was only what they called a "sustaining series"; there was no commercial sponsor, so we didn't have the budget for a full orchestra. But we did have a great quintet led by Johnny Guarnieri, a masterful pianist who'd played with both Lester Young and Frank Sinatra. *Steppin' Out* was a joy.

My career has covered the whole history of television. It's wild to think about how much it's evolved since 1950. I've worked with all the greats of the medium—Edward R. Murrow, Ed Sullivan, Dave Garroway, Jack Paar, and Steve Allen. I did the first *Tonight Show with Johnny Carson,* and I did the first *Merv Griffin Show*. I've kicked off a lot of new television shows in my time, and it's an honor I'll always be proud of.

⁜

I went back into the studio on July 14, 1950. This time I worked with arranger-conductor Percy Faith. The folks at the label were looking for a song to build upon the success of "Boulevard of Broken Dreams." There was a song floating around at that time that had been a country hit for Red Foley on Decca, and for Kitty Kallen and Richard Hayes on Mercury, a semireligious tune called "Our Lady of Fatima." My producers thought I should try recording my own version, since it was a proven hit.

In those days, "cover records," the recordings of songs previously made popular by another artist, were standard industry policy. What usually happened was that a smaller label would have a hit, like pianist Francis Craig doing "Near You," with a little outfit called Bullet Records. When it started selling, RCA got into the act and "covered" it with their own instrumental version by staff arranger Larry Green. Sometimes white artists "covered" Black artists, or mainstream artists "covered" country artists. Normally the big label's profits would leave the independent label's in the dust, so the majors were always on the lookout for successful independent tunes that one of their artists could cover.

One of the things I liked about Mitch was that he didn't believe in making "cover" records, particularly the kind in which the original record was mimicked note for note, nuance for nuance. Mitch always said that he would rather spend the same energy creating original hits. But this was early in Mitch's career at Columbia, before he became a power figure at the label, so when Columbia's sales department wanted another hit, Mitch obliged by getting Percy and me together in the studio to record "Our Lady of Fatima." It was a hokey tune, but it was an important record for me because it was the first time Percy and I worked together.

The song caused little fanfare when it was released, and Columbia sent me right back into the studio. I could sense that the label was becoming concerned, and we both knew that I needed another hit to keep my career moving forward. Although my live engagements were going well, I wasn't selling records. I released eight singles between August 1950 and January 1951, and none of them went anywhere. "Boulevard of Broken Dreams" was a big enough regional hit for me to get jobs on the road as far away as Ohio and Pennsylvania, but nothing had broken through on the national level.

By the spring of 1951, I was told that if I didn't get a hit soon I'd be dropped from the label. I went into Percy's office and he said, "In this next session you really have to deliver. We have only three songs ready, so we need another song." I remember that he looked through a bunch of sheet music on his desk, grabbed a song, and said, "Well, let's do this one." That song was "Because of You." I was doing a lot of dramatic singing on my early records like "Sing You Sinners" and "Boulevard," but Percy said to me, "Just relax. Use your natural voice and sing the song." I took his advice.

When "Because of You" was released, the record company didn't have much confidence in me. But then something interesting started happening: the record didn't get on the radio right away, but people were playing it on jukeboxes so often that it started to build momentum, one nickel at a time. It was unusual for a song to become popular on jukeboxes before it got on the radio, but this one did. Listeners from all around the country began calling their local radio stations and requesting "Because of You," and it reached number one on *Billboard* magazine's pop chart on June 23, 1951. It stayed on the chart for thirty-two weeks— ten weeks at number one. I finally had my first major hit record.

It was amazing. Everywhere I went that summer I heard the song blaring from car radios, and record stores set up speakers outside and played the song to attract customers. My family was thrilled, of course, and couldn't stop telling me how proud they were that I had made it. It was wonderful.

"Because of You" sold a million copies, and *Billboard* put me on the cover with Mitch Miller and Harry Siskind, owner of one of the country's leading jukebox companies. Suddenly my songs were being played everywhere, and my records were selling. I was really enjoying my success, but the funny thing was, I couldn't help thinking that I had jinxed myself when I took that monthlong trip to Miami right after my initial success with "Boulevard." It taught me never to take a vacation when the public is clamoring for you.

⚓

We recorded fifteen more songs that year. Those sessions turned out to be a gold mine. "Cold, Cold Heart" also hit *Billboard*'s number one spot, and three other songs from those sessions were all in the top twenty: "I Won't Cry Anymore," "Blue Velvet," and "Solitaire." That was kind of the moment of truth for me. All of a sudden I had to deliver, and I did. I felt the way I imagine a baseball player feels when he hits a home run when the bases are loaded.

When Mitch first played me Hank Williams's "Cold, Cold Heart," I have to admit I didn't think I should sing it. In those days country artists still used the old-time fiddle, and I told Mitch that I couldn't do it. He told me just to listen to the words and music, pointing out how beautiful the ending was: "Why can't I free your doubtful mind / And melt your cold, cold heart?" He convinced me, and I recorded it. The song started out slowly at first, but it caught on, and it kept climbing the charts until it was number one.

I'd never heard of Hank Williams before then, though I soon learned that he was the single most important figure in all of country music. Back then there wasn't the "crossover" between different styles of music that there is today. If you listened to country music, you probably never heard pop music, and vice versa. Williams had reached the top of the country ladder in 1949 when he joined the cast of the Grand Ol' Opry, and by then virtually all of his records were hits in the Bible Belt and the Midwest. All you have to do is listen to Hank's records to understand why he was so popular. He was the greatest.

Thanks to "Cold, Cold Heart," Hank's songs finally caught on with the rest of the country. This was the first time a country song had crossed over to the top-forty mainstream chart—it even became an international hit. I never met Hank in person, but one day he called me on the phone and said, "Tony, what's the idea of ruining my song?" He obviously had a sense of humor. We sold two million copies of "Cold, Cold Heart," and I'm sure he did quite well by it. Later, Hank's friends told me how much he loved my recording and said that whenever he passed a jukebox, he'd put a nickel in and play my version.

Hank died in 1953 when he was only twenty-nine years old. A few years later I had the privilege of being invited down to Nashville to pay homage to his memory on *The Grand Ol' Opry* TV show. In those days they were very strict about what was authentic country music and what wasn't: just violin, bass, and guitar. Anything else, including drums, was off limits. When I passed out my arrangement to the Opry musicians, one of the guitar players put the arrangement aside and said, "You just sing and we'll follow you." So I sang it the same way I always did, and they accompanied me beautifully.

Mitch customarily reserved Monday afternoons to audition new material, and songwriters and demo singers lined up the entire length of the hall outside Mitch's office. When songwriter Bernie Wayne got his chance to play "Blue Velvet" for Mitch, he got as far as the first line, "She wore blue velvet..." when Mitch interrupted and said, "How about Tony Bennett?" Bernie said, "Don't you want to hear the rest of the song?" and Mitch answered, "Quit while you're ahead!"

I was on a roll. With a second hit single I was getting a lot of bookings and having a great time on the road, but the one thing that made me unhappy was Columbia wouldn't let me use my musicians when we recorded. Mitch and Percy Faith insisted on using their guys, who were great, but I was building up a rapport with my trio that's hard to duplicate with studio musicians. My great drummer Billy Exiner had been with me from the beginning, but it wasn't until 1955 that I was able to have him at my Columbia recording sessions.

Billy was something of a legend among musicians: he'd never even touched a drumstick until he was twenty-four years old. When he was a merchant seaman, he was at a dance when the drummer, who had to leave the stand, asked him to take over. He did, even though he'd never played before. He eventually became one of the great drummers of all time.

My pianist throughout 1951 was a fine musician from Boston named Jack Medoff. When Jack left in 1952 I was able to get Gene di Novi, an old friend of Billy's. I knew Gene from Charlie's Tavern and the other musicians' hangouts in New York. He'd been one of the original bebop pianists on Fifty-second Street in the late forties. Back in those days there were only a few piano players who could handle the new music, and Gene was one of them. He had the honor, at a very young age, of playing with jazz giants like Charlie Parker, Dizzy Gillespie, Benny Goodman, and Lester Young, just to name a few.

All my records were hitting the charts at the same time. I was on a real lucky streak. While "Because of You" and "Cold, Cold Heart" were still hot, I was booked into the Paramount as a headliner. This was the first time I was the main attraction, and I was thrilled. I was on the same bill as Louis Prima and his Orchestra, featuring Keely Smith and the Vanderbilt Boys, and the movie feature was *The Flying Leathernecks*, starring John Wayne.

The shows were more fun to watch than they were to perform in, let me tell you: I did seven shows a day starting at ten-thirty in the morning—I'm still numb just thinking about them! There were at least three distinct audiences coming in to see the shows. In the morning we had kids, some who had probably ditched school the way I had in the early forties. In the afternoon came the senior citizens, and then in the evening the young lovers and married couples. Bob Whitman and Nat Shapiro, managers of the Paramount, insisted that we do material that would appeal to everybody, not just one age group, so we had to find songs that everybody loved. Today it's completely the opposite. I dislike the concept of demographics—targeting certain segments of the market—because it puts everyone in categories. There's no reason that if you sing good songs the whole family won't like them. On this subject, Duke Ellington always quoted Toscanini: "Music is either good or it isn't. It's not someone's opinion."

I was set to open on September 19, 1951. Ray Muscarella and Sid Ascher, the press agent he'd hired, were determined that this would be a big deal. Ray owned a whole fleet of trucks as part of his family's wine business, and he had them all specially wired for transmitting sound. The trucks made a parade starting in Little Italy, playing "Because of You" as loud as they could all the way to the Paramount in midtown Manhattan. You could hear it in Astoria and Brooklyn! It got louder and louder as the trucks approached the Paramount, and by the time they were parked in front of the theater, it was a virtual Tony Bennett wall-of-sound.

Apart from his sound trucks, Ray used other publicity stunts to promote the Paramount appearance. He hired sky-writers to write "Tony Bennett—New York Paramount" across the Manhattan skyline, and on opening day I gave away American Beauty roses and handkerchiefs monogrammed "Borrowed from Tony Bennett" to the first five hundred girls. It was really quite a show. I was overwhelmed by what was happening to me: everybody knew who I was, and young girls mobbed me wherever I went.

The greatest thing about that gig was getting the chance to work with Louis Prima, another of my show business heroes. He was terrific. I always called him "The Chief." Prima was a genius of a showman, a wild man on stage that you just couldn't take your eyes off. Louis grew up in New Orleans, and he had been surrounded by gambling all his life. He knew more about it than anyone I've met, before or since. When they started building casinos and resorts in Vegas, Louis was the one who showed them how to do it. He told them where to put the casino, where to put the lounges, where to put the showroom, how to make it work. But they weren't loyal to Louis. When he came to them and wanted to open his own golf course in Vegas, they wouldn't help him out. That broke his heart.

People wondered why I was so happy to follow a strong act like Louis Prima. In fact, there are a lot of big stars, and I'm not going mention any names, who always make it a point to get a weak act to open for them; that way the "big star" can feel confident the audience can't wait for him to go on.

I've had Duke Ellington, Count Basie, Lena Horne, and the great drummer Buddy Rich in front of me on the bill. Of course they knocked everybody out, but I've worked hard at being able to follow the best in the business, and I realize that the best way to win over an audience is to give them something great right off the bat. I believe the audience deserves the best from start to finish. Every time I opened with a very dynamic act like the Step Brothers, the Nicholas Brothers, or even Louis Prima, by the time I got on stage the crowd was wide awake and at the edge of their seats. They're all thinking, "What's gonna happen now? How can anybody follow what we just saw?" Then, I just came out and did it. If the program is strong all the way through, from the first act to the last, then the public never feels cheated.

I know how important it is to reach the kids—then and now—and I was the first entertainer I know of to make a point of playing at high schools. I played three schools a day in Chicago, New York, or wherever I happened to be performing. I'd sing a few songs and then tell the kids how much I enjoyed playing for them, and I thanked them for listening to my records. It was a great way to reach an audience that otherwise would never get a chance to see me perform live.

But I was once so badly mobbed that I really got scared. I had agreed to appear at a graduation at a girl's school in Brooklyn. They were holding the ceremony in the Botanical Garden. The young ladies hadn't been informed beforehand that I was going to be there, and as soon as this very proper teacher got up on the stand and said, "Girls, don't get too excited, but we have Tony Bennett here..." the "ladies" went wild and started chasing me all over the park. They tore my clothes, took my cigarettes and everything that I had in my pockets, and made me run for my life. I had to hide in a little stone house in the park. They had me trapped like a rat!

All this attention, of course, meant that I really had made it. The first thing I did with the money I was making was buy a house for my mom. It was a nice place at 76 Valley Road in River Edge, New Jersey, and I felt so proud that I'd finally achieved my life's ambition: getting my mom to stop working. That's all I was interested in. Everything else I've done ever since has essentially been a free ride. I would have stopped singing altogether after "Because of You" and "Cold, Cold Heart" if I hadn't loved it.

But do you know what? Life is funny. When my mom was working, she was never sick a day in her life, but she fell apart the minute she stopped going to her job every day. I thought I was doing something great for her, but it was more like a curse. She couldn't afford to get sick during the years that she was struggling to take care of my father and raise her family, but I guess once she was able to relax, it hit her all at once. She was like her brother, our uncle Jim, who had been a cab-driver. It wasn't until the end of his life that he found out he'd had two heart attacks and never even felt them. He just knew he had to show up the next day for work.

If she'd kept working, maybe she'd have stayed strong. My mom was never the same. Mary and her husband, Tom Chiappa, moved in with her in River Edge, and for many years they took care of her. Mary set up my office for me, now that things were really under way, and she worked for me through most of the fifties. She's very gregarious and always great to everyone she meets. She organized my first fan club, "The Bennett-Tones," even before I was with Columbia Records, and after everything started happening for me Mary kept track of the day-to-day business. I can't say too often how much I love her. We also hired a very nice woman named Natalie Sanders as her assistant to help out around the office.

After the success at the Paramount, I was booked to appear in Miami, Chicago, Cleveland, and Buffalo. I did some further touring with Jan Murray and Rosemary Clooney, and as Mitch had predicted, my price had gone up considerably. In 1950 I was getting a hundred dollars a week, but after the success of "Because of You" I was commanding over three thousand dollars a week, top dollar at that time. Rosie and I played the Capitol Theater in Washington in October 1951, and the local press sent out their "inquiring photographer" to do a story on us. The novice reporter was a young woman named Jacqueline Bouvier, who later became Mrs. John F. Kennedy.

My asking price went up so fast that one sharp club owner was able to take advantage of it. I first worked for Ben Maksik's Town and Country, which was sort of the "Copacabana of Brooklyn," in early 1951. To get the gig, Ben insisted I come back later in the year and work at the same price. I took the deal. After all, you never know what will happen, right? And then a few months later "Because of You" became a hit. Ben called in my contractual obligation in August, when I was really soaring. People lined up around the block to see me, but all Ben had to give me was the one thousand dollars that he'd paid me six months earlier, a third of what I was getting everywhere else. It was Christmas in August for Ben.

Of all these early gigs, my biggest personal triumph was playing Chicago, and that was entirely due to Nat "King" Cole, a wonderful man and a great artist. I don't think people fully comprehend the extent of his brilliance. He was a magnificent piano player, and he could sing like an angel. Songs like "I Realize Now," "Embraceable You," and "It's Only a Paper Moon" are mesmerizing. Nat and I had the same agent, Buddy Howe, of General Artists Corporation (GAC). I came into the GAC office one day and there Nat was, all six feet and change of him. I told him I'd just come from visiting my mom in New Jersey. He asked, "Did you take a limousine?" I told him, "No. I don't use a limo. I took a bus in." He was shocked that I had all these records on the chart and I was taking the bus in from my mom's house. That knocked him out and we became friends.

At this time I was very big in New York City, but I hadn't made a dent in Chicago. It happened that Nat was booked into the Chez Paree there, but he had to cancel when he was asked to sing at the White House. He needed to have someone fill in for him, so he told the owners of the club, "Get Tony Bennett." I did the show, and I went over big.

The Chez Paree was an important gig for me. I was on the bill with Sophie Tucker, one of the all-time great ladies of show business. I'll never forget the opening night with the Step Brothers, Ford and Hines, and Sophie Tucker. The show hit so big that Sophie told us, "You guys can relax, because our contract's gonna be picked up, and we'll be here all month." And sure enough, I spent the whole month there. Miss Tucker had been such a big headliner for so many years that she always insisted on top billing. But I wanted to get at least equal billing. We resolved it by writing "Sophie Tucker and Tony Bennett" on one side of the marquee and "Tony Bennett and Sophie Tucker" on the other side. The club very carefully arranged to drive Sophie in from the "correct" direction, so she never saw the side that gave me top billing.

The audiences in Chicago were wonderfully receptive to me. They'd never seen me before, but they knew my records, and called out requests. Sophie used to stand in the wings and monitor the opening acts to make sure we didn't grab any extra stage time or go over too big with the audience. One night I wound up staying on stage for longer than my allotted time, and Sophie was fuming. When it was clear I was going to keep singing, she marched up to my road manager and hollered, "Tell your friend to get off stage!"

I met and fell in love with a young woman named Patricia Beech in July of 1951. I was singing at Moe's Main Street in Cleveland, Ohio, and one night she came in with a date. I could see her from the stage—she was sitting ringside—and I was taken with her beauty. After the show her date asked me to join them at their table, so of course I took that opportunity to introduce myself to her. I found out that she was from a little town south of Cleveland called Mansfield and that she had just graduated from high school and moved to Cleveland. Even with my newfound fame and all the attention I was getting, that night was the first time I'd met someone I wanted to see on more than a casual date.

That night was probably Patricia's first time in a nightclub. She was a big jazz fan, though, and used to listen to radio broadcasts by the famous disc jockey "Symphony Sid" Torrin. He played jazz records all night long, and as a teenager she'd stay up and listen to his show. She'd heard my singing before, but didn't own any of my records until after we met. She loved art, and had come to Cleveland in the hope of being admitted to that city's excellent art school. I was twenty-four and she was eighteen.

I managed to get her telephone number, and since I was in Cleveland for a couple of days doing promotion, I called her the next day and asked her out. That Saturday we had our first date, an unusual one since I didn't have a lot of free time in those days: we spent the day picking out neckties for me to wear on stage. She had great taste! We hung out together as much as we could, but soon I had to leave Cleveland and get back on the road. For the next couple of months we had a long-distance relationship. I called her every day, and we talked on the phone for hours about jazz and art and all kinds of things. She always came to my shows when I was playing around Ohio, which was a big market in those days, so we got to see each other quite a bit. But not enough.

Two months after we met, I invited Patricia to come and visit me in New York in time for the big show at the Paramount. I wanted her with me so that she could get a taste of what my life was like. She'd never been to the city before, and the only address she had for me was the Paramount Theater, so when she arrived she took the bus from Newark Airport right into midtown Manhattan. She was astonished to see thousands of screaming bobby-soxers surrounding the theater and clamoring for me. There were so many kids they had to be held back by police barricades. She had no idea it would be like this—the only place she'd seen me perform was in Ohio, and I guess I neglected to mention that New York City would be a little different. So different that Patricia almost didn't get in to see me because the police thought she was just another teenage Tony Bennett fan and they refused to let her backstage. She was standing there at the stage door trying to convince the doorman that I'd invited her to the show when Billy, my drummer, happened to walk by and he rescued her. What a welcome Patricia had that day!

Soon after, I convinced her to move to New York City so we could be together more often. She found a job working for a broker on Forty-fourth Street as a gal Friday. I was on the road a lot that year, but New York was always my home base, so I got to see her a lot more often than I would have if she

In a Hirschfeld sketch

Sketch of the Cole Porter Suite
at the Waldorf-Astoria

My sketch of me at the 100th anniversary of the Royal Albert Hall

Sandra Bennett

With Liza Minnelli and my daughters, Joanna and Antonia

With my best friend, Susan Crow

Me and Boo in Central Park

Dae, me, and Danny at the Village Vanguard, 1981

With Ella Fitzgerald

With Don Ienner and Michele Anthony

With Tommy Mottola

Painting, my other love, in New Orleans, 1997

Portrait of me by my mentor,
Everett Raymond Kinstler,
the most distinguished
portrait painter in America

With Count Basie

Performing on the very first *The Tonight Show with Johnny Carson*

With Bill Evans

With
Duke Ellington

Maurice Chevalier taught me, "Have champagne after
a show, and not before. If you put on a bad show,
you'll blame the liquor instead of yourself."

With Judy Garland

Harry Belafonte, Martin Luther King, Jr., and me in Selma, Alabama

MARTIN LUTHER KING, JR.

April 5, 1965

Dear Mr. Bennett:

The march from Selma to Montgomery was 50 miles. It was a long walk, but it is a symbol that those who have suffered deprivation and brutality can make their voices heard and that freedom will one day be not a cry in the dark, but a living, breathing proclamation that we have overcome, and that a whole nation has turned to a new course.

My good friend, Harry Belafonte, told me of the difficulty you had in rearranging your schedule so that you could perform at the Rally.

I speak for myself and for the courageous 300 marchers and all the other people who came to St. Jude's to be spurred on to those final miles to the capital in Montgomery. Your talent and good will were not only heard by those thousands of ears, but were felt in those thousands of hearts, and I give my deepest thanks and appreciation to you.

With warmest good wishes,

Martin

Martin Luther King, Jr.

mlk:c

Mr. Tony Bennett
271 Next Day Hill Court
Englewood, New Jersey

P.S. It was really good seeing you in Montgomery. S.C.L.C. could not make it without friends like you and neither could I. I hope our paths will cross again soon

Frank and me hanging out at Nathan's

For Tony —
The Best g.d.
Pop Singer I've
ever heard!
I Love Ya —
Frank Sinatra '86

Compliments from
the master,
Frank Sinatra

Presenting Louis Armstrong
with my portrait of him

Cary Grant provides an introduction to
Senator Robert Kennedy, 1967

With Bob and Dolores Hope in 1994

At the White House with President Clinton, 1996

With the Red Hot Chili Peppers at the 1993 MTV Music Awards

THANKS!!

TO TONY
FROM BART
and Matt Groening

Animation cel from *The Simpsons*

With Sophia Loren

had stayed in Ohio. While I was on the road with the band, Patricia stayed at Jack Medoff's empty apartment in the West Seventies until she found her own place at the Henry Hudson Hotel on West Fifty-seventh Street. It wasn't very long before I decided that I wanted to marry Patricia, and I wanted to propose to her in a dramatic way. I was headlining the Paramount again for the Christmas holidays, and I thought that New Year's Eve would be the perfect night. So during my show I announced my intentions to the world, which was a surprise to Patricia since I'd never actually *asked* her. I was fortunate that she wanted to marry me as much as I wanted to marry her, otherwise that would have been the most embarrassing night of my career.

My manager, Ray Muscarella, was also very surprised, although not as pleasantly. He didn't like the idea that his star client would have a wife, or that somebody else would be more closely involved with me than himself. He believed that if I married I wouldn't be as attractive to all the young female fans who, he thought, harbored the fantasy of someday marrying me themselves.

Ray's attitude toward Patricia was one of the major reasons that Ray and I eventually split. He constantly did little things to discourage me from marrying her. One day she was on her way to meet me at a club when she noticed that some guy was following her. He waved a wad of money at her and tried to force her to take it. He said, "Hey, lady! I won it at the track. I don't need it. I don't want it. Here, you take it." It was frightening and bizarre. Of course she didn't take the money, and when she got to the club, Ray and his brothers were hanging around waiting for her. She told me what had happened, and we figured that it was a stunt Ray had pulled—I guess he expected her to walk into the club holding a pile of bills, tell a ridiculous story about a strange man who had given the money to her, and somehow compromise herself in my eyes.

Ray pulled his biggest stunt on my wedding day. Patricia and I were originally set to get married on February 11, 1952, at St. Patrick's Cathedral in New York City, one of the most spectacular churches in America. But Ray decided we should get married on the twelfth. We didn't know why, but Patricia and I agreed. Well, it turned out that Monday, February 12, was Lincoln's Birthday, which meant that all my teenage fans would be out of school and able to show up at the church on Fifth Avenue, create a huge scene, and turn our wedding day into a publicity stunt. Ray arranged for thousands of screaming girls to mob the church; he even supplied black mourning veils for them to wear! It was so crazy that Patricia had a hard time getting into the church—the girls didn't want to let her up the steps—and Patricia never forgave Ray for it.

We honeymooned at Nassau in the Bahamas for a week, and when I got back my first gig was at Copa City in Miami with Sophie Tucker and Jack Carter. That March we visited Patricia's family in Mansfield, Ohio, and I invited everybody to come down when I played the Loew's State Theater in Cleveland. We had a great time. Patricia traveled everywhere with me, and for the first few years of our marriage we were always on the road, though we did get an apartment at Riverside Drive and Eighty-sixth Street. This was our first real place together, and we spent our time there when we weren't traveling.

By 1952 I felt I had matured both as a performer and as a person. I was a married man, I'd proven that I could create hit singles, and I was ready for the next stage in my development as an artist. I wanted to try something beyond the familiar Tony Bennett–Percy Faith sound that had given me five chart hits in 1951. Mitch had a knack for finding these snappy little novelty tunes, things like Rosemary Clooney's "Come On-A-My House," Frankie Laine's hit "Hambone," Doris Day's "Sug-arbush," Jo Stafford's "Chow Willy," and Guy Mitchell's "Pittsburgh, Pennsylvania." All of these songs were hits, but I wasn't interested in singing that type of song. Yet Mitch kept trying to push these kinds of tunes on me, and as much as we liked each other, there was always tension between us. I wanted to sing the great songs, songs that I felt really mattered to people.

Rosemary Clooney, who was recording for Columbia at the time, felt differently about this than I did. Like me, she knew from the time she was a child that she'd make her living singing. But she couldn't have cared less if she was in Maysville, Kentucky; Cincinnati, Ohio; or if she was on the road with Tony Pastor. Essentially it was just a job to her. And so for her the object of this job, like any other, was to please the people who signed the checks. When Mitch Miller gave her a song called "The Canasta Song"—she told me that she couldn't believe how bad it was, that it was just *awful*—she didn't think about it; she just did it. She worked for Mitch, and she sang whatever he told her to.

Rosie told me that when Mitch played her "Come On-A-My House," she hesitated. She asked him, "Do you think this song is a song that people will understand? And do you think that if they hear me sing this, that they'll realize I'm a singer who can do other things too?" Mitch explained the situation to her in his own sensitive way: "If you don't want to sing this song, don't bother showing up at the session tomorrow, or ever again."

Rosie was amazed that I stood up to Mitch, but she respected me for it. She knew I wasn't being disrespectful to him, or obstinate, or hard to deal with. She understood that I just could not sing a song I didn't like.

Fortunately, Mitch and I came to an understanding. We were still doing four tunes per recording session at that time, so we worked out a deal. He picked two songs and I picked two songs. Of course, even then there were certain songs he'd come up with that I just couldn't do. But on the other hand, not everything that Mitch picked was a novelty. He often showed me that he still knew a thing or two about good songs. As a result I ended up having some great sessions with Mitch. But I always had the sword out, and I was always verbally dueling with him.

I'm not saying that I was always right. I absolutely hated "Rags to Riches" the first time I heard it in 1953. They really had to tie me down on that one. But Mitch laid down the law. "I don't care what you hate. You *have* to record this," so I went along with him. Thanks to Percy's innovative arrangement, which included what he called a "double tango" in the instrumental break, I had another colossal hit and a gold record. More importantly, I grew to like the song and to enjoy singing it. Years later "Rags to Riches" was in Martin Scorsese's hit film *Goodfellas* and it became popular all over again.

There was one source for new songs that both Mitch and I agreed on. When I first came to Columbia, Cole Porter's lawyer, Jack Spencer, was trying to interest the label in me at the same time they were negotiating for the rights to *Kiss Me, Kate*. By 1953, the situation had reversed itself. I became so hot as a pop singles artist that all the Broadway producers and composers came running to Mitch pleading for me to record one of their songs.

In 1953, there was a huge newspaper strike in New York that lasted so long it actually closed down two or three newspapers permanently. Reporters couldn't review openings. The producer of *Kismet* had a brainstorm. He compelled Columbia to have me record "Stranger in Paradise"—then had New

York radio stations play it over and over again weeks before the opening. It hit the charts in November, making it all the way to the number two spot. On opening night in December, when the audience heard "Stranger in Paradise," it stopped the show cold. Word of mouth had made the song—and the show—a smash hit.

Over the years ninety different artists have recorded "Stranger in Paradise," but my version remains the biggest. It was also the first record of mine to go over really big in England, and I sang it the first time I played there in 1955. In England the song has been recorded ninety-six times, but the public eventually made mine number one.

In 1956, Jule Styne came to me with "Just In Time," the big song from his forthcoming show, *Bells Are Ringing*. The Columbia people told him, "If you want Tony to record a single of 'Just In Time,' you'll have to let Columbia Records have the cast album." That was standard policy for Columbia. Jule said, "I want Tony. No one else!" So that was that. I recorded "Just In Time" in September. I had a hit with the song and the show opened at the Shubert Theater on November 29.

We eventually collected twelve show tune singles for my 1962 album *Mr. Broadway*. I did many more Broadway show tunes over the years—enough to fill a two-CD set. I think probably the most important part of my recording legacy is that I had the privilege of introducing all those wonderful show tunes to the general public.

My habit of recording songs from Broadway shows also endeared me to Goddard Lieberson. I would record a new Broadway song, and Columbia in turn got the cast album, which became the foundation of their catalogue. Goddard was a friend of both Rex Harrison's and Alan Jay Lerner's, and when he heard about the show *My Fair Lady*, he took Columbia's involvement in the Broadway scene one giant step far-

ther. He persuaded William S. Paley to put some of Columbia's money into the show, and Columbia was rewarded a
thousandfold.

The show was the biggest hit in the history of Broadway
up to that time: Columbia not only made a fortune with their
original cast album (which they rerecorded in stereo in 1958
with the British cast); it was the biggest-selling cast album of
all time, selling five million copies by the 1960s. When the
producers of the show sold the movie rights to Warner Bros.
for five million dollars, Columbia Records made out like a
bandit. So did Goddard. *My Fair Lady* had opened on Broadway on March 15, 1956, and Goddard became president of
Columbia Records that June.

With more and more hit records, my bookings got better
and better. In April 1952, I opened at the El Rancho in Las
Vegas for the first time.

Las Vegas was just getting started as a major entertainment town in the early fifties. The first hotel-casino had
opened in 1941, featuring the now-standard showrooms,
restaurants, and entertainment lounges. The Strip contained
only two or three hotels in the forties, among them the Desert
Inn and the El Rancho, and I-95 was just a dirt road. But what
followed in the fifties was a construction boom that gave us
the glitzy gambling and entertainment capital we know and
love today. Vegas thought big right from the start, and by the
time I opened there, the Strip was packed with clubs and casinos and was already legendary. If you played Vegas, you knew
you were famous. The underworld controlled just about every
club and casino, but that was not news to me or anybody else
who played there. It was a wild place where the attitude was
"anything goes!"

Eventually, I worked all the big hotels in Vegas: the El
Rancho, the Sahara, the Sands, the Dunes, the Riviera, Cae-

sars Palace, you name it. Those were sensational days. Entertainers like myself, Dean Martin, Frank Sinatra, Sammy Davis, Lena Horne, Count Basie, Duke Ellington, Noel Coward, Marlene Dietrich, Harpo Marx, and Louis Prima really made that town happen. Playing Caesars Palace regularly came about because of my friend Dave Victorson. When I first started making it, Dave came to see me and told me, "I'm flat broke. I have to go to L.A. and try my luck." I asked him how much he needed. He said, "Five hundred dollars." So I gave it to him. About seven years later I got a call from Dave. He said, "You're coming to work for me." "What are you talking about?" I asked him. He told me he was the entertainment director for a new hotel called Caesars Palace, and remembering that favor cemented our long-term association.

My big opening of that year was in October at the Copacabana in New York City. All the superstars—Frank Sinatra, Nat "King" Cole, Ella Fitzgerald, Jimmy Durante, and Joe E. Lewis—played there. Vegas generally took its booking cues from the Copa then, and at first neither venue was too keen on what they called "record acts," which they figured were a bunch of fly-by-nighters who wouldn't bring in the right type of customer. They preferred old-line show business legends like Sophie Tucker. Once I got out on stage, I won them over.

One of the great things about my first engagement at the Copa was getting to work with Joe E. Lewis. Today he's primarily remembered as the character Frank Sinatra played in the classic movie *The Joker Is Wild*, in which Frank introduced the song "All the Way," but in his day Joe E. Lewis was an immensely popular and well-respected comedian. It was a real honor to be on the same bill with him. I felt like an amateur opening for a giant like Joe, but he was great to me. Being inexperienced, I couldn't handle the crowd at the Copa; they never stopped talking, and I didn't yet know how to hold a difficult audience like that. Joe gave me some great tips on how to grab the audience's attention. When he found out that I was going to Texas, he wrote the critics in Houston and Dallas before I got there and told them to check me out. He was a real gentleman.

⚜

By 1953, I was on the road pretty much full-time. Along with my musicians I was traveling with a radio promotions man from Columbia Records named Danny Stevens and my road manager, Dee Anthony. Toward the middle of the year my piano player Gene di Novi left me to do a solo gig at an important cabaret in New York called the Show Spot.

I made an unusual choice for my next accompanist, the remarkable guitarist Chuck Wayne. I remembered when I first heard Bing Crosby in the early thirties he had a brilliant guitarist named Eddie Lang. I liked the soft, intimate sound that a guitar brought to the songs. Chuck was an accomplished musician and could conduct the band for me as well as any pianist I ever had.

Chuck and I had a lot of wild times on the road. One night in Florida I was asleep when the phone rang around eleven-thirty PM. It was Chuck and he said, "There's a guy downtown who's really bad-mouthing the hell out of you and our act. Should I take care of him?" I said, "Wait a minute; I'll get dressed and come with you." So we walked into this club, and there was a comic on stage. Sure enough, when he saw us come in, he started dumping on us: "Ah, there's that Italian kid crooner Tony Bennett and his sidekick ukulele player Chuck Wayne. They think they're hot stuff just 'cause they're from New York City." It started out pretty mild, but he went on rapping us big time. By the time the set was over, Chuck and I were really steamed up and we went backstage to jump the guy. We walked right over to him and pushed him up against the wall. I put my hand around his neck, and Chuck put his knee in his crotch. Then I said, "Don't ever mention us again. Ever." He said, "You got it. You got it. You boys are serious." "You better believe it," I told him, and walked out. Well, I found out later the comedian's name was Don Rickles. That was at the very beginning of his career—nobody had even heard of him then. That type of insult comedy was completely new, and a lot of people, myself included, found it shocking. He was like Howard Stern today, pushing the limits of what's considered acceptable. Chuck and I laughed about the whole thing because our bark was always much bigger than our bite, but to this day Don only has nice things to say about me.

Luckily, my legion of bobby-soxer fans did not lose interest in me after I got married. In fact, my two most ardent admirers, Molly Siva and Helen Schulman, became even more determined to pursue me. For months on end, whenever I'd go anywhere in public in New York City, they were there. I'd be sitting in a restaurant, having a bowl of soup or something, and I'd look up to find them staring at me through the window. When they found out I was getting married, they sent me telegrams by the hour pleading with me to change my mind. They'd wait at the stage door at the theater where I was appearing, and when the show was over, they'd follow my cab home. When Patricia and I got back from our honeymoon, they camped out on our doorstep for days.

During one engagement at the Roxy, I gave a total of seventy performances. Molly and Helen were there for at least sixty-eight. There was a building across the street from the theater that had an unoccupied office facing directly into my dressing room. Molly and Helen convinced the owner to lend them that office space for the month. There was a huge poster of me in front of the theater, and somehow the two of them managed to make off with it. They filled their special room with sandwiches, bottles of soda, and that enormous poster, and basically lived there. Most importantly, they had a phonograph and copies of all of my records that they blasted so loud that the neighborhood heard nothing but Tony Bennett for the entire month.

Once they took a bus all the way to Asbury Park, New Jersey, to hear me perform. They missed the last bus back and wound up stranded and came crying to me in my dressing room. I called their parents and assured them that everything was all right; then Patricia took them down to the local hotel and got them a room for the night. Another time they showed up for a performance at the Copa, but they'd drastically underestimated how expensive that famously high-priced nightspot could be and again wound up coming to me. I was happy to help them get into the show. Anything for such loyal, dedicated fans!

In those days, syndicated newspaper columnists occasionally invited celebrities to fill in for them. Once in 1954, when Dorothy Kilgallen took a vacation, I wrote one installment for her as a "guest columnist." I devoted the entire column to the exploits of Molly and Helen, and that column inspired a novel by Nora Johnson called *The World of Henry Orient*, in which two schoolgirls become obsessed with a concert pianist (somehow they figured a classical musician was funnier than a pop crooner). The gag is that he's always trying to make it with some chick, and these two little girls are forever following him around and messing up his plans. It was a very funny book and was later made into a film starring Peter Sellers as Henry Orient (me!), as well as a 1967 Broadway musical entitled *Henry, Sweet Henry,* starring Don Ameche.

⌗

That June Patricia told me she was pregnant. Things couldn't have been better. My career was in full swing, and now I could look forward to starting a family. Since our apartment wasn't big enough to accommodate the new arrival, Patricia and I decided to look outside the city for a bigger place. We found an apartment at the Briar Oaks apartment complex right off the Henry Hudson Parkway a little north of the George Washington Bridge in Riverdale, New York. We lived in apartment 1012 in the first tower, a spacious four-room spread. This was much different from anywhere else I'd lived, and the view of the Hudson River and the New Jersey palisades was spectacular.

My first son, D'Andrea, was born on February 3, 1954. We were so pleased when he arrived, and Patricia wanted to choose a very special name for him. She liked the name "Andrea," but didn't want the baby to be called "Andy," so we weren't really sure about it. But then I thought of my singing teacher Pietro D'Andrea, of whom I was very fond, so we decided to put a "D" in front of "Andrea." Patricia started in right away calling him "Danny," and I also liked the idea that I could call him "Danny" because once on Fifty-second Street I had heard the great Art Tatum play "Danny Boy" so beautifully that it always stayed with me. So that's how he got the name he goes by today.

It was thrilling and at the same time a little bit frightening to think that I was now a father. Great responsibility comes with being a parent, and I didn't want to miss a day of my son growing up. I was determined that we stay together even though my career required extensive travel. Patricia agreed and we traveled with Danny from the time he was three weeks old.

Traveling was quite different then than it is today. We were all basically still kids. I was twenty-eight and Patricia was only twenty-two, and we were traveling with the whole crew. We went from city to city, often performing in one town one night and opening in another town the next. We did get to travel by plane, but again, this was back in the fifties. The planes were prop jobs, they barely flew above the clouds, and we were subjected to some pretty bumpy rides. On top of that it took twice as long as it does today to get anywhere.

We'd pack up our luggage, the baby, and all the musicians every day, get into cabs, and rush to the airport. We'd invariably arrive at the last minute. Now remember, I was traveling with some pretty hip jazz musicians, and we were all known to partake in a little recreational pot smoking; everyone but Patricia, that is. I remember one time when Patricia was learning how to make my mom's special spaghetti sauce. My mom came over to our house and showed Patricia her secret ingredients: a package of aluminum foil filled with a "stash" of herbs. Coming from a small town, Patricia had never seen oregano before and in her astonishment she thought, "Oh, my god, Tony's mom uses pot in his favorite recipe!"

The musicians' "extracurricular activities" made the organization a little less than organized. Getting everybody up and going in the morning was quite a feat. On top of that, the stand-up bass, which is about six and a half feet tall, was always too big to fit in the cargo compartment of the plane and had to have its own seat, and this was always a last minute hassle. But somehow we never missed a show in all those years, and we had a great time.

I had two more top-ten hits in 1954, Hank Williams's posthumous hit "There'll Be No Teardrops Tonight" and a novelty tune—Mitch's idea, of course—called "Cinnamon Sinner." I was especially fond of a song I recorded that year called "Funny Thing," which was credited to the excellent lyricist Carl Sigman and a little-known composer named "Arthur Williams." Actually, "Arthur Williams" was a pseudonym adopted for publishing reasons by the great tunesmith and my great friend Jimmy Van Heusen. Van Heusen had also written "Somewhere Along the Way" in the same undercover fashion, and though I also recorded that, the hit on that 1951 classic belonged to Nat "King" Cole. I thought "Funny Thing" was a great song and a likely hit, and I was disappointed when it didn't go anywhere.

At this point in my career, I became dissatisfied with just trying to turn out one pop hit after another. I wanted a hit record as much as anybody, but I knew that there was more to music than trying to beat out all the other pop singers for a top spot on the charts. I had wanted to do an LP ever since I signed with Columbia, but Mitch Miller felt that the public was really only interested in singles. Capitol, Decca, and other labels were starting to release full-length albums and were doing well with them; in fact, George Avakian, who ran Columbia's jazz division, had released albums a couple of years earlier. But Mitch really missed the boat. It wasn't until the advent of stereo sound in 1956–57 that Columbia really got behind LPs.

I was already singing a lot of jazz numbers live, and I continued to plead with Mitch and everybody else at Columbia to allow me to record a full-length jazz album. Finally, perhaps out of fear that I'd leave the label, they relented and let me have my way.

I started recording that album, *Cloud 7,* in August 1954. Two years earlier, Columbia had released an LP called *Dedicated to You,* but that was only a collection of hit singles and not an original album. *Cloud 7* was, to use a latter-day term, a genuine "concept album," and it was one of Columbia's first twelve-inch long-playing records.

Among the great musicians I was able to bring to that session were my old friend and idol, the great Al Cohn, alto saxophonist Davey Schildkraut, who like me was a big fan of Charlie Parker, and drummer Ed Shaughnessy, who later became famous as the linchpin of the *Tonight Show* band. I also brought back Gene di Novi on piano. Columbia had never wanted me to use Gene when he was officially part of my touring band in 1952 and 1953 because they thought he was too much of an upstart bebopper.

The most important player on *Cloud 7* was Chuck Wayne. He worked out all the arrangements with me, and we featured his sensitive guitar work on every song. Chuck was also smart enough to clue me in to the fact that one of the songs we included on the album, "My Reverie," was actually based on classical composer Claude Debussy's "Reverie." So here I was, a pop singer, doing an album that had both jazz and classical inspirations.

We did *Cloud 7* very inexpensively, using just six musicians on each of the two recording sessions, the first in August, the second in December, 1954. *Cloud 7* included the song "While the Music Plays On," which Miles Davis later told me was one of his favorites. It was released in February 1955. *Cloud 7* wasn't a smash hit like "Because of You," but then I wasn't expecting it to be. This was a record I wanted to make to show the world that I was capable of doing something beyond hit singles. It was a long-term investment in my career, not a fast-buck hit. Though Mitch wasn't thrilled with the album, he wasn't opposed to doing something a little high-minded once in a while.

As far as I was concerned, *Cloud 7* was a triumph. It proved that I was ready for some major changes in my career.

"Beat of My Heart" session

I parted company with Ray Muscarella in 1955. My career really got started during the early years with Ray, and though I appreciated how much he had helped me, I questioned some of the engagements that were being presented to me—they weren't exactly the kind of career moves that I wanted to be making. I didn't feel that I had my finger on the pulse of my career, and I wanted to have more control over my own destiny. I had my lawyer negotiate an agreement with Ray that gave him ten percent of everything I earned for the next five years. Even then, Ray was reluctant to let me go, but the offer was a very generous one, and my lawyer convinced him to take the deal. I made sure I never missed a payment, and when the five years were finally over, I felt a new freedom. My sister Mary stepped in and managed my career.

As a result of the success of "Stranger in Paradise" in the U.K., where it went all the way to number one, I was invited for the first time to appear there.

I must say that the circumstances under which I visited Europe were much more agreeable than they had been in my previous visit during the war. But my first "tour" consisted of only two cities, Glasgow, where I played for a week at a theater called the Empire, and Liverpool, where I played a week at another club called the Empire. This wasn't my English dream tour, not yet. English commentators at the time thought it was unusual that I didn't perform in London, but I did lay down some good groundwork. I filmed what I believe to be the first music video—I was shot walking in Hyde Park along the Serpentine while my recording of "Stranger in Paradise" was played. The clip was distributed to all the local TV stations in the U.K. and America, where it was aired on shows like Dick Clark's *American Bandstand.*

I also made my first of many appearances on Perry Como's show around this time. Como's NBC variety show was a Saturday night institution. He was by far the most successful singer on television, and his shows were beauties. The first time I met him I went to one of his rehearsals. Don't forget I was a kid who grew up on the streets. He took one look at me and said, "Come with me." I thought he was taking me to lunch. He walked me down to Tenth Avenue and Fifty-eighth Street and took me into St. Paul's Church. Perry led me right to the confessional and said, "All right, now step in!" That was part of Perry's great humor—always doing the unexpected, but always the right thing.

I went over well on the Como show, so much so that in 1956 NBC decided to let me take over his time slot as host of the summer replacement show. It was a great opportunity for me, and an intimidating challenge. When Perry did the show, it was a big production with great sets, a huge budget, all kinds of big name guest stars, and a full vocal chorus. I soon realized I wasn't going to get any of those big budget advantages, including the high-powered guest stars who could pull in the ratings. To make things even tougher, they stuck me on an empty stage with a ten-piece band. I was still a little jumpy about going out on stage in general, but the idea of having to appear in front of an audience, with very little assistance, really made me nervous.

It occurred to me that maybe Frank Sinatra could give me some advice. He was always my number one hero, and I figured if anybody knew what to do in the spot I was in, it was him. He was in New York that summer, sharing the Paramount bill with the Tommy Dorsey orchestra and one of his own movies, *Johnny Concho.* I told my friends I was going to go backstage at the Paramount and talk to Sinatra. Some of them told me it wasn't a good idea—that sometimes he was unpredictable. But I didn't care what they said. I believed in my heart that he would have some good advice for me.

I went over to the theater and asked for permission to see him. He said yes, and they led me back to his dressing room. The door opened, and there was Mr. Sinatra. He looked at me and without batting an eye said, "Oh, hello, Tony, come on in." So much for the cynics. I told him about my predicament, about how nervous I was. He said not to worry about that, people don't mind when you're nervous. On the contrary, he said, it's when you're not nervous that you're in trouble. If you don't care about what you're doing, why should the audience? When people see how much this means to you, they'll adore you. They'll see that you really want to please them, he told me, and they'll support you. Frank Sinatra taught me a great lesson, one that I carry with me to this day. I learned that anxiety is a very essential part of performing. "Will the lights work? Will I remember the words?" I focus on these elements when I do a show, and as a result I get butterflies, but that's part of being a good performer. In the end, I got through that TV series fine. Three summers later, in fact, I was again invited to star on *Perry Como Presents,* another summer Saturday hit.

My second son was born on October 15, 1955. Patricia went to the hospital in the middle of the night, but by the time the baby was born, it was morning and the sun was shining. We took that as a good omen and named him Daegal, a Scandinavian name Patricia liked that means "day."

By this time we were on the road all the time, and Danny was getting to the age where he suffered from the lack of a stable home environment. He'd begun walking and talking before he was a year old, and believe me, he hit the ground running. Nobody could keep up with him. His feats became legendary within the entertainment community. In fact, the comic Joey Bishop did a bit about how Danny totally exhausted Joey's pet dog! When the new baby came, we felt that Patricia needed to stay at home with the kids, especially since I was scheduled to start an extensive tour that would last until the end of January. Not being together was a big adjustment for all of us. Having two children running around a small apartment was more difficult than we had expected, and after the tour, Patricia and I decided it was time to get a house out in the suburbs where the kids could spread out.

Englewood, New Jersey, was only a few minutes away from my mom's house, and Tony T. had recently moved there, so it seemed like the perfect place to look. In the spring of 1956 we decided to rent a house in the nearby town of Tenafly while we looked for a lot to build a new home.

By summer we'd found a beautiful two-acre piece of property that had once been part of the Morrow estate. (Anne Morrow eventually married Charles Lindbergh.) There was little else on the property except the original carriage house and a big old red barn. It was perfect: all this space, and close to midtown Manhattan. That was a very important consideration for me—since I'd grown up in the city, I'd never learned to drive, and I had to be able to get back and forth easily. From here, I could jump into a cab and be there in twenty minutes. About a year later we rented another house right around the corner from Tony T. in Englewood, hired an architect, and started construction on our new home.

My annual appearance at the Copacabana was a magical engagement. I'd played the Copa at least three times before, but this one was the charm. Although I was still doing some of my hit songs in the set, the main emphasis was on a collection of standard tunes that I performed with a traditional fifteen-piece swing band. I put together the greatest group of songs you could possibly imagine, choosing songs like "Taking a Chance on Love," arranged by Neal Hefti; Duke Ellington's "I'm Just a Lucky So and So" and Sammy Fain's "I'll Be Seeing You," arranged by the legendary Gil Evans; and "Always," arranged by Don Costa (whom Sinatra called "Mr. Music"); most of the other tunes were arranged by Marion Evans. These guys were the cream of the crop, the best of the up-and-coming jazz and vocal arrangers on the New York scene, and all of them went on to become leading lights in the field of orchestration. It was a kick to sing those orchestrations! I loved them all, and I featured them in my act for many years.

I got tremendous reviews, and every celebrity in town came by to check out the show. I went on to tour that show around the country, and the material got really tight. I was anxious to get home to spend some time with Patricia and the kids. My road manager, Dee Anthony, and his wife, Harriet, had just had their first daughter, Michele, so it seemed to be a good time for all of us to take a break from the road and begin work on a new album. I was still desperately trying to persuade Columbia to continue to let me do complete albums, but since the live show was so successful, Columbia agreed to let me make an album based on that material. This became *Tony*, my second original album.

We were going to tape the album live at the Copa, but we couldn't get good enough sound recording in the club, so we moved to the studio. Frank Laico and I set it up in an unusual way. Instead of having the musicians sit around in a circle, the way most big band records were made, we set up the band in a regular bandstand arrangement. I stood in front of the band and sang, just as I did during live performances.

All the guys—Marion, Gil, Neal, Don—did a tremendous job on the orchestrations for *Tony*, but you'd never know it from reading the front or back cover of that album. At that time Columbia was heavily pushing Ray Conniff. He was going to be the new Percy Faith, their next big name in instrumental pop music. Ray conducted the sessions, and he did a good job, but it burned me up that none of the others received any credit on the cover. Over the next few months I was embarrassed when I ran into them. They'd always ask me why they didn't get credit. I felt terrible about it.

Tony was released in January of 1957 and was more warmly received than *Cloud 7*, but the main order of the day was still making pop singles. My favorite one of the era was "Ca, C'est L'Amour," one of Cole Porter's songs, the kind of hip song I was happy to sing. I just loved that record; it was a great song and a mellow Neal Hefti arrangement. Goddard Lieberson sent me a very nice letter—the first he ever wrote to me—saying, "If you keep making records like this, you'll be with us forever." If only Goddard's successors at Columbia had shared those sentiments.

I did a tour in Cuba in January of 1957, and Patricia came with me. Our decision to have Patricia and the boys stay home while I was on the road was beginning to put a tremendous strain on our marriage. This trip was an attempt at a compromise between my work and our life together at home. But it was the last time Patricia went on the road with me.

I was booked into the Sans Souci nightclub outside of Havana for an extended run. I was excited about playing there because I'd heard how enthusiastic the Cuban audiences were and how much they loved American jazz. The first night I was singing, I was interrupted by the audience. At first I thought I was being heckled, but then I realized my audience had found out that Zoot Sims was jamming in the lounge next door, and they were whispering, "Zoot, Zoot, Zoot!" during my show! They loved him so much that after his show they carried him away on their shoulders. We didn't see him for two days, and he even missed his plane back to the States!

Cuba was in the beginning stages of the revolution, and because this wasn't officially acknowledged by Cuba, or by the rest of the world for that matter, American entertainers were still performing in the casinos and nightclubs around the island—which, by the way, were primarily controlled by the underworld.

I discovered that in show business sometimes you can't help running into a political situation head-on. I'd picked a particularly bad time to go to Cuba because the discontent of the Cuban people was explosive. What had started out as a small guerrilla rebellion was becoming a full-fledged revolution. The rebel army, led by Fidel Castro, was in a state of war against the dictator Fulgencio Batista. It wasn't even safe to go to restaurants because rebels randomly shot up any place where they thought government officials or members of the bourgeoisie might be. They'd spray the dining room with machine gun fire, and if a visiting American happened to be eating there, it was too bad for him. The rich placed armed guards in front of their houses, and government buildings were heavily protected, and every day we heard about a new rebel attack or about a body found washed up on the beach.

My closest call with danger came when a bomb went off on stage in the middle of a show. Fortunately, I wasn't on stage at the time, but the chorus line of thirty-five girls was in the middle of their number. The explosion reduced the cinder block wall of the club to rubble, injuring every one of the chorus girls. None of them were killed, thank God, but some were permanently maimed or disfigured. Many were never able to dance again.

Patricia and I visited them in the hospital. One young woman was desperate to get her baby out of Cuba and safely back home, and Patricia offered to bring the child back with us. The woman was grateful but ended up making other arrangements. She never forgot us, though, because just a few years ago, a middle-aged woman recognized Patricia on the street and walked up and embraced her. She turned out to be the same chorus girl we had tried to help forty years ago!

A few days later, Patricia had driven herself into Havana at night to see the ballet. As she was driving back to the hotel, she lost her way on a long road between two towns. Two soldiers emerged from the trees. It was hard to tell if they were rebels or part of Batista's army, but they forced her to pull over and pointed their machine guns through the car windows on either side of her. She had no idea what was going on—she didn't speak Spanish and they didn't speak English. They kept asking her questions that she didn't understand, and she just sat in frightened silence. Fortunately, they let her drive on.

When she got back to the hotel, she was in a complete panic. We knew that we were pushing our luck by staying so we decided to pack up and leave immediately. The next morning the sheriff's house right across from our hotel was blown up. To make matters even worse, when we got to the airport, we learned that a hurricane was about to hit the island and that all the planes and boats were grounded. We found a pilot who was willing to risk the flight to the States, and Patricia said, "Let's go. We're better off taking our chances with the hurricane than staying here." The takeoff was frightening but we arrived home safely.

My first gig after Cuba was at the Americana Hotel in Miami Beach. It was a very special engagement because I got to play with one of my favorite people, the blind accordionist and singer Joe Mooney. Joe was already a major star in his own right, but he was kind enough to come on over to the Americana and play the accordion for me during a few of my sets. A couple of weeks later he served as my official accompanist when I played at the Miami Copa.

At rare moments in life a pure musician like Joe comes along. When he played, it was the most sublimely musical thing you could imagine; he put you right in heaven. He sang just right, his intonation was perfect, and he had tons of feeling. He wasn't loud, so he never attracted a big crowd, and as a result, he never got the recognition he deserved. Shirley Horn is like that, and so are Milt Jackson, Ruby Braff, and Joao Gilberto. They each have a sound that's as precious as a string of pearls or a rare diamond. And fortunately they've made records that audiences will enjoy forever.

While I was down in Miami I met the crew from the performance group the Vagabonds. I've had some crazy friends in my life, but I have to say the Vagabonds were the greatest. What wild times! They were like four maniacs on stage, doing music and comedy and shtick all at the same time. At one time they were bigger than Martin & Lewis. Tillio played the accordion in a unique way, using only the black keys and avoiding the white keys entirely. He never spoke on stage, doing everything in pantomime, and he was a total deadpan, just like Buster Keaton. The "Vags," as *Variety* used to call them, had their own showroom in Miami, which was sold out all the time.

Tillio, my closest friend of the bunch, was one of a kind. He had a comic mind that was as funny and sharp and as far-out as Lenny Bruce's, although today he is totally unknown, except to other performers. I used to watch them on Arthur Godfrey's television show—Godfrey loved those guys so much that he had them on as often as he could. At that point they were making more money than any act in show business and they were just tremendous. I brought them with me on the Como show whenever I was host.

I first met them in the Miami airport when I was getting off the plane and they were getting on to go back to New York. They recognized me, we started chatting, and Tillio told me they were going to New York to do the *Ed Sullivan Show*. When I left New York there had been three feet of snow on the ground, and Tillio was wearing a mohair suit with no overcoat. He told me he was coming back to Florida the day after the Sullivan show, so I said, "Take my coat, and give it back to me when you get back to Florida."

Well, that did it for Tillio. The fact that I loaned my coat to a stranger really meant the world to him. From that day on I became his main man. If I got a telegram that read "Bing Crosby called," I knew that Tillio was in town. Every time he took a plane ride, I got a statement in the mail from some insurance company informing me that he'd had taken out a policy and had named me the beneficiary. Tillio was the kind of guy who if he borrowed your car put all new tires on it before he returned it.

I was having a lot of fun, but I also had business to take care of. In 1957, my guitarist Chuck Wayne decided to move on. I needed a new accompanist, and was lucky enough to get pianist Claude Thornhill, but only for one month. When he left I held auditions at Nola Studios in New York. The first guy who showed up was okay, but the second guy, Ralph Sharon, just had to hit a few notes for me to know he was the piano player for me. Ralph said he'd played for Carmen McRae and Chris Conners and Johnny Hartman, and that's all I needed to know. He got the job instantly. Claude passed my songbook on to Ralph, and he stayed with me for the next ten years.

Hooking up with Ralph was one of the best career moves I've ever made. No one understands me more than he does, and we've become as close as brothers. Ralph is my idea of the perfect accompanist. He's a beautiful musician, and even more than most great players, he really knows how to perform with a singer or a soloist. He doesn't show off like a lot of other guys, playing lots of extra notes or fancy runs. After all, it's the emotion behind the music that's important. It takes a special person to support a performer and make him look good. I like to communicate the song simply by telling the story. Count Basie played that way, and that's why what he did worked so well. Ralph has that same gift.

Ralph's mother was an American who married an Englishman and settled in London. He was born and raised there, but in the early fifties he moved to America to pursue his musical career. He'd played gigs around London during and after the war, including little clubs where both Django Reinhardt and Stephane Grappelli (Europe's most famous jazzmen of the time) informally sat in. Ralph's talent was impossible to miss. He's the only musician I know who started at the top: when he was just twenty years old, Ralph's first big-time professional gig was as the original pianist with Ted Heath and His Music,

England's leading jazz big band. He stayed with Heath for two years, recording and broadcasting for the BBC.

Ralph left Heath to play with a small band led by clarinet player Frank Weir, a rather special position to be in, because the great pianist George Shearing was also in that group, only he was playing accordion at the time. Ralph is virtually the only piano player in the world who can boast that he played piano for George Shearing! In 1949 Ralph began recording as a bandleader in his own right, doing sessions for some British labels. For several years, he was voted the most outstanding jazz pianist in Britain by the readers of *Melody Maker*, the *Down Beat* of England, and he played at their all-star recording sessions.

By 1953 Ralph had decided to try to make it in the country that invented jazz and came to New York City. He made a series of albums with such major American stars as Howard McGhee, Teddy Charles, Kenny Clarke, Charles Mingus, J. R. Monterose, Milt Hinton, and Jo Jones. Ralph's album of original compositions, *Around the World in Jazz*, featuring Eddie Costa, Lucky Thompson, and Oscar Pettiford, was recorded in January 1957, just a few months before he joined me.

During my first recording session with Ralph I was practically forced to record what is probably my least favorite hit song, "In the Middle of an Island," and he had the pleasure, such as it was, of witnessing my worst disagreement ever with Mitch Miller. As I've said, if Mitch brought me a song I really didn't like, I'd simply refuse to do it. He'd keep pushing me, and I'd keep turning him down, until one of us relented. But in the case of "In the Middle of an Island," neither one of us would let up. He was absolutely determined that I record it, and I was equally determined not to go anywhere near that terrible song.

Mitch had worked up a big arrangement with a vocal group and four guitars. He said, "You should show the world what a varied palette you have. It's only going to be one side of a single. Am I going to have you put out a bad record?" I didn't answer that.

Mitch didn't let up on me, and everybody was standing around waiting for me to do something. It was still early in my career, I was still an amateur, and I hadn't gotten over the fear that I might be dropped from the label, so I began to sing the song halfheartedly. I suddenly developed a throat problem, and said I couldn't complete a take. But Mitch wasn't buying any of it. He told me, "Come on, just give me one take all the way through and we can all go home." So I thought, "The hell with it!" I took off my jacket and tied it around my waist like a grass skirt, started doing a hula dance, and managed to get through one take. That's all I would do. To my great annoyance it actually got in the top ten. But I've never received one request for that song in all the years I've been performing since.

That was the last time I sang something I really couldn't stand. Mitch was gradually phased out of A&R, and fortunately none of my other producers were as aggressive as Mitch in pressuring me to go against my own judgment, but they still tried. All through the sixties Columbia gave me a hard time. Even Goddard Lieberson, as high-minded as he was (this is the person who recorded John Gielgud's *The Ages of Man*), started in on me. I went to a big board meeting with Goddard and the rest of the top brass, and they were trying to put me in a certain musical pocket, one I didn't want to be in. Goddard and Mitch were emphatic, telling me, "We know what's best for you; we know what you should do," and so on and so forth. I answered them very calmly. I said, "I have just two words for you: 'Frank Sinatra.'" It broke them all up. By 1957, Sinatra was again the biggest thing in show business, and Columbia had let him leave.

Meanwhile Ralph was encouraging my jazz inclinations. He took a look at my whole repertoire up to that point and saw that Columbia was trying to put me in a certain commercial niche by having me record one ballad after another. He thought I needed to diversify. He told me, "You can have six hits in a row, but if you keep doing the same thing over and over, the public will eventually stop buying your records." I always had some swinging numbers in my act, and now with Ralph on piano, Billy Exiner on drums, and Don Payne on bass, I was doing a lot of numbers with the trio. Mitch Miller claimed that every time I got a hit single I wanted to sing jazz. Well, I figured that every time I did one for Columbia, I was entitled to do one for myself. *Cloud 7* came after my hits "Rags to Riches" and "Stranger in Paradise." Ralph said I should always do the unexpected to survive and to remain interesting to my fans. Once "In the Middle of an Island" made it onto the charts I felt free enough to start work on *Beat of My Heart,* the most ambitious jazz project of my career.

Ralph and I wanted to make a jazz statement in a big way, and I came up with the idea of recording an album of standards that put the spotlight on different kinds of rhythm by using all the great jazz drummers I could find. We talked the concept over during our first few months on the road, and gradually it all came together. The first recording date was in June 1957, with Chico Hamilton. I was delighted with the results, particularly with the tongue-twisting, super-percussive title track, "The Beat of My Heart." Mitch came to the first recording date, but was unusually quiet. Maybe he hoped he was giving us enough rope to hang ourselves. But when the album came out, an army of jazz fans said, Hey, this guy knows how to swing. A whole new audience accepted me—in fact, I still get my biggest reactions at jazz festivals the world over.

Between the June and October recording sessions for *Beat of My Heart*, I decided to try my hand at acting in the Kansas City production of Cole Porter's *Silk Stockings*. I was still gigging around the country, of course, and my live shows were going great, but I wanted to do something a little different. I hadn't been in a "show" since I starred in *On the Town* back in Germany in 1946! I had a great time. Later that year I starred in the Chicago production of *Guys and Dolls*. It was a great experience. The show was well done, took off right away, and was sold out for a month. Unfortunately, I made the mistake of playing Sky Masterson instead of Nathan Detroit. The reviewer's headline read "Tony Bennett, The Wrong Sky." If I had played Nathan Detroit, I could have made it work— his dialogue had much more humor in it.

Guys and Dolls was done in the theater-in-the-round format. Patricia brought Danny and Dae to see one of the performances, and they were fascinated with how it all worked. As the actors entered and left the stage, we'd have to carry all the props and scenery on and off with us; it was wonderful to watch how the stage manager organized the chaos. When we got back home, the boys put on their own play using the same concept, with sets and costumes they'd built out of cardboard. It was quite elaborate, especially considering they were only three and four years old. It was one of the first indications I had that Danny was interested in show business and stagecraft.

When I got back to New York, we did three more recording sessions in October, and that more than finished the *Beat of My Heart* album. For our first October session we had trumpeter Nat Adderley, Al Cohn on tenor, and Art Blakey as featured drummer. For the next date, Ralph indulged his passion for writing for trombones, and we had four, led by the wonderful Kai Winding, who flew in from Chicago for the occasion. We were also lucky enough to get Jo Jones, Count

Basie's greatest drummer. The last date featured my regular percussionist Billy Exiner; two giants of Latin American rhythm, Sabu and Candido; and Ralph brought in five flautists led by Herbie Mann. Not too shabby! The album was released in November and went over well with the critics and the jazz public.

When I played the Copacabana again in February 1958, I brought Herbie Mann, Sabu, and Candido along with me. I put cards on all the tables that read, "It's great to be appearing at the famous Copa again. This time I'm being abetted by some wonderful musicians I thought you might like to meet." And then I listed all the guys. We went over so well at the Copa that I took Candido on the road with me, playing the Chez Paree in Chicago, the Town and Country in Brooklyn, and the El Morocco in Montreal.

After the success of *Tony* and *Beat of My Heart*, I was finally allowed to make albums regularly, even though the vibe at Columbia was that I was wasting my time if I put my energies into anything but hit singles. I followed *Beat of My Heart* with a more conventional pop vocal album called *Long Ago and Far Away*. That was the first of three albums of lovely standards I did with arranger Frank DeVol. Frank was a great guy and a fine orchestrator. The album is a nice mixture of slow ballads, with a few slightly jazzy numbers thrown in, like "So Far," which ends the album with a beat. Those sessions with Frank yielded a couple of hit singles, "Climb Ev'ry Mountain," which I sang on Hugh Hefner's TV show *Playboy's Penthouse*, and "Till," another big hit for me on the English charts.

⁜

It was always my dream to perform with Count Basie and Duke Ellington, the greatest bandleaders of all time. I was particularly keen to do an album with Count Basie, and in 1958 I got my chance to make not only one album with him, but two. No star singer had ever recorded an entire album with Basie before, and Basie was all for doing an album with me, but we had to contend with his record label, Roulette Records, and Morris Levy, who ran it. Levy was a classic ruffian who wheeled and dealed any way he could. He was notorious for scamming artists, and unfortunately Bill Basie was a gambler who ended up borrowing a lot of money from Levy. In the typical "owing your soul to the company store" scenario, it was rumored that after a while Basie was simply put on the payroll, like the rest of his band, and never got a cent of the royalties from his compositions or recordings.

Morris Levy agreed to my recording with Basie for Columbia as long as we agreed to make a reciprocal record for Roulette. Basie and I decided that we'd record the Columbia album live and the Roulette album in the studio. But getting Mitch Miller to approve this was another story.

He was totally opposed both to my working with Basie and to my appearing on Roulette Records. He said, "No way. What do you want to be on a junk label like Roulette for?" Mitch's own career as a recording artist was starting to take off around this time. He had a hit single with "The Yellow Rose of Texas" that was steadily climbing the charts, so I decided to bide my time and wait for the record to reach the top. I got Mitch's approval the day his song hit number one. Mitch told me that if I made this record, it would ruin my career, but he was feeling so great about reaching number one with "Yellow Rose," he finally gave in.

We decided to do the live album for Columbia first, and worked out the details with the Latin Casino in Philadelphia. Ralph orchestrated and arranged the entire album. Although I'd talked with him on the telephone I didn't meet Count

Basie until our rehearsals began. It was an amazing experience, the fulfillment of a dream, and I'll never forget it. We hit it off right away, as though we always knew and understood each other. At one point Basie turned to his band, pointed at me, and said, "Anything this man wants, he gets!" I was floored.

We opened at the Latin Casino in Philadelphia on November 28, 1958, and did tremendous business. There was barely room in that tiny club for Frank Laico to set up his console, and he finally had to rig it up in the basement kitchen. I thought the recording came out wonderfully, but stereo recording had just been discovered and Al Ham, the producer, was unhappy that we had recorded in mono. It was his call, so the following month, we rerecorded the album in the studio in stereo, adding the crowd noise and applause to make it sound "live." But of all things, Ham put the audience applause in the wrong places. What a mess! We titled the album *In Person!* and released it in early 1959. I never understood why we didn't release the live version. The whole attempt at fabricating an audience was in bad taste. As a result I've always been partial to the second album, the one we recorded for Roulette. It was originally released in 1961 as *Count Basie/Tony Bennett: Strike Up the Band*, but Levy was such an opportunist that over the years he licensed the recording to anyone he could, and as a result the album appeared under an endless number of titles, including *Basie Swings Bennett Sings*.

Those two albums were the beginning of a beautiful personal and musical relationship with the Count. Over the next twenty-five years we worked together many times and hung out together whenever we got the chance. I'd gotten in the habit of bringing home my musician friends at all hours of the night, and Patricia got used to expecting the unexpected. One night she woke up and wandered into the living room in her nightgown, where she saw not only Bill Basie himself but all sixteen members of his band sitting around jamming. Not your usual domestic scene!

We once played the Academy of Music in Philadelphia, and our combined act was so hot the audience went absolutely crazy. We got ten standing ovations—it was phenomenal. After the show Basie and I were standing in the parking lot and a white guy came up to Basie, threw him a set of keys, and said, "Hey, buddy, get me my car, will ya?" He thought Basie was a parking attendant! The Count replied, "Get your own car; I'm tired. I've been parking them all night." Basie always had a great sense of humor, and working with him was truly one of the highlights of my life.

Beat of My Heart and my two records with Count Basie earned me a whole new audience: true jazz fans. Jazz critics question my validity as a jazz artist, and I don't label myself as one. But personally I love jazz more than any other form of music. It's spontaneous, honest, and natural. Every civilization is known by its culture, and jazz is America's greatest contribution to the world, and I've always surrounded myself with jazz performers because they understand that the *moment* is the most important thing: they improvise, they reinvent the music every night. I know how to improvise too. I sing in the tradition of Bing Crosby: if I like a song, I sing it, and I never sing a song the same way twice.

⚜

My most vivid memories from the late fifties are the great years I spent in Chicago. Those were tremendous days. My favorite Chicago hangout was the Black Orchid. It was owned by Paul Raffles, and it was the hippest place in town. He hired singers and brilliant comics like Larry Storch and Jack E. Leonard, there was a chorus line of scantily clad girls, and he always had a great piano player like Ace Harris in the lounge.

When the show was over, we'd go to Paul's apartment and jam until morning.

I met Hugh Hefner around this time. He was on the scene, just getting started with *Playboy*. He liked to hang out at the Black Orchid, and though he was basically a shy, introverted guy, he knew a good thing when he saw it. His plan was to take all the fun we were having in Chicago in those days and mass-produce it in his magazine, in his clubs, and on his TV show. He refined his idea into a million-dollar concept that's still going strong today. I got to know Hugh during those nights at the Black Orchid, and I was a guest on his TV shows, *Playboy's Penthouse* and *Playboy After Hours*.

One night after my show at the Chez Paree I was hanging out with the guys in the band. Suddenly there was a banging on the front door of the club and some guy yelled, "Open up! FBI!"

Two agents muscled their way into the club, lined us up against the wall, and frisked us, but there was nothing to be found. We were really shaken up and figured the incident would hit the papers the next day.

The next night, we were at a party at Hef's place when in walked Lenny Bruce with his arms around those two "FBI agents." The whole thing was a joke! Lenny wanted to get us, and he did.

When I think back to my days in Chicago, I can't help but remember my great friend, the miraculous piano wizard Erroll Garner. The Chez Paree had a joint within a joint, a little piano room in the back called the Key Club, where Erroll would play until all hours. He loved playing the piano so much that even after the regular audience went home, he kept playing for the bosses, the entertainers, and the chorus girls.

We often met in his studio at Carnegie Hall and jammed for hours, and sometimes we hooked up when we were on the road.

One time he told me he thought I should open my show with the song "When You're Smilin'." I told Erroll that everybody opens with that song, but he wouldn't take no for an answer. I didn't give in, though, because I felt sure the song was overdone, so I turned his request down. At the same time, I heard everybody raving about Judy Garland's new live album from Carnegie Hall. I bought the record. It starts with an exciting announcement, "Ladies and Gentlemen, Judy Garland..." There are deafening cheers and Judy begins singing, in ballad tempo, "When You're Smilin'..." Once again I learned my lesson.

Erroll was a great musician, and his classic album *Concert by the Sea* showed Columbia just how well a jazz album could do. Before then everybody thought 75,000 was a good figure for a pop (let alone jazz) album to sell. But *Concert by the Sea* sold 250,000 copies. That was an astonishing figure for a jazz album, and it helped Columbia reach a whole new legion of fans.

I made my next album, *Hometown, My Town*, with the great orchestrator Ralph Burns. This and other albums I made with Ralph are a great example of the musical scene that was flourishing in New York in the late fifties and early sixties. This was the time when all the very best musicians were working in the city. Many of them—like Al Cohn, Urbie Green, and Zoot Sims—had started with Woody Herman and other big bands, and when they came off the road, they settled in New York. I'd see them in the recording studios, in the pit bands on Broadway, and jamming in the jazz clubs.

It's significant, then, that our first album together had New York City as its theme. It consisted of only six songs, some of which directly refer to the Big Apple, but most simply reflect a New York mood. I wanted a rich, lush, orchestral sound, but I didn't want anything that sounded like "easy listening" music. I knew Ralph Burns was the perfect guy for the job.

He had an apartment on Fifty-fifth Street and Seventh Avenue, and I'd go up there every day and we'd work out the songs on the piano. And that's the way I still work with Ralph Sharon today: we sit at the piano, figure out the tempos, the keys, and how the orchestration should go, and then we present it to the orchestrator and he does the rest. I told Ralph Burns that this might be the only "pop vocal" album he'd ever do where the overall quality of each track was the most important thing. I didn't want to worry about making a commercial album filled with the standard three-minute pop songs. This was to be an album with no limitations.

I included some of the songs from *Hometown* in my live appearances. I did "Skyscraper Blues" and "The Party's Over" when I played the Copa in March 1959. It was customary to introduce fellow performers who were out in the audience, and on opening night Joey Bishop, whom I'd recently worked with at the Sands in Vegas, and many other performers were in the house. I introduced them all, and they stood up and took a bow. I started a song, and I looked over and saw Jack Carter sitting ringside and realized I hadn't introduced him. So I decided to do it during the instrumental break in the middle of "Skyscraper Blues." I gave the usual spiel: "Ladies and gentlemen, there's a great comedian in the house tonight. How about a big round of applause for Jack Carter!" When I went back to the song, the next line was "When you're walking in the streets of New York and you haven't got a friend in town..." I sang that right after introducing Jack, and the whole place collapsed in laughter! Sorry Jack!

Patricia and I finally moved into our first house. I was looking forward to having a home to return to for some sense of stability, and I thought it would do Patricia and me some good. It was a beautiful sanctuary. We designed the house after the style of Frank Lloyd Wright, building it mostly of redwood and glass. We were literally surrounded by nature. I had an art studio and a recording studio built in the basement, so I had a place to jam with my colleagues.

In the early part of 1960 I recorded two more albums with Frank DeVol; *To My Wonderful One* and *Alone Together*. Later on that year I did my first, and for many years my only, songbook album, *A String of Harold Arlen*. The son of a cantor, Harold grew up in Buffalo. He became the musical director of the Cotton Club and originally wrote many jazz compositions. But his pop songs were dramatic and right up my alley. Arlen was known for the jazzy quality of his melodies, but Mitch thought it would be novel to give his songs a lush, symphonic treatment. He brought in Glenn Osser, a veteran record and show orchestrator, and his charts were just right. I felt free singing to Glenn's arrangements. We used a big orchestra of mainly classical players, and they really enjoyed the recording session. That's the only album I ever made where the musicians actually applauded after each take. Glenn and I did some singles together, and he came up with a lovely, quasi-oriental treatment of Richard Rogers's "Love Look Away," the lament from *Flower Drum Song*.

I loved "When the Sun Comes Out," and I thought that was a perfect opener for the Harold Arlen album. Then again, you can't go wrong with any of Harold's songs. His songs are perfect for an interpretive performer like me; I just love the tools he gives me to work with. You can give virtually any treatment to an Arlen tune. They can be sung dramatically or "straight out," exactly as written.

Harold's attitude was the opposite of Richard Rodgers's, who always insisted that his songs be performed exactly as he wrote them. Harold loved improvisation. He said, "Hey, change it anyway you want, as long as it works." Anything you did was okay with him as long it pleased the audience. That was the most important thing to him. I've sung the music of so many wonderful composers that I'd rather be diplomatic and not name any one of them as the best, but I'd be lying if I said the songs of Harold Arlen didn't occupy a very special place in my heart. He was a very debonair man, with a thin "French style" mustache, and he always kept a fresh flower in his lapel; he was the consummate artist. He wrote his own music, sat down and played a mean piano, and performed his own songs as well as anyone.

In 1963 Harold wrote a song with André Previn's wife, the lyricist Dory Langdon, called "So Long Big Time," and I recorded it with Ralph and Marty Manning. Harold hadn't attended any of the tapings for *A String of Harold Arlen* three years earlier, but he came to this session, probably because this was a new song. We were working with the song when Harold interrupted and started showing me more things I could do with the lyric, how I wasn't getting enough out of it, how I could emphasize certain words. I liked what Harold told me so much that when the album, *The Many Moods of Tony,* came out, I gave Harold credit on "So Long Big Time" for conducting his own composition.

I always wanted to be unpredictable, and so for my next project, I decided to go in the opposite direction from the big orchestral albums I'd been doing lately and cut an intimate piano-vocal album with Ralph Sharon. We booked time in the studio and pored through music books, trying one tune after another. The arrangements were spontaneous, and we finished each song in one or two takes. In one afternoon we laid down sixteen tunes—which must be some kind of record—twelve of which made it onto the album, which became 1961's *Tony*

Sings for Two. Mitch Miller showed up at the start of these sessions, furious that I was really going through with it. When he saw that there was no dissuading me, he turned to Frank Laico and said, "I'm leaving. I can't support this." *Tony Sings for Two* turned out to be one of my finest records ever.

Ralph Burns and I got together again to do some singles, including "Smile," and for our next album we changed gears again. Instead of the lush, ballad-style arrangements we had used on *Hometown, My Town,* we switched to a cookin' jazz sound. The album is called *My Heart Sings,* and I simply love Ralph's writing on this one. It's really beautiful music.

By the end of the fifties the music of Elvis Presley, Chuck Berry, and disc jockey Alan Freed dominated the radio air-waves. Rock and roll music was being forced on the American public. I was fortunate that my own string of hits in the fifties more than established me as a household name and enabled me to make the kind of quality records that I needed to make in order to assure that I'd be considered a lasting artist. Little did I know that Ralph Sharon had my biggest hit of all time sitting at home tucked away in his dresser drawer.

In the studio

CHAPTER EIGHT

George Cory and Douglass Cross were an aspiring song-writing team living in New York in the mid-fifties. Like most songwriters, Cory and Cross were always hanging around singers and their accompanists, trying to get them to listen to their new tunes.

They met Ralph Sharon when he was playing around town, and frequently gave him some of their songs, hoping that he'd pass them along. One particular day Cory and Cross bumped into Ralph on the street, and true to form, handed him some more songs. Ralph promised he'd take a look, but our lives being as hectic as they were, he simply stuck them in a dresser drawer and forgot about them.

We were home in New York for a brief stay in mid-1961. We would be heading to Hot Springs, Arkansas, and then moving on to the Fairmont Hotel in San Francisco. Ralph was packing, looking through his dresser for some shirts, and he saw the batch of songs that Cory and Cross had given him two years earlier. On the top of the pile was a song called "I Left

163

My Heart in San Francisco," and Ralph took it along since that's where we were headed.

Off we went to Arkansas, where we played a great gig at a nightclub called the Vapors Restaurant. (When I was visiting the White House recently, President Clinton told me that he actually saw that show. Since he was too young to get in, he stood outside the club and watched my performance through the window!) After the show, Ralph took out the song, read it through, and decided it was good. We went down to the piano at the hotel bar, and he played it for me. I thought it was a great song. What really impressed me was that after I sang it through only once, the bartender setting up said, "If you guys record that song, I'll buy the first copy." You might say that was our first rave review.

I was happy to have a special song for my San Francisco show, because I'd never performed in that town and had heard that if the audiences didn't know you, they didn't warm up to you quickly. Ralph wrote up a great chart and I sang it on opening night at the Fairmont Hotel. It really went over like gangbusters. It might have ended right there, but as fate would have it local Columbia reps heard the song at rehearsal that afternoon and loved it. They wanted me to record the song, feeling that sales in San Francisco alone would make it worth my while.

The important thing was that I loved the song, and that meant more to me than how well it would sell in one market or another. I asked Marty Manning to flesh out Ralph's chart, and he wrote a beautiful orchestration. On January 23, 1962, I recorded "San Francisco" in one take along with a song called "Once Upon a Time," from a Ray Bolger show called *All American*.

The next day Ralph called Cory and Cross. They were knocked out to hear that I had recorded one of their songs. Columbia quickly released the single using "San Francisco" as the B-side, since I was positive that "Once Upon a Time" was the surefire hit. I even put that song in my show and plugged it like crazy. But Columbia reps stopped me in my tracks because requests were pouring in from all over the country for "San Francisco." They immediately rang me up and told me that the public was reacting like crazy to the B-side. So I started plugging "San Francisco."

"I Left My Heart in San Francisco" was a "grass roots" phenomenon: it literally came from nowhere, it was written by two unknown songwriters, it wasn't from a show or a movie, and the record company didn't spend millions of dollars promoting it. People responded to it because it was a great song, not because some record company exec was telling them what to like. Even Goddard Lieberson called and said, "You're never going to stop hearing about 'San Francisco' for the rest of your life. As long as you keep singing, you'll be singing this song." I had big hits before, but this song was off the map. The record sold thousands of copies a week for the next four years, became a gold record, scored me my first Grammy, and in short, became the biggest record of my career. In fact, it hasn't stopped selling, and although the record stayed on the charts for twenty-five months, it never reached number one. San Franciscans now treat me like an adopted son and often tell me that the song has done wonders to increase tourism in America's most elegant city.

Cory and Cross eventually moved back home, where they built a lovely mansion in Clearlake, a posh suburb of San Francisco. Ralph and I went to visit them a couple of times, and they showed us press clippings from around the world. One mentioned that karaoke bars in Japan were using the song to help Japanese people learn English!

The song also helped make me a world citizen: it allowed me to live, work, and sing in any city on the globe. It changed my whole life. I was especially touched by an article I read one Sunday in *The New York Times* near the end of the Vietnam War. It described lonely, homesick soldiers sitting around a campfire singing "I Left My Heart in San Francisco." When I'm asked to name my favorite song, you can bet I don't hesitate. The wonderful response I always get from the audience makes the song fresh and new for me every single night. When people ask me if I ever get tired of singing "San Francisco" I answer, "Do you ever get tired of making love?" That usually leaves them speechless.

The unprecedented success of "San Francisco" and the constant touring intensified the strain on my family life. Try as I might, I couldn't get the two worlds in sync. After months of trying to pull things together, Patricia and I felt it was best to separate so I moved into an apartment in the city on East Seventy-second Street. Patricia and I hoped that we'd gain perspective by stepping back and giving each other a little breathing space. But being away from my family devastated me. On one hand my career was flying higher than ever, but emotionally I was hitting rock bottom. I was very lonely. So I threw myself into my work.

If I thought I was busy before, I really didn't know what busy was until after "San Francisco" hit big. I didn't have a manager, and by this time my road manager Dee Anthony and I had gone our separate ways. It was getting more and more difficult to handle the day-to-day business with Columbia, which was still trying harder than ever to get me to record novelty songs. I didn't have someone to speak on my behalf, so out of necessity I had to deal with all the executives at Columbia myself, which was in retrospect not the best way to handle matters. I found it's always best to have somebody I trust take care of the business, leaving my head clear to concentrate on my work. "Trust" is the operative word here, and I just couldn't find someone I felt could do the job.

I'd pretty much gotten into the habit of doing without producers. I'd do a take; then I'd walk into the control room and use Frank Laico as a sounding board. Eventually Frank set up the studio the way I liked it, and we ran the sessions ourselves from start to finish. It was ridiculous that I had to go through this, but things once again worked out for the best. It gave me freedom to do what I wanted to do. In addition to *Tony Sings for Two*, I released one more album in 1961, *My Heart Sings*. But in 1962, I made four albums: *Mr. Broadway, I Left My Heart in San Francisco, On the Glory Road* (Ralph and I taped twelve tracks for this album, but Columbia never released it), and a live album called *Tony Bennett at Carnegie Hall*.

When "San Francisco" was peaking in early 1962, I was invited to appear at Carnegie Hall for the first time. Carnegie Hall had never featured a "pop" singer like myself as a solo performer. It was unprecedented. To my surprise, Columbia backed me completely. Goddard said, "You've got to play Carnegie Hall, and we'd love to make a record out of the concert."

I wanted everything to be right. I called my old army buddy Arthur Penn and asked him to help me stage the show. He very graciously agreed even though he'd just directed his Oscar-winning film *The Miracle Worker* and wasn't exactly staging shows anymore. He brought in Gene Saks, the famous Broadway director, and together the three of us worked out what would be done at Carnegie Hall. I asked Arthur what songs he thought I should sing, and he said, "Sing whatever you want. All I'm going to do is make sure nothing distracts you. I'm going to make a nice environment for you on the stage." Under his direction Gene Saks gave the whole theater a truly spiritual look with his elegant, understated lighting.

Carnegie Hall never looked better. My dear old friend Arthur really came through for me.

I put everything I'd been studying for the last twenty years into practice for that show. During the fifties I'd opened with swingin' numbers like "Sing You Sinners" or "Taking a Chance on Love," and sometimes I didn't grab the crowd right away like I wanted to. One night when I was hanging with Count Basie I was talking to him about this, and he said, "Why open with a closer? Start with a medium-tempo number like 'Just In Time,' and give the audience a chance to settle in." He understood that if you ease the audience into your world, later on you can hit them with an up-tempo number and it will be twice as effective. With that in mind I decided to start with "Lullaby of Broadway," slightly slower than usual, and then do "Just In Time," just like Basie suggested. By my fourth number I'd go way up with "Fascinating Rhythm."

Now that I had figured out how to open the show, I needed something really special to close with. I'd start out with old favorites, but I wanted to end with something that nobody had ever heard me sing before, something unexpected. Tony T. suggested the spiritual "Glory Road."

Ralph had never heard this tune before I laid it on him, and the score went on for pages—the song is nearly nine minutes long! But Ralph managed to arrange it for me, and did his usual bang-up job. Two weeks before the concert, I was in Chicago in a bistro on Rush Street called the Living Room. Ralph was rehearsing day and night in preparation for our Carnegie Hall show. The jazz vocal trio Lambert, Hendricks, and Ross were working across the street and Jon Hendricks and I ended up jamming in every joint on Rush Street. By the end of the two weeks I was ready for opening night.

The concert was held on June 9, 1962. Backstage I had a healthy case of the butterflies and reflected on Sinatra's advice about the jitters. From the minute I hit the stage all the nervousness disappeared, and I knew I was gonna nail it. I'm proud to say the concert was an absolute triumph. Candido added to the success of "Glory Road" by playing a wonderful solo in the middle of it that drove the crowd wild. In fact, I had a whole percussion section with me on that night. In addition to Billy Exiner, Candido, and Sabu, I had Eddie Costa on vibes and Bobby Rosengarden on timpani. I was able to put together the most amazing orchestra imaginable, including Al Cohn on tenor, Frank Rehak on trombone, guitarist Kenny Burrell, and trumpeter Nick Travis, who had been with me in the 314th in the army. These men were the absolute greatest players of a great era.

"Glory Road" went over better than I could have hoped for, but the biggest hit of the concert was, not surprisingly, "I Left My Heart in San Francisco." Ralph is fairly unflappable, so when he told me he thought the show was a real winner, I knew I had hit the mark. Mary later told me that when the show was over, the audience was cheering for me to sing an encore of "San Francisco," but I was already in my dressing room and didn't hear what they were saying. If I'd known, I certainly would have obliged.

My whole family was in the audience that night. I was particularly proud that my mother was there; that made me feel like a million bucks. It was the biggest night of my life. My mom couldn't believe how far I'd come. She was sitting between Mary and Tom, and as the crowds were cheering for an encore, she kept turning to Mary and asking, "Why don't they let Anthony go home and rest? He must be exhausted after two and a half hours of singing." She was so precious, she meant everything to me.

Columbia was able to get *Tony Bennett at Carnegie Hall* released by the end of August. We got the greatest sound on our album, better than any other album I'd recorded. Frank

Laico did a terrific job, not only recording the music, but beautifully capturing the enthusiasm of the crowd.

I wouldn't give up nightclubs for a while, but now that I had a faithful audience I wanted to encourage them to go to places like Carnegie Hall, to all the beautiful concert halls across the country, which are my favorite places to perform.

That same great year President Kennedy invited me to the White House to appear with the leading modern jazz group of the era, the Dave Brubeck Quartet. The occasion was a special concert held on the White House lawn in honor of journalism students, and there were thousands of press people there. I'd done some campaigning for Kennedy during his run for president, and it was a glorious day for me. Kennedy was always kind and generous to me throughout his years in office and I later became one of the twelve founding fathers of the Kennedy Center in Washington, D.C.

Later that year I appeared at the White House with Count Basie. The windows had luxurious green velvet drapes with rich tassels. Basie grasped the tiny ball hanging from a tassel, pinched it between two fingers, and said to me under his breath, "My taxes paid for *this*." A typical Basie line. What a little devil he was.

Between 1960 and 1961 I'd been in and out of every major American city at least six times. I was on the road constantly, and I only made it back to New York to make records during the day and work the Copa, the Waldorf-Astoria, or the Town and Country in Brooklyn at night. In 1962 I was away from home even more. Obviously there wasn't much time to try to patch things up with Patricia, but I stayed in touch with her and the kids by telephone as much as I could. I felt we were making some headway toward a reconciliation, and so we decided to give it another try and I moved back into the house in Englewood. I was relieved.

In addition to my jazz excursions I became part of another musical trend that year. I was working at the Copacabana in Rio de Janeiro for the first time. I wasn't yet well known in South America. There were only twenty-five to fifty people a night in a thousand-seater house—boy, did I have the blues—so I decided to sing my heart out. The audiences were really wonderful and inspired me to do my best. I played for two and a half hours every night. At least a thousand people say they saw me at the Copacabana while I was there—talk about word-of-mouth! Now every other year I perform to huge audiences there.

I fell in love with Rio. I still have great affection for that city and long to return. The beaches are forty miles of the whitest sand you can imagine, and Sugarloaf Mountain is one of the most spiritual places I've ever seen. In fact I recently did a painting of that very spot that I feel is one of my most successful. The whole country is filled with music and poetry. Each language has a philosophy, and there's something about the rhythm and the sound of Portuguese that's so poetic and truthful, and the people are full of life and love.

One morning my bass player, Don Payne, woke me up and said, "You've got to come down to the beach right now." Right there on that beautiful beach was where I met Joao and Astrud Gilberto, singing and playing. Later they introduced me to Antonio Carlos Jobim's songs and there was no turning back.

Bossa nova was a new soft and swinging rhythm very closely tied to jazz, and I fell in love with it instantly. Billy Exiner got excited about it because it was a whole new beat for him too. When I came back to the States, I opened in San Francisco and told the San Francisco disc jockeys about my discovery, and they raved. Bossa nova spread across the country like wildfire.

Once when Joao Gilberto was in the States I invited him to my home in Englewood and he brought his five-year-old son with him. We had a jam session in my basement studio, and Joao took out his guitar and started singing as his son lay on the floor playing with a toy. It was a beautiful day; the sun was shining down on all of us through the window. I looked at his son, and the little boy was quietly crying. I asked what was wrong, and Joao asked him in Portuguese. He said something to his father that I'll never forget. Joao translated it for me: "I hope this day never ends." I felt the same way.

In the early sixties I'd frequently appeared on Hugh Hefner's TV show *Playboy's Penthouse.* Cy Coleman had written and recorded an instrumental opening for Hef's TV series. Cy Coleman and Carolyn Leigh had long been my favorite composers of that period. I'd done their songs "Firefly," "Walk a Little Faster," "On the Other Side of the Tracks," "It Amazes Me," and many others. I thought this new song was very catchy and wanted to sing it, so I called Cy to ask if there were lyrics. He told me there were, but he said if I liked his "Playboy's Theme," he had another song that had a similar groove that he thought I'd like even better.

That song was "The Best Is Yet to Come." Cy played it for me and I agreed that it was a great tune. I recorded it the next day. I couldn't get any of my usual top-drawer arrangers on such short notice, though I did find a writer who was able to turn it around overnight. The next day he dropped by the studio and unceremoniously dumped the chart on me about an hour before the session and then split. We didn't have a conductor, but Cy was there and when we started going over the orchestration, we realized it wasn't what we wanted, so Cy rewrote it. When it was finally finished we knew we had a winner. "The Best Is Yet to Come" became one of my biggest all-time hits, and the next in a series of wonderful songs I had on the charts in the early sixties.

Another big number from 1962 was "I Wanna Be Around," a Johnny Mercer tune that I had the honor of introducing to the world. What a thrill when I found out that Johnny said my version was his favorite interpretation of any song he ever wrote.

"I Wanna Be Around" has a particularly interesting history. The song was originally conceived by a lady in Youngstown, Ohio, named Sadie Vimmerstedt. Sadie wasn't a professional songwriter, but she was a fan of great songs, especially Johnny's. One day she came up with two lines: "I wanna be around to pick up the pieces / When somebody breaks your heart." She thought they sounded like they belonged in a Johnny Mercer song, so she sent them to him along with a letter explaining how she thought the lyrics would make a good song. She had no idea exactly where Johnny lived, so she addressed the envelope, "Johnny Mercer, Songwriter, Los Angeles, California," and somehow the letter got to him.

Johnny agreed that the two lines made an ideal opening for a song, and he proceeded to write one (one of the rare instances when Johnny wrote the music as well as the lyrics), and then asked me to sing it. We recorded it in October 1962. I had Marty Manning arrange the song and conduct the band, and Ralph played a great piano part.

Johnny very generously gave Sadie fifty percent of the publishing rights to the song, and she did very well indeed. For years I got postcards from Paris, Italy, and Spain; she was able to leave her job and travel for the rest of her life.

Both those songs wound up on my next album, *I Wanna Be Around,* which was released in March 1963. One of my favorite songs on that album was the opening track, "The

Good Life," a French tune by singer-songwriter Sacha Distel. I love the philosophy of that number, which is why I chose it for the title of this book. It's intriguingly ambiguous: what does he mean by "The Good Life"? Is it to be single and unattached, or is it to have somebody and not be alone? The conflict between the two ideas makes it exactly the kind of lyric I love to do. My old friend Duke Niles, the last of the old-time song pluggers, gave me the first crack at this song in America, and I've always been grateful to him.

Immediately after that record was released I decided to record a trio record for the first time using Ralph on piano, Billy Exiner on drums, and Hal Gaylord, who had by this time replaced Don Payne, on bass. We recorded twenty-four songs, and I chose Benny Carter's tune *When Lights Are Low* for the album's title, because of the intimate connotation.

I found a wonderful illustrator named Bob Peak to do a picture of me for the cover, and it came out great, but I got flak from Columbia over the artwork. It was a battle every step of the way. The woman who ran the art department really blew her top! She told Goddard Lieberson, "If the artist starts telling us what to put on the album cover, I'm out of here." She really wreaked havoc for me, and when it was all over, Bob's illustration was out and I received quite a scolding from the front office for upsetting the art department. Bob later did the cover for Barbra Streisand's *Funny Girl*, the cover for *My Fair Lady*, and the poster for *Apocalypse Now*. He was a great illustrator, and became one of the industry's favorite graphic artists.

In April, a week or so after we finished recording *When Lights Are Low*, Columbia decided that they wanted another live album, this time from the Las Vegas Sahara, with Ralph and conductor Louis Basil. Frank Laico flew in with all of his remote recording equipment, and he spent all day setting up. Milton Berle, Danny Thomas, and Mickey Rooney were all in the audience that night, and they came right up on stage and started kibitzing. It was hilarious, and the crowd went crazy. It's all on the tape, but nobody's ever heard it because Columbia has never released it! That year we also recorded and released *This Is All I Ask,* my third and last full album with Ralph Burns.

The following year I got the chance to work with Judy Garland for the first time when she invited me to sing on her CBS television special. It was the beginning of a long and treasured friendship. Just like everyone else in America, I'd fallen in love with Judy in 1939 when I saw her sing "Over the Rainbow" in *The Wizard of Oz.* She was always a fantastic entertainer, and like Louis Armstrong, Frank Sinatra, and Jimmy Durante, one of my major artistic influences. Judy was only a few years older than me, but since she'd been a child star, I'd been her fan my entire life.

I first met Judy in 1958 when she came backstage after my show at the Ambassador Hotel in Los Angeles and congratulated me on my performance. It was a thrill that never wore off. She was a true original, full of life and fun. She was intelligent, a one-of-a-kind lady, and a great artist, but sadly, she led a very troubled life. As we got to know each other, Judy told me stories about how badly she'd been treated when she was making movies at MGM. She was just a kid, but they gave her all kinds of uppers and other drugs so she could finish one of those high-energy movies in just five weeks. She also had to deal with the sexual advances of the executives and all kinds of verbal and psychological abuse. She had a reputation for sometimes being out of control, but how can you grow up normal if that's how you're forced to spend your childhood? It's such a shame, because she was so wonderful.

Judy told me there were only two people in her entire career who were really good to her: Lionel Barrymore and Mickey Rooney. No one else befriended her during those early years at MGM. She told me Mickey would fight like crazy for her, and wouldn't tolerate anybody insulting her. One night he ran into the famous society girl Brenda Frasier, and she made a lousy remark about Judy. Mickey pulled her hat over her face and pushed her into an ash can. The next day it made front-page news.

Over the years, Judy talked to me about all aspects of her life and career, and once she said to me, "You know, I've never had money in my hand. Someone always gives a check to my accountant and he pays the bills." One time, backstage before one of Judy's shows, the promoter kept asking me, "What can I do that would make her happy? What would she like?" Remembering what she'd told me, I suggested he give her some of her fee in cash, that she'd get a big kick out of that. He said he'd do it. I went to her dressing room after the show, and there she was, jumping up and down on the couch, playing with the money, throwing it up in the air, rolling around in it—acting like a little kid. She said, "Tony! Look what I got! I got money. It's the first time in my life! I've got money!" It was wonderful to see her so happy.

She gave me an interesting piece of advice one night. She said, "You always have to do only the finest songs, but then every once in a while it's okay to sing a number that just hits the back of the house, like 'Mammy'—give 'em a real show stopper, one that everybody digs." She had a really good point. That's why I don't mind singing a song like Cy Coleman's "Firefly," which is a real crowd pleaser.

I went to see Judy every chance I could get, of course, but what surprised me was the number of times she came out to see me. It was always a pleasure to look out into the audience and see her. When *Billboard* did a special tribute issue called "Twenty Years of Tony Bennett" in 1968, Judy contributed an interview in which she talked for a whole page about how much she enjoyed watching me perform. Imagine how thrilling it was for me to read that she thought I was "...the epitome of what entertainers were put on earth for. He was born to take people's troubles away, even if it's only for an hour. He loves doing it. He's a giver." It's the best compliment I've ever received.

I don't know if Judy treated everyone she knew so well, but she always made me feel special. There was a really "in" club in Hollywood called the Daisy. Judy wanted to check it out, so I escorted her there. We ran into the Rat Pack—Dean Martin, Sammy Davis, Peter Lawford, and Frank Sinatra. They knew Judy was in trouble with drugs, so they gave us the cold shoulder. She turned to me and said, "Don't ever forget this: someday they'll regret that it was you instead of them that I was with."

I was opening at the Waldorf-Astoria in Manhattan, and as I was walking through the wings, about to go on stage one night, the stage manager stopped me and told me I had a phone call. I couldn't imagine what could be so important that he'd interrupt me at such a moment, but when he said, "It's Judy Garland," I grabbed the phone. She said, "Tony, I'm in my room at the St. Regis Hotel. There's a man here and he's beating me up!" She was crying and sounded terrified. We all knew Judy had a tendency to exaggerate, but she sounded desperate, and I believed her.

I told her, "I'm about to go on stage, Judy. I don't know what I can do." Then I thought: I'll call Frank. I put in a call to the Fontainebleau in Florida, where Sinatra was appearing, and explained the situation to him. He said, "I'll call you back in fifteen minutes." The second I got off the stage, the stage manager told me there was another call from Judy. I picked up the phone and she said, "I wanted help, but this is ridiculous! There are nine hundred cops downstairs and five lawyers in my room!" Frank certainly took care of the situation for her in grand style.

He'd just finished making a movie called *The Detective* with my old friend Abby Mann, and since they wanted it to be as realistic as possible, they'd worked closely with the New York City Police Department. All the police loved Frank, so they rallied to Judy's aid when he asked for their help. Sinatra called me back later and said, "Is that all right, kid?"

I was glad that Judy knew she could count on me when she needed a friend, since many people in her life did nothing but take advantage of her. The last time I saw her was in London in April 1969, when I was there doing a TV special with Count Basie. After the show she came backstage to see me, and the last thing she said to me was, "You're pretty good!" She died two months later. I've never gotten over it. She was so kind, so talented, such a dear friend. When I look back, it's hard to believe that most of the time she was just trying to hold on for dear life.

By the time 1964 rolled around, America was becoming a hotbed of activity on all fronts. Like everyone else, I was shocked and appalled by Kennedy's assassination. It was a sad time for this country, the end of the age of innocence. We had survived the Cuban missile crisis, but the Cold War and the threat of a nuclear confrontation still hung over our heads. The papers and the television were filled with news of Dr. Martin Luther King's fight for civil rights. It was hard to comprehend the injustice and the discrimination that was going on right here in our own backyard. I was sympathetic to the movement and I did whatever I could to help the cause.

At the same time America was experiencing a new wave of rock music called "the British invasion." I'd managed to get through the first wave—the Presley phenomenon—relatively unscathed, and now they were cramming the airwaves with the sound of a new group called the Beatles, and the marketers were hard at work creating what would soon be dubbed "Beatle-mania." Rock music was becoming big business, and Columbia quickly jumped on the bandwagon. They signed bands called the Byrds and Paul Revere and the Raiders; I thought the world was losing its mind. This music was starting to take priority over artists like Barbra Streisand and Johnny Mathis, and I became more determined than ever to find songs that would break through the rock and roll hype like a blade of grass through asphalt. My efforts paid off. I found hit songs like "When Joanna Loved Me," by Jack Segal and Bob Wells, and introduced it on my album *The Many Moods of Tony.*

I also had hits with two songs by the great British lyricist Leslie Bricusse: "Who Can I Turn To," cowritten with Anthony Newley, and the title track to my 1965 album, *If I Ruled the World (Songs for the Jet Set),* which he wrote with Cyril Ornadel. That album also included a song that's always been very special to me: "Sweet Lorraine." I dedicated it to Nat Cole, who had died a month earlier in April 1965. I was heartbroken when I heard that Nat had passed away. Bobby Hackett and I were working at the Palmer House in Chicago, and it seemed appropriate to pay tribute by recording Nat's signature tune while we were in his hometown. (Bobby, whose instrument was normally cornet, surprised us all by playing ukulele on this record; his buddy Joe Marsala played clarinet.)

I have a lot of fond memories of Nat. I was fortunate enough to be working in Las Vegas when he was playing the Sands around the time of his big hit "Rambling Rose." Since we were always working on the same nights, I couldn't catch his show, but I visited him during rehearsals. I was standing in the back of the room in the shadows while Nat was going over his cues one day. Jack Entratter, who ran the Sands, was there too, and I heard Nat tell him that he planned to walk through the audience while he was singing. But Jack Entratter objected, so I stepped out of the shadows and said, "Don't worry, Nat, you have the number one song in the country. Do whatever you want." They turned to me and both cracked up laughing.

The Sands treated Nat like the king he was. Jack threw him a special party, and I was privileged to be invited. It was held in one of the big ballrooms upstairs, and Nat's wife, Maria, his kids, and his extended family were all there.

During dinner Nat said to me, "I've got a big item for you. There's a theater that's opening up in Los Angeles next year, and I want just you, Ella Fitzgerald, Count Basie, and me to perform. Nobody else. Put it on your calendar." Every couple of months he'd call me and ask me, "Are you blocking that date off?" I didn't even know which theater it was, but it didn't matter; I was happy to sing anywhere Nat asked me to. It turned out to be the Dorothy Chandler Pavilion, and Nat's friends owned the place and wanted him to open it with a spectacular show. He had it all planned: Basie would open; then I'd come out and close the first half of the show with the Basie band. The second half would feature Ella and Nat with Basie, and then we'd all close the show together with a big jam session.

About three weeks before the show was scheduled to open, I was talking to Dean Martin. I asked him how Nat was doing, since I hadn't spoken with him for a while. Dean told me that Nat had cancer and that it was bad. He died a few days later.

The show at the Pavilion was turned into a memorial for him. Sinatra took over the planning, and it was huge. It seemed like everyone who had ever known Nat was on the bill.

Since I'd been out on the road with Basie for a while, and the music was really tight, I was looking forward to doing a half-hour set with him, but there were so many stars on the bill I only did two numbers. It was an exciting night, and the audience went wild. I think Nat would have been proud of the show.

⊹

Unfortunately, I've run into far too many incidents of racism involving the many great Black musicians I've worked with throughout the years. It's a shame that a genius like Nat had to be subjected to discrimination, but as I knew from my experiences in the war, racism could be disgustingly blatant. I once went to see Nat in Miami and I invited him to come join me at my table after the show. He told me he wasn't allowed in the dining room, that if I wanted to see him I'd have to go backstage. When the Americana Hotel opened in Miami in the mid-fifties, Duke Ellington and I played the first show. The hotel threw a big press party, but, of all things, Duke wasn't allowed to attend. In fact, the band couldn't even stay at the hotel; they had to bunk in some dingy joint in another section of Miami.

I'd never been politically inclined, but these things went beyond politics. Nat and Duke were geniuses, brilliant human beings who gave the world some of the most beautiful music it's ever heard, and yet they were treated like second-class citizens. The whole situation enraged me. That's why when Harry Belafonte called me up and asked me to join Martin Luther King's civil rights march to Selma, Alabama, in 1965 I accepted.

I'd known Harry since the late forties when we met at New York's Hanson's Drug Store on Fifty-second Street, the hangout for struggling musicians and entertainers. At that time it was anybody's guess as to which of us would make it, but none of us had any doubts about Harry. We knew he was going to be a big star. He was virtually the only entertainer in the fifties who had the courage to make social statements, and he continued that crusade through the sixties, right up to the present time.

Harry told me that the march had been planned by Martin Luther King to draw national attention to the fact that Blacks were still being denied the right to vote. Dr. King thought it would be a good idea to have some celebrities on the march to attract some media attention and to entertain the marchers at the end of each day, so he also invited my old pal Billy Eckstine, Leonard Bernstein, Shelley Winters, Sammy Davis Jr., Adolph Green, Betty Comden, and other popular performers of the day.

When the march started, I had a strange sense of déjà vu. I kept flashing back to a time twenty years earlier when my buddies and I had fought our way into Germany. It felt the same way down in Selma: the white state troopers were really hostile, and they were not shy about showing it. There was the threat of violence all along the march route, from Montgomery to Selma, some of which was broadcast on the nightly news and really helped to make the country aware of the ugliness that was still going on in the South. Billy and I were really scared. Fortunately Harry was there to reassure us, and the way he kept his cool was an inspiration.

One night, early into the march, the performers put on a show and I sang a couple of numbers. We were in the middle of a clearing, and there was no stage available, so a local mortician volunteered eighteen heavy wooden coffins for us to use as a stage. It was bizarre to be singing on top of a pile of coffins, but we made do with what we had. Twenty years later Abby Mann asked me to re-create that scene for his TV miniseries *King*.

The fifty-four-mile march lasted from March 7 to March 25. Neither Billy Eckstine nor I could stay for the entire march, but while we were there we tried to act cool and pretend we weren't terrified by the violence that surrounded us. We shared a room in a broken-down hotel. When it was time to leave, we hurriedly packed up our stuff and headed out. The next day when I was in New York, Billy called me from L.A. and said, "Where are my f——— pants?" We were so nervous when we were packing up to leave that I put on his pants and he put on mine—he's six feet two, and I'm five feet nine—but we didn't even notice.

One of Dr. King's supporters, a white woman from Detroit who had three children, took Billy and me to the airport when it was time for us to leave. We were horrified to learn that she was murdered by anti–civil rights men on her drive back to Selma.

I'm enormously proud that I was able to take part in such a historic event, but I'm saddened to think that it was ever necessary and that any person should suffer simply because of the color of his skin.

Fortunately I could continue to express my sentiments in song. A year after the Selma march Carmen McRae came to me with a song called "Georgia Rose." It was a 1921 vaudeville tune that Black entertainers loved to sing, a lullaby about a Black woman singing to her baby as she rocks him in his carriage. One of the lines goes, "Don't be blue because you're Black." It's an affirmative song, and its message is that Black is beautiful. Carmen and Ralph Burns had recorded it for Decca, but the company pretty much sat on the master and no one heard it. I fell in love with the song, and I got Ralph to write a new arrangement for me that we recorded in June 1966.

Columbia released it right away, but they claimed that someone from the NAACP had called to complain about the song, which was absurd, because the song was nothing if not pro-Black. I later found out that the story wasn't true at all; the NAACP had never called Columbia; it's just that the label wanted to stay away from anything even remotely controversial that could hurt sales down South. Columbia suppressed the single, although I did include it on my album *A Time for Love* in 1966. The whole incident still irritates me.

On April 23, 1965, I reached a pinnacle in my career: that was the week that Frank Sinatra told the whole world that I was his favorite singer. He put it like this, in *Life* magazine:

> For my money, Tony Bennett is the best singer in the business. He excites me when I watch him. He moves me. He's the singer who gets across what the composer has in mind, and probably a little more.

That quote changed my whole life. After fifteen years there were still some people in the industry who didn't take me seriously, who thought I was just a flash in the pan. Well, not after the Chairman of the Board named me his number one. From that point on, Sinatra's audience began to check me out. It was probably the most generous act that one artist has ever done for another.

Frank had long since proven himself the biggest booster I'd ever had. When I was working with Duke Ellington at the Americana Hotel in 1960, Frank found out that there was a convention of hotel owners in town. He and Joe E. Lewis rounded up every hotel owner they could find—at least fifteen of them—and brought them all in to see my act. From that one show I got bookings in places like the Waldorf-Astoria in New York, the Hilton in Las Vegas, and the Palmer House in Chicago for the next twenty years. What great guys they were to do that for me. I wish more entrepreneurs and artists today were as generous as they were.

When the *Life* story came out, I knew it was a great honor, but it was a responsibility as well. From that point on, I

New York Yellow Cab No. 1, oil on canvas, 30" x 24"

Sunday in Central Park, oil on canvas, 30" x 40"

Homage to Hockney, oil on canvas, 36" x 24"

Florence, watercolor, 12" x 16"

Mountain of Two Brothers, Rio, watercolor, 14" x 20"

Golden Gate Bridge, SF, watercolor,

Monet's Gardens No. 2, oil on canvas, 30" x 40"

Duke Ellington—"God Is Love," watercolor, 14" x 20"

had to work even harder to live up to Frank's praise. That really made me buckle down and apply more discipline and technique to my singing.

⊹

For years I'd been asked to do films, but since they always wanted me to play an Italian gangster, I just wasn't interested. But in 1965, I was offered a role in a film called *The Oscar*. It was based on the novel of the same title by Richard Sale and was a story about double-dealing and back-stabbing in Tinseltown. While Paramount Pictures was in the process of casting the film, producer Clarence Greene and director Russell Rouse happened to catch me on television. They thought my personality would translate well to the big screen, so they contacted me to see if I'd be interested in playing Hollywood agent Hymie Kelly. I was. They flew me out to California, where I passed my screen test and started production on the film.

It was loaded with great character actors, many of whom had won Oscars for their work in the past—Stephen Boyd, Elke Sommer, Milton Berle, Eleanor Parker, Joseph Cotten, Jill St. John, Edie Adams, Ernest Borgnine—in fact, I was the only unknown quantity. I was thrilled to meet all those wonderful artists.

During a break in filming, I met a young woman named Sandra Grant. She knew some people who were working on the set, and we gradually became friends and started to see a lot of each other. Sandra was a beautiful aspiring actress and we had a lot of things in common. I was still married to Patricia, though by now things had really fallen apart. One day Patricia called me at my hotel and Sandra answered the phone. We were officially separated from that moment on.

I once again threw myself into my work. The filming went well, and when we finished the picture we had a grand premiere party, a black-tie event at the Riviera in Las Vegas. The entire cast and all the Paramount executives attended. Mike Douglas was host and later ran a tape of it on his television show.

The Oscar premiered at the Civic Auditorium in Santa Monica. But it was not a success with the critics. The reviews of my performance were okay, and though I did get offers to make other movies, my heart just wasn't in it. Acting just didn't hold the charm for me that performing, making records, and painting does. In fact, I learned from that experience that I should only work on something that I have a real passion for.

The best thing about *The Oscar* was the theme song that Percy Faith had written, called "Maybe September," which I recorded for the original soundtrack album. Later I rere-corded it with the great musician Bill Evans. The whole movie-making process, though, inspired me to make my next and all-time favorite record, *The Movie Song Album.*

So many of the songs being written for films were great and I thought it would be fantastic to record a whole collec-tion of them—and even better if I could get all the original composers to conduct. I had a lot of old friends, composers, and orchestrators like Neal Hefti and Quincy Jones whose work I loved, and who were now breaking into movie writing. So I got ahold of them.

After hearing about the project, a music publisher con-tacted my producer Ernie Altschuler with a new song by Johnny Mandel called "The Shadow of Your Smile," from a film called *The Sandpiper.* I loved "The Shadow of Your Smile," and also "Emily," which Johnny had already written for a James Garner–Julie Andrews comedy called *The American-ization of Emily,* so I enlisted him as my overall musical direc-tor on the album.

In addition to Johnny's two songs, I got Neal Hefti and Quincy Jones to arrange and conduct their songs "Girl Talk" (from *Harlow*), and "The Pawnbroker" (from *The Pawnbro-ker*). Luiz Bonfa also played guitar on his songs "Samba De Orfeu" (from *Black Orpheus*), and "The Gentle Rain" (from *The Gentle Rain*). I asked Al Cohn to do scores on three older film songs, "Smile," "The Second Time Around," and a swinging treatment of "The Trolley Song" that had an out-standing tenor solo by Zoot Sims. Except for the three selec-tions conducted by Neal, Quincy, and David, Johnny conducted the rest of the album with Tommy Flanagan, Jimmy Rowles, and Lou Levy playing piano on different cuts.

"The Shadow of Your Smile" was my big song from the album, "Emily" had a lyric by Johnny Mercer, and when Man-del got the commission to do "Shadow of Your Smile," he brought the melody to Mercer, who turned him down flat. He thought it reminded him too much of "New Orleans," an old Hoagy Carmichael song. Mandel then went to Paul Francis Webster, who'd already written words for several Oscar-win-ning songs, including "Secret Love" and "Love Is a Many-Splendored Thing." He provided a lovely lyric for "The Shadow of Your Smile." Mercer regretted not working on "Shadow," even before it won the Academy Award.®

It's a great song, and it became one of my all-time most requested numbers. It hit the charts, and it meant a lot to me that I performed my version at the Oscars in 1966 and it won the award.

Both *The Movie Song Album* and Sinatra's *Life* magazine story climaxed a great era in my career. I had the honor of singing "If I Ruled the World" at a command performance for the Queen Mother of England. After the song, Bobby Hack-ett, who was playing with me at that time, leaned over to me and whispered, "What do you mean 'if'?"

With Joanna, fourteen months old,
for my album cover of "Something"

CHAPTER NINE

*A*lthough my career was at a high, my private life was falling apart. Christmas of 1965 was the lowest point in my life. Patricia and I were split up, I wasn't welcome at my home in Englewood, and I spent the holiday in a lonely room at the Gotham Hotel. Being away from my boys was devastating to me.

I was alone in my hotel room and feeling sorry for myself, when I heard music. I thought I'd left the TV on, but it was off. Then I thought it was my portable tape recorder, but that was off too. I finally realized the music was coming from the hallway, and when I opened the door a choir was singing the Burton Lane–Alan Jay Lerner song "On a Clear Day (You Can See Forever)." Duke Ellington was giving a concert of sacred music at the Fifth Avenue Presbyterian Church, and he'd heard from Louis Bellson I was in a bad way, so he sent the choir over to cheer me up. It was his Christmas gift to me, the most beautiful I have ever received. It was a moment that made me believe in people, no matter how difficult things might become for me.

My relationship with Sandra Grant continued to grow, and we became a couple. After I left Englewood and moved into the city in 1966, Sandra joined me. We lived on Riverside Drive for two years, then moved over to East Seventy-second Street.

But things weren't perfect. It was a difficult relationship from the start, filled with the classic pushing and pulling that comes when two strong-willed people get together. Initially things were exciting, because Sandra took a great interest in my career. This really appealed to me, since I always felt better when I had somebody on my side watching out for my best interests. For a long time it had been my sister, Mary, but she had become too busy raising her own family to take care of my busy career.

Sandra wanted to take on more responsibility than I was comfortable giving her. It's a rare couple who can remain emotionally close while arguing about the day-to-day running of a career—especially in show business. At least I've found that to be the case, and that's the way it was for Sandra and me. It was a really difficult time for me personally, and I don't think it would have been easy for any woman I was involved with.

⌗

After all those years of sparring with Columbia, I finally started to feel secure. I thought I was out of the woods—until I realized just how much rock and roll was dominating the scene. In 1966 an attorney named Clive Davis—originally head of business affairs for Columbia Records—took over as president of the label. It was the first time that someone without any musical background was put in charge of a record company. He took a trip to the Monterey Pop Music Festival in 1967, and when he returned he traded in his Brooks Brothers suits for Nehru jackets and love beads and signed Janis

Joplin. He began to insist that all his artists record rock and roll tunes and was convinced that nothing else would sell. At one point he was even trying to convince Barbra Streisand to record an album of Bob Dylan tunes. The whole thing was ridiculous and resulted in chaos for most of Columbia's top-selling artists.

It was a tough time for all traditional pop singers, and it took the recording industry years to adjust. But I continued to have a string of hits, and to perform to packed houses wherever I went. It was all about perception, and about the inability of the record companies to come up with some creative ideas to market my music properly. But I knew that never compromising my music would ultimately be the key to my success. Count Basie calmed me down when I asked his advice about whether I should change my act. He quickly replied, "Why change an apple?" His comment reassured me that I was on the right course.

What was happening at Columbia, and to me in particular, wasn't due simply to Clive Davis. I had nothing personal against the man; if it hadn't been Clive giving me a hard time, it would have been somebody else. The record companies thought that rock and roll was all anybody would ever want to hear from that point on: that's the way the industry was headed; he was just the guy in the driver's seat. When it occurred to the major labels that they could make a real killing with rock music, they gradually lost interest in anything else, including classical artists. Despite my proven success, there was never a time while I was at Columbia that they said to me, "You know what you're doing. Go ahead, keep making the records you've been making." Instead, they always insisted they knew what was best.

What was ironic about the whole thing is that there were a lot of first-rate traditional pop songs being written in the late sixties—enough so that I could still fill album after album. For instance, Johnny Mandel and Paul Francis Webster, after winning the Oscar for "The Shadow of Your Smile," wrote two more songs together, "A Lonely Place" and "A Time for Love," and I recorded them in 1966 for my album, *A Time for Love*. I also included "Georgia Rose" and "Touch the Earth" by the wonderful singer and piano player Jeri Southern. These were wonderful songs, so I just couldn't understand why Columbia insisted that I do what I considered second-rate material.

A Time for Love also included two tracks from the best recording session I ever had with the great trumpeter Bobby Hackett. I was in London to do another command performance for the Queen Mother. We had British arranger Johnny Keating for the show, and the orchestra consisted of one hundred violin players, a rhythm section, and Bobby Hackett.

The performance was televised by the BBC, and since it was such an incredible experience—singing with Bobby and one hundred strings—I wanted to put it on record. The next day we all went into the studio and laid down "Sleepy Time Gal" and "The Very Thought of You." I still get a thrill when I listen to those records. Bobby also played behind me on "The Shining Sea," another song written by Johnny Mandel and Peggy Lee. He was determined to achieve a particular sound for his solo, and to do this he needed a special mouthpiece. He said, "If I can get that, I'll get a sound you won't believe," and he looked everywhere for one. He eventually found it and he did get the tight, beautiful sound he was looking for. Last Christmas my current guitarist, Gray Sargent, gave me that very mouthpiece. Bobby once made an album of love ballads conducted by Jackie Gleason. Every record company turned it down, saying it was too slow, then Capitol

Records reluctantly agreed to release it, and it sold millions of copies.

Bobby introduced me to Louis Armstrong. They were great friends, and he and Bobby spent hours listening to classical music together. They both lived in Sunnyside, Queens. When Bobby and Louis came over to my house to meet me, Louis turned to me and said in that raspy voice of his, "I'm the coffee, but Bobby's the cream."

Louis was a genius; he practically invented jazz single-handedly. When classical trumpet players first heard him play, they ran to their teachers and asked, "How'd he do that?" And the teachers replied, "We don't know." Louis was an original! People adored him. Bobby and I remained Louis's loyal friends and fans for the rest of his life. In 1970 we had the honor, along with Miles Davis and Ornette Coleman, of being part of a big tribute choir of jazzmen and celebrities who sang and played behind Louis on his last album, *Louis Armstrong and His Friends*.

I once did a painting of Louis and presented it to him in London. He took one look at it and said, "You out-Rembrandted Rembrandt!"—a typically humorous thing for Louis to say. He hung the painting in front of the desk in his study so he could look at it every time he sat down. He showed the painting to anyone who visited him and he'd say, "Here's a painting a boy who lives in my neighborhood did of me." I loved that man.

⁂

Ralph Sharon's wife, Susan, had asked him to get off the road and relocate to San Francisco. Living in California made it a lot more difficult for Ralph to hook up with me for gigs, since I was based in New York and air travel wasn't as sophisticated as it is now, but we managed.

While I was filming *The Oscar* we weren't doing many live shows anyway, so it didn't affect us too much. I wanted the trio and myself to keep in shape while I was doing the picture, though, so I called my friend Hugh Hefner and he got the trio a gig at the Playboy Club in Los Angeles, and I came by and sat in whenever I could get off the set. Ralph and the trio did two albums for Columbia during this time, a collection of jazz instrumental versions of my hits, and an interpretation of the latest Richard Rodgers musical, *Do I Hear a Waltz?* With everything he was doing Ralph soon became well-known enough to get his own local music show on San Francisco TV. He was really settling in.

After the movie was finished it was time to get back on the road, but Susan was still pressuring Ralph to stay home. When Hugh Hefner opened a new club in San Francisco in the spring of 1966, he asked Ralph to become permanent musical director, and it seemed too good an offer to turn down. We were both terribly broken up over his leaving.

I had a number of pianists while Ralph was away. The most famous was Tommy Flanagan, one of the most marvelous accompanists of all time. He'd spent many years on the road with Ella Fitzgerald and didn't really want to commit himself permanently to another singer after that. Who could blame him? But he did agree to play with me for a little while, and I was thrilled to have him.

He was with me for my most ambitious television project yet, *Singer Presents Tony Bennett*, a special that we taped for ABC at their studio in Brooklyn on May 3, 1966. It was produced and directed by Gary Smith and Dwight Hemion. I'd first met Dwight in the early fifties when he was camera director for Steve Allen and I was doing a guest spot on Steve's show.

I'd had other offers over the years to do television specials, and while some of the things the producers proposed were interesting, they weren't for me. But then I met Al di Scipio. He ran the Singer Sewing Machine Company, and was sponsoring the upcoming show. I said yes to ABC because Al, as producer, gave me as much creative freedom as any artist could ask. I told them I didn't want anybody writing phony dialogue for me; I just wanted to sing and be spontaneous with how I presented each artist. Al heard my request, and the next day he handed me a script. I opened it and found only blank pages. Someone like Al comes around only once in a lifetime.

I added a couple of personal touches too. The show was going to be a combination of my big hits and my current repertoire, and I wanted to change some of the arrangements to make room for instrumental guest stars. I assembled six of the greatest jazz soloists ever: Bobby Hackett on "Because of You," Buddy Rich on "Fascinating Rhythm," master vibraharpist Milt Jackson on "Lost in the Stars," guitarist Gene Bertocini on "Quiet Nights of Quiet Stars," Candido on "The Moment of Truth," and flautist Paul Horn and his quintet on "The Shadow of Your Smile." I thought that using jazz guys would give the show a feeling of freshness and spontaneity, and I was right. To top it all off, Ralph Burns served as conductor and musical director, and the band featured such luminaries as Richie Kamuca, Frank Wess, Joe Wilder, Urbie Green, and Quentin Jackson.

At one point we broke away from the concert format to go into a little "travelogue" that featured rear-projection shots of me walking around San Francisco. As the audience saw these images on screen they heard me singing "San Francisco," "Just In Time," "A Taste of Honey," and "Once Upon a Time." During the photo shoot for this segment, they tried to get a picture of me sitting on a rock overlooking the sea, but one wave hit real big, knocking me over; it was worth it because it gave the audience a good laugh.

After Tommy Flanagan moved on I found a wonderful pianist named John Bunch. John was playing in Buddy Rich's new big band, and he totally knocked me out. When he finished his engagement with Buddy I asked him if he wanted the job as my musical director, and he said, "Are you sure you want me? I haven't worked with many singers, and I've never conducted at all." But John had played with all the great big bands, including Benny Goodman, Maynard Ferguson, and Woody Herman. He could swing, and he had an elegant touch, and that was more important to me than anything else. Gentleman John Bunch was the man for me.

Sometimes when we were off for a few nights in New York, John took a gig with some local act. One night he told me he was playing for Zoot Sims and Al Cohn down at the old Half Note, and invited me to come down and check it out. Naturally, I went, and when Zoot saw me in the house, he introduced me to the crowd and said, "Tony, why don't you come up and sing a song with us?" That was all I needed to hear! I jumped up on stage and started singing without even waiting for John to give me a piano introduction. John later told me that I'd started singing the song in the same key that Zoot and Al usually played it in, without having been given a pickup note or a downbeat. I guess I felt the vibe. I loved the way they played; to me they're the most intelligent, romantic people in the whole world.

Around the same time Ralph left the group, my drummer Billy Exiner had to leave too. He hadn't been well for years and was never really healthy the whole time I knew him. He'd been badly injured during the war, and the doctors were never able to get all the shrapnel out of his back. It was an incredibly painful injury, and he became addicted to morphine and other painkillers for the rest of his life. Still he was one of the most brilliant philosophers and kindest people I ever knew.

By the mid-sixties Billy's ailments had developed into Berger's disease, a circulation disorder that slowly cripples the limbs. He finally had to cut out in order to take care of himself. He got the best medical care, but it wasn't enough to save his life. He died in 1985, and I still miss him. I've had a number of drummers since Billy's been gone, including Sol Gubin, Joe LaBarbera, Joe Cocuzzo, and my percussionist of the last five years, the amazing Clayton Cameron. They are all ace players, but I'm not exaggerating when I say that Billy has never been replaced. He was closer to me than anyone.

After Billy, the drummer I had most often in the sixties was Sol Gubin, and I was glad to have John Bunch and Sol with me on my next album of jazz standards, *Tony Makes It Happen,* which we taped in late 1966 and early 1967. There was a song on the album, "Country Girl," a tone poem by Henry Wadsworth, that was special to me because it was the first time I recorded a piece of music by Robert Farnon. Bob had written the song for a British music competition, and though it didn't win, it got more attention than the tune that actually did. It's a gem.

As touching a tune as "Country Girl" was, Bob's number one asset was that he was one of the greatest orchestrators of pop music. Sinatra dubbed Farnon "The Guv'nor." Recording with him was one of the high points of the late sixties for me. His music gives me the chills.

I had met Bob Farnon in early 1952, when I was playing the Casino in Toronto. He then came to the United States in 1954 to work with his friend Don Walker on the orchestrations for *The Girl in Pink Tights.* Tony T. found him a house right next door to my mother's in River Edge, New Jersey.

Even back then, Bob wanted us to record together, but I had such reverence for his work that I told him I wasn't ready. I just didn't feel like I had developed enough as an artist to make an album with him. I thought I'd have to wait about twenty years before I sang with Bob, and I was pretty close, because we didn't work together until 1967.

We decided to do a Christmas album together. The title, *Snowfall,* was inspired by Claude Thornhill's most famous composition and struck me as a beautiful title. We taped six tracks in New York and four tracks in London. The project inspired Bob to work at his highest level, and his orchestrations were superb. I especially liked "Christmasland," an original song Bob and his brother Brian wrote for the album.

The New York recording session for *Snowfall* was amazing. Farnon had conducted for American singers before, like Sinatra and Sarah Vaughan, but this was the first time he'd actually come to the U.S. to do it. The clique of New York orchestrators who'd studied Farnon's writing—including Don Costa, Marion Evans, and Torrie Zito—all showed up at the session.

Everybody wanted to know how Bob worked, and the second he left the room the curious arrangers rushed up to the podium to study his score.

Quincy Jones threw a party for him, and every musician and orchestrator in New York City was there. There were so many celebrated music makers in that one room that Quincy cracked, "If a bomb goes off in this apartment, there won't be any more records made!"

We went an hour overtime at the London session. Paul McCartney had booked the studio after us, but he was very obliging and agreed to wait until we were finished. I had met

Paul a number of times before that; in fact, in 1965 I had presented the Beatles with their first award at an annual New Musical Express event. I recently ran into Paul at a party at David Frost's house in London. For years people have been coming up to me and saying, "My mom thinks you're the greatest!" and my automatic tongue-in-cheek response is always, "Tell her she has good taste." When I met Paul, my good friend Susan told him that my son Danny is a big fan of his. He responded with the same line that I always use, "Tell him he has good taste." From the beginning, I always felt Paul was the one in the group with real star power.

I was delighted with *Snowfall*, but Columbia didn't share my enthusiasm. They thought the title was too "uncommercial," and again they didn't like the cover illustration, which I'd had Bob Peak do. Columbia had nixed the one he did for *When Lights Are Low*, and again, they balked.

That Columbia didn't put any effort into promoting *Snowfall* was hardly a surprise. "For Once in My Life" had been my last hit single, and by 1967 it seemed that the company was ready to wash their hands of me. I was still making records for them, but they weren't doing much about trying to sell them. Judy Collins tells a Duke Ellington story that I think applies particularly well to what was going on with me at this time. In the early sixties Duke was having trouble with Columbia. They asked him to come into their offices and sat him down and told him they were going to drop him from the label because he wasn't selling enough records. Duke thought for a moment and responded, "I guess I must be mistaken. I thought I was supposed to make the records and YOU were supposed to sell them." Right on, Duke. That sums up my situation in a nutshell.

Clive Davis took particular pride in getting what he called "middle of the road" artists—a term I dislike—to "cover" contemporary hits. In his book, *Clive: Inside the Music Industry*, he admits that he'd come up with a formula for figuring out exactly how many copies an album of cover tunes could sell and then went about making records according to that formula. He told me the only way he'd get behind me was if I agreed to record some of the current material he was pushing. I couldn't do that, so we were at a stalemate.

In fact, all my recent albums, *For Once in My Life, Yesterday I Heard the Rain,* and *Something* contained wonderful new songs by great songwriters like Cy Coleman, Johnny Mercer, Richard Rodgers, Stephen Sondheim, Jule Styne, Leslie Bricusse, Anthony Newley, Michel Legrand, Sammy Cahn, Jimmy Van Heusen, Marilyn and Alan Bergman, Jack Segal, Bob Wells, and Gene Lees. They were all writing wonderful contemporary songs, but Columbia didn't see it that way.

I had no objection to doing songs that were already hits, provided I thought they were good and that I could sing them with a different interpretation. I recorded a number of Burt Bacharach hits, but I did them in my own style. I had Torrie Zito write me a swinging big band version of "What The World Needs Now," which I thought was really on the money, and it went over big every time I sang it. I even sang it once on the *Ed Sullivan Show* with Duke Ellington's orchestra.

I was doing three albums a year, and all this pressure started bringing me down. On top of it all, I'd been separated from Patricia for close to three years, and we couldn't seem to reach an understanding. Although the last thing I wanted to do was get involved in a nasty legal battle, attorneys entered the picture. I was served with divorce papers. After that, all I heard was "See you in court."

In 1968 I celebrated my twentieth anniversary in show business, and I did a tour with Duke Ellington and his Orchestra. We opened a series of twenty-five concerts at the New York Philharmonic on March 3, and it was a sellout show. In fact I was selling out concert halls all over the world, so when Columbia claimed that they weren't able to sell my records, I couldn't help but wonder what they were doing wrong.

I'd first worked with Duke about ten years earlier, at the Bal Masque, part of the Americana Hotel in Miami, a dream come true. When I was a kid one of the greatest shows I ever saw featured Duke Ellington, Ethel Waters, and the tap dance trio Tip, Tap, and Toe. It was absolutely tremendous, and I was hooked on Duke's music from then on.

Ralph hoped to realize a long-held dream of his during that engagement at the Americana, but it didn't exactly work out that way. Since he was a jazz arranger and composer himself, he'd always wanted to have a look at Ellington's music, so early one morning Ralph went down to the rehearsal room to sneak a peek. He looked everywhere, but there wasn't a page of written music to be found. Later Ralph asked Duke's great baritone sax player Harry Carney about it, and Harry said, "Oh, we don't have music. We know all our parts." When Duke wrote something new, the band had to learn it. They were playing the most intricate, intense music you've ever heard from memory!

Whenever I worked with Duke—or with Basie for that matter—I deliberately violated some advice that Louis Prima had given me years earlier in Vegas. He'd said, "Whatever you do, wherever you work, make sure you get top billing. Go ahead and work a smaller room, but even if it's a sawdust joint, be the headliner." But I went against his great advice where

Basie and Ellington were concerned because I wanted to show respect for them. The only other times I settled for second billing were when I played with Bob Hope and Frank Sinatra, and I'm sure I don't have to explain why.

Duke was a mystic. He told me that after he'd read the Bible, he knew everything he needed to know. We were on a plane together once and he told me a story about writing an upcoming concert of sacred music. When he started working, he called his writing partner, Billy Strayhorn, in New York and told him he wanted to start the concert with a musical motif inspired by the Book of Genesis. A month later he called Billy to see what he had come up with. Amazingly, they had written the exact same notes to the same opening words, "In the beginning there was God."

Another time, Duke and I were both working in Boston and staying at the Somerset Hotel. I was hanging out in my room with Bobby Hackett, who was talking about how he'd really love to have a jam session. The phone rang, and it was Duke. He said, "I'm downstairs and I have a song for you. Come to the Grand Ballroom." When Duke began playing he realized that the middle octave of the piano was shot. But that didn't deter Duke: he played for us anyway, using the remainder of the keyboard. That song was "Love Scene." He played a whole hour for us, everything he could think of. I looked over at Bobby, who was so moved he was quietly crying tears of joy.

Duke had a lovely habit of sending me a dozen roses whenever he'd written a new song. It was a beautiful gesture from a great man, and it later inspired me to do a watercolor painting of Duke in front of a bouquet of roses, which I entitled "God Is Love." To this day it's one of my favorite paintings, and though I always show it, I would never sell it. In fact, it's the only one of my own paintings I've hung in my home.

I've sung so many of his songs over the years, including "I'm Just a Lucky So and So," "Sophisticated Lady," "I Let a Song Go Out of My Heart," "Don't Get Around Much Anymore," "Love Scene," and "Reflections," to name only a few. I've concluded many concerts with a special medley of Ellington songs, always climaxing with "It Don't Mean a Thing (If It Ain't Got That Swing)." When the great Louis Bellson was playing with me, that medley was a feature for him, and we still do it today to spotlight my wonderful drummer Clayton Cameron. Few people know that Duke composed more music that anyone else in the history of music, including ballet suites, tone poems, sacred concerts, and popular songs.

We got together whenever we could, whether it was on the road, in a club, or staying up all night jamming. Duke and I celebrated his seventy-second birthday together. I was working at the Waldorf-Astoria that night, and Duke was out in the audience. I introduced him and he came up and played a few numbers, charming the entire room. I brought out a huge cake, and everybody sang "Happy Birthday." What a night!

By 1968 my life was in a complete uproar. My divorce battle with Patricia was raging in the courts, and in April, Sandra told me she was pregnant. My mom started to get really sick and became bedridden; all I could do was think back to the time when we were all in Astoria and she worked so hard to take care of us. Now the tables were turned. I ran back and forth between New York and Jersey to see her whenever I could. After every visit I rode back to the city thinking it might be the last time I'd ever see her. It was about as much as I could take.

My first daughter was born on January 9, 1969. At the suggestion of my friend and television producer Dwight

Hemion we named her Joanna, inspired by my song "When Joanna Loved Me." I'd always thought that was a lovely song and an enchanting name. Joanna was a beautiful child and it was really exciting and comforting to have a new daughter in my life.

In the late sixties, a new pop star's career lasted about a year and a half; as soon as he started slipping, the label would drop him and move on to the next guy. It got to be like a supermarket. I called those kind of artists "overdogs" because they were so heavily promoted they couldn't lose. It didn't matter whether or not they had talent or how long they lasted; they were forced down the public's throats.

After much disagreement, Clive Davis convinced me to do the kind of record he wanted. The album was called *Tony Sings the Great Hits of Today,* a collection of contemporary cover tunes. I started planning the record by listening to as many current hits as I could stand. I mean, some of these songs made me physically ill. Even Clive Davis says in his book that I became so nauseous before the first recording session that I literally threw up.

Wally Gold was the producer, and the poor guy was in the difficult position of having to serve as a buffer between me and the company. These songs just weren't my style. The only good thing to come out of that project was that we hired the great orchestrator Peter Matz. He was perfect for the job.

Clive made sure to promote *Great Hits* so well that it sold more than my other recent albums had. I thought it was pretty corny because first he got me to do it his way, and then he printed up more copies of that album to make it look like the public was demanding it. Give me a break!

It wasn't long before he wanted a follow-up. But there was no way I would go through another *Great Hits of Today* session—I just couldn't do it. Instead I took the George Harrison song "Something" and made it the title song on my next album.

Peter once again did the orchestrations for *Something*, and this time everything turned out right. All twelve songs were my kind of contemporary songs, the best the times had to offer.

I ended the *Something* album with Louis Armstrong's last hit, "What a Wonderful World." Instead of just covering the song, I made it into a tribute to him, ending the song by imitating him: "Yeah, Louis Armstrong was right. It's a wonderful world." The album was released in October 1970. For the cover, I chose a shot of me cradling infant Joanna in my arms. It's the best album cover I ever saw.

At the end of 1971 my divorce with Patricia became final. For all practical purposes my relationship with Patricia had been over for years, since that lonely Christmas in 1965. Patricia and the boys stayed in the house in Englewood, and as hard as it was to accept, I was determined to stay involved with my boys, and though at times it was tough to work everything out, I didn't disappear from their lives.

While the pressure at the label continued to mount, I hired Derek Boulton, an Englishman, as my manager. Derek was also Bob Farnon's manager; we'd met when I was working with Bob and we hit it off right away. We both agreed that it was time for me to put the "two shows a night" phase of my career behind me. I'd been doing nightclubs for twenty years. It was time to graduate to venues like Carnegie Hall, the Palladium, Royal Festival Hall, and Royal Albert Hall. When I worked in Vegas, the rooms were the size of concert halls, and I'd been gradually expanding my stage show so by this time I was using a thirty-two piece orchestra. I was also showing back-projection film clips during my performances, like scenes from the city of San Francisco, or scenes from Chaplin's film *City Lights* when I performed "Smile." Mr. Chaplin was so impressed with my version of "Smile" that he mailed me the last ten minutes of his film *Modern Times,* in which Chaplin gives a flower to Paulette Goddard and walks down the road into the sunset.

The old-time clubs like the Copa and Chez Paree were on their way out anyhow, since by the late sixties all the action had moved to Vegas. I was happy with my decision to stop playing the small nightclubs, and on Saturday, October 9, 1971, I gave a concert at Carnegie Hall. I was working with Bob Farnon, who conducted the fifty-piece orchestra and included some of his original compositions as well as his imaginative orchestrations of other works, like his wonderful suite based on Gershwin's *Porgy and Bess.*

The first half of the show went great, but by my second or third number of the second half, I could see that the audience was getting up and leaving. Then I noticed a funny smell in the air. At first we thought it must be a fire, but eventually we figured out that somebody had sabotaged the concert by putting a stink bomb into the ventilation system.

Once we knew there was no fire, everybody calmed down. It was a warm autumn night, so the audience went outside while the Carnegie management cleared the air. After ten minutes everybody came back for the rest of the show—not one person gave up and went home. The great opera singer Richard Tucker was in the audience that night and came backstage and encouraged me to relax. His talk inspired me to come back out and sing my heart out! To this day I don't know who it was that tried to break up my concert with a stink bomb, although I figured it was one of "the boys" trying to put a scare into me: it didn't work.

Things were pretty much still at an impasse with Columbia, even after the release of *Great Hits of Today* and *Something*. We were soon embroiled in another disagreement, this one because of my longtime friendship with composer Alec Wilder.

Alec wrote "serious" concert pieces, mainly for chamber groups. I especially loved his song "While We Were Young." He was a great wit, and a fixture on both the jazz and cabaret scenes and I'd met him in the early fifties. I had been doing his songs ever since.

In the late sixties, I introduced Alec to friends of mine in England, Ken and Renee Gordan, whose young son liked to write poetry. Alec was so taken with the boy's poems that he decided to set them to music. The Vietnam War was on everybody's mind back then, and the boy's poems addressed the war from a child's point of view: why he didn't want his father to go into battle, why war was bad for children. Alec's idea was to compose an octet around this boy's recitation of his poems. He eventually included other children's poems, and by the time he finished *The Children's Plea for Peace* it had music for a full orchestra, a children's chorus, and a narrator.

I was determined to record it. I wanted the part of the narrator, and Alec planned to compose some pieces for me to sing as well. He was thrilled that I wanted to do it. But when I brought the idea to Columbia, they immediately decided the piece was too controversial and too uncommercial—without ever hearing it. So I had to explain to Alec that Columbia just wouldn't go for it, and he never quite forgave me for not getting that composition recorded. He later wrote about his life and criticized his closest friends: Whitney Balliet, Marian McPartland, and yours truly, and he let me have it in print for not coming through on *The Children's Plea for Peace*.

But I had fought like crazy to record *Plea for Peace*. I fought, and I kept on fighting. I stormed out of the studio one day after an argument with Clive and his cronies, and on my way out I heard one of them say, "We gotta get rid of that wop!" The proverbial straw broke the camel's back: I went to Columbia brass and said, "I want out. I don't want to play this game anymore. I don't want to make the records that sell the most, I want to sell the most records that are the best I can make. The public deserves it."

After some long and loud negotiations we finally worked out a deal we both could live with. I was to give them two more albums, which I'd produce myself, and that would fulfill my contractual obligation to them. I decided to do both of these projects with Bob Farnon, and the first album would be live.

The Royal Albert Hall was celebrating its one hundredth anniversary in 1971, and Derek arranged for Bob and me to perform at one of the special concerts being given to commemorate the centenary. The London Philharmonic Orchestra was featured, and I supplemented them with fifteen of the best jazz musicians we could find in London, like the fabulous drummer Kenny Clare. The program included a lot of my big numbers, as well as some standards.

It was a sold-out concert, and one of the most exciting nights I've ever enjoyed in show business. The audience went wild; it sounded like all of Britain was there. We made arrangements for the BBC to videotape the concert, directed by Yvonne Littlewood, and Derek worked out a deal for NBC to broadcast it in the United States. It got top ratings. When it came time to design the album cover, I chose my boyhood friend Rudy DeHarak. His design was based on a black-and-white image of me taken off the TV screen. It was great.

On November 15, 1971, I had my final recording session for Columbia Records. It consisted of a single song, "The Summer Knows," the theme from *Summer of '42* by Michel Legrand and Alan and Marilyn Bergman. It was a fine song, and after twenty-two years it was an appropriate way to conclude a long relationship. Sandra and I were finally married in December of 1971. I was relieved because I really wanted the three of us to become a family. I had to believe that everything in both my personal and professional lives was going to work out for the best.

With a collection of my albums

CHAPTER TEN

9 left Columbia Records voluntarily because I wanted to create a catalogue that would be a legacy for my fans. I wanted to make records that would stand the test of time. I'm not concerned about the criticisms of the pencil pushers at the record company; the public is my only critic. I go by their reaction, and if their reaction to my live performances was any indication of how they felt, then I was doing something right. My goal was to become the consummate concert performer.

I looked around for another record company. My manager Derek Boulton worked out a deal for me with Mike Curb, head of A&R in the American division of Polygram Records. They offered me more than Columbia had, and promised that the rights to the masters of my albums would eventually revert back to me. According to the terms of the new contract, my albums would be released on the Philips label in England, and on MGM/Verve in America.

I started my recording contract with MGM/Verve the same way I ended with Columbia: by making the best album I possibly could. Once again I worked with Bob Farnon. The album, *The Good Things in Life,* began and ended with a wonderful title track by Leslie Bricusse and Anthony Newley from their musical *It's a Funny Old World.* I thought this song really expressed the way I'd been feeling for the last few years, and ending the album with a reprise of the same song was a musical concept that appealed to me.

I went back to England in 1971. Derek had made a lot of show business contacts there over the years, my new record company was located in London, and we figured that concentrating on that market for a while would be time well spent. So Sandra, baby Joanna, and I packed up and left for what would turn out to be a yearlong stay. Ted Lewis, the famous vaudevillian and bandleader had told me—this was before I'd ever played England—"Do yourself a favor. Play England every year. The fans there are unlike anywhere else. They're loyal. They never forget you."

Mr. Lewis was right. I'd gone back in 1958 to do a television broadcast, *Sunday Night at the London Palladium,* and I'd made my proper London nightclub debut at Pigalle, in Piccadilly in 1961, to smash reviews. Each time I toured the British towns—London, Manchester, Liverpool, Harrogate— my fans came out to support me. My recording sessions for MGM/Verve were done in England, and between sessions I did a provincial tour with a big band featuring Kenny Clare on drums, Arthur Watts on bass, and my pianist John Bunch, who'd accompanied me from the States. All my engagements were "standing room only." In February of 1972, I gave concerts all over England and set a record when tickets for the shows sold out in thirty-five minutes. It was truly rewarding to be so enthusiastically welcomed by the British public. England has been good to me over the years; I've done six royal command performances, and I go back to perform as often as I can. In fact, my biggest fan club, or "appreciation society," as they like to call it, is based there.

I taped a television series—thirteen half-hour shows done in a concert format—at Talk of the Town, a restaurant theater in London. The guests were fabulous—I had Annie Ross, Matt Monro, and one night I had both Sarah Vaughan and Billy Eckstine. You can't get any better than that! Every show featured one segment that took place outside the studio: a camera followed me while I went sightseeing with Joanna, and these scenes were accompanied by some gorgeous instrumentals by Bob Farnon.

I worked hard while I was in England, but I also took some time out for my personal life, something I hadn't done in years. Sandra, Joanna, and I took in the lovely English sights and got to spend some good times together. I'd been painting whenever I could, but it was during this year in London that I really started to get serious about it. I found a wonderful professor of art, John Barnicort, who gave me private instruction. I was staying in a flat next to the American embassy in Grosvenor Square, and he'd come over to my place and give me some lessons on technique. I became more serious about painting than I'd ever been, and I've never looked back. I was determined to become a skilled painter, no matter how hard I had to work at it.

I took up tennis too. Whenever we got to a new town, the first thing John Bunch did was find out where a game of tennis was going on. I'd never really played before, but I'd enjoyed watching the game as a kid, and the fact that John felt so passionate about it really got me interested. John's girlfriend Chips (who'd been raised by Winston Churchill) took me to a very nice tennis court the first time I played. I later found out that it was center court at Wimbledon! Soon I started taking professional lessons, and it wasn't long before I was hooked.

Today I play at least twice a week. Whenever I'm in New York, I head out to the courts at the East River Tennis Club in Astoria, usually with my drummer Clayton Cameron—who plays tennis better than he plays the drums, which is saying a lot!

I also had some time to tape another television show, a one-hour TV special at the Palladium with the fabulous Lena Horne. To me Lena is synonymous with class, and when someone proposed the idea that she and I should do a concert together, I jumped at it. The show was produced by Lord Lew Grade, and featured John Bunch on piano and the great English drummer Jack Parnell. After the show, we toured our act around England during 1972 and 1973, toured the States with the package in 1974 and 1975, and then brought it back to the Palladium in London in 1976.

Nineteen seventy-two was a rough year for Lena. Within a very short period of time she'd lost the three most important men in her life: her father, her son Teddy, and her husband of twenty years, Lennie Hayton. Yet you'd never know it from looking at her. She was probably the most professional performer I've ever worked with. She never missed a show and she always gave one hundred percent. Lena taught me a lot about discipline. Even at rehearsals she was thrilling to watch. I'd never seen that kind of intensity in anyone before, that determination to do everything just right.

I thought it would be more effective to start with something subtle, so we opened the show singing two songs together, usually "The Look of Love" and "Something." Then Lena and her conductor, Robert Freedman, did a forty-five minute set together, which included some of her perennial hits. After intermission, I performed. Lena and I then closed the show together with a medley of Harold Arlen songs that was seventeen minutes long. What a night!

John Bunch moved on in the fall of 1972 and Bernie Leighton replaced him for a few months and played on my second MGM/Verve album, *Listen Easy*.

Then Torrie Zito took over and stayed with me for six years, as my pianist, conductor, and orchestrator. Over the years we worked together on three albums, *Once in My Life*, *Yesterday I Heard the Rain*, and *I Gotta Be Me*.

While I was with MGM/Verve, Columbia tried to patch things up with me, particularly after Clive Davis left in May of 1973. They approached Derek and offered a very generous deal: an imprint label within Columbia—which meant that I would be running my own record label, deciding what albums I wanted to make, and bringing in other artists to record for me. But I wasn't ready to go back to Columbia yet.

When I returned to the States in late 1972, my old buddy Dave Victorson was running the Las Vegas Hilton. He offered me an eighteen-month contract, giving me the run of the house, letting me put on whatever kind of shows I wanted— all because I once helped him when he was down on his luck.

So in May 1973 Dave and I had installed an 109-man phil-harmonic orchestra in the Hilton. I can still see all those men up there on stage: we'd flown them in from all over the coun-try, the most spectacular band that ever played Vegas. Bob Farnon did the orchestrations, and Louis Bellson joined us on stage. It was a fantastic show.

When I was ready to go back on the road, I put together the great trio that worked with me all through the 1970s: John Giuffrida on bass; Chuck Hughes and then, for most of the decade, Joe Cocuzzo on drums; and Torrie Zito on piano. Joe is a world-class drummer, particularly sensitive when playing with singers. We'd first worked together back in 1969 when I was on tour with Louis Bellson. Louis was going out to play and conduct for his wife, Pearl Bailey, and I needed a drummer right away for an upcoming show at the Shoreham Hotel in Washington. Joe Soldo—who hired musicians for me when I was on the road—heard that Joe was available, and he came in and played the whole show for me without a rehearsal. After the show I told him, "You know what? I just had Louis Bellson play for me all last week, and tonight you're there with the best of them." That was my way of saying, "Welcome aboard." Joe played for me pretty regularly between 1969 and the start of my "English period" in 1971, and then came back and joined my trio in 1973.

My main focus in late 1973 became the brilliant trumpet playing of Ruby Braff. I'd known Ruby since 1951 when I first played Chicago. Ruby heard George Barnes and Bucky Pizzarelli playing at the St. Regis Hotel in New York, and he sat in with the two guitarists. He loved the way that combination sounded, and suggested to George that they start a group. They gradually worked out a lineup of two guitars, a trumpet, and a bass. When I heard about this group, I had to check them out. I thought they were great, and Ruby said to me, "Why don't you come and sing a couple of tunes with us, and relax for a while, you know?" I was singing almost exclusively with big bands then, and even with a good sound system I always had to belt it out to be heard above the music.

I liked the groove I got into with this intimate group so much that I did two special concerts with them at Alice Tully Hall in New York. Ruby and George played the first half instrumentally, and then I came out in the second half and sang with them—two entire evenings of Rodgers and Hart. Two weeks later I recorded twenty-four Rodgers and Hart songs with Ruby and George, with Frank Laico as engineer. It was later released as *Tony Bennett: The Rodgers and Hart Songbook*.

On April 7, 1974, Sandra gave birth to our second daughter. We named her Antonia, in keeping with the long tradition of Antonios and Antoinettes in the Benedetto and Suraci families. Many years later I asked Bob Wells and Jack Segal, who had written "When Joanna Loved Me," to write a song for Antonia, since I wanted to honor both of my daughters in song. They came up with a beauty, and I recorded "Antonia" in 1989.

I now had two beautiful daughters and we moved to Los Angeles and started living the glamorous Hollywood lifestyle— the good and the bad. We had the big beautiful house in Beverly Hills, the celebrity friends, and the endless round of parties.

On top of everything else, the seventies drug scene was getting out of control. At every big party I'd go to, people were high on something. Cocaine flowed as freely as champagne, and soon I began joining in the festivities. At first it seemed like the hip thing to do, but as time went on it got harder and harder to refuse it when it was offered. Compounded with my pot smoking, the whole thing started sneaking up on me.

Sandra thought that I might want to get back into making pictures, but I just didn't have a passion for it. Cary Grant set me straight about that. He loved the idea that I traveled all over the world doing concerts, and one time he said to me, "Tony, what you do is beautiful, the way you go out and meet the people where they live. Making movies would be boring for you. You sit around for hours while somebody changes a lightbulb. You were right not to get mixed up in it." He actually envied me for being able to work in front of live audiences all over the world. What a life, what an education. There's nothing like performing.

I got to see a lot of Cary Grant during this period of my life. There were some actors that I had infinite admiration for, and Mr. Grant was one of them, so it was nice to be able to count him among my friends. One day I got a call from Cary and he'd seen my painting "South of France" when I showed it to Johnny Carson on *The Tonight Show*. He told me, "I want to buy that painting!" I was thrilled that he liked it, and I told him I'd be happy to give it to him as a gift, but he insisted on buying the painting, and he hung it in his home in the Hollywood Hills.

But the greatest thing about living in L.A. was the chance to get to know two of my biggest idols, Fred Astaire and Ella Fitzgerald. Fred was well over seventy by the time we got acquainted, but he was still very active. Every morning he'd take his daily constitutional, and he'd walk right past my house. He was so graceful he actually looked like he was floating as he strolled by.

My friend the dancer John Brascia introduced me to Fred Astaire. Fred told me that he was no longer athletic and that he only acted and wrote songs these days. We were sitting in a little art studio I had, completely separate from the rest of the house, and listening to the local jazz station. I had to go back to the main house for a few minutes to answer the phone. When I returned, I caught Fred Astaire dancing to a song on the radio. It was tremendous. He stopped as soon as he noticed me and his face turned red. He asked me who that was singing the blues, and I told him Big Joe Turner. Fred said, "It's always been that way. When I hear the right beat, I just *have* to dance." Where was my video camera when I needed it?

As I got to know him better, I found out about how he rehearsed. He always got involved in the process and contributed his own ideas. His official choreographer was Hermes

Pan, but essentially Fred co-choreographed all of his dances. Hermes told me the secret of Fred's genius was that he knew what to leave out. In other words, it wasn't what he did in the dance, it was how he eliminated extraneous movements and made everything look so economical and effortless.

One time I was talking to one of the owners of the MGM Grand in Las Vegas and I happened to mention I was friendly with Fred Astaire. He was flabbergasted. "Do you really know Fred Astaire?" he asked. When I assured him that I did, he took out a blank check and wrote Fred's name in the "pay to the order of" line, leaving the amount blank. He handed me the check and said, "You tell Mr. Astaire that if he'll play a week here in Vegas, he can fill in any amount he likes. He doesn't even have to dance. I don't care what he does." I took that check to Fred, but I wasn't surprised when he passed on it.

I grew up listening to Ella Fitzgerald, and I never, ever dreamed that I'd become her friend. We first met in 1952 on the occasion of my mother's birthday. I told my mother I'd take her to any show she wanted to go to, and she surprised the hell out of me when she said, "I want to see Ella Fitzgerald!" Ella was working at Birdland, and I never thought I'd see my mother in Birdland in a million years, but there we were, and we had the greatest time.

Ella came up to us after the show and introduced herself—as if she needed an introduction!—and I told her it was my mom's birthday. Ella wished her a special day and told her she was honored that she'd chosen to spend it watching her perform. Then Ella turned to me and said, "I love your recording of 'Blue Velvet.'" I couldn't believe it—Ella Fitzgerald saying that to me! I carry that memory around with me as a badge of honor.

I got to know Ella very well in California. She was a great human being. I often told her she was the best singer I'd ever heard in my life. She said, "No, no, everybody's good! There are so many wonderful singers out there." Ella was a truly humble person. When she toured with the Count Basie band, she could have flown first class like most stars do when they work with the big bands, but Ella preferred to stay with the boys on the bus; she would never play the star and leave them. The two of us spent decades crisscrossing the country, and we frequently ran into each other. It didn't matter where she was going or how many times she'd already played a particular town. She loved her audiences and couldn't wait to entertain them.

Ella wasn't just a singer; she was a real musician, and her voice was her instrument. When she sang without words, it wasn't just scat-singing; it was a remarkable kind of nonverbal communication. She sang all over the world—China, Germany, South America, Africa—and never worried about the language barrier. When Ella scatted, the whole world understood and cheered her on.

We always spent Christmas with her. I took Joanna and Antonia over to Ella's house every Christmas Eve, and she'd cook up a storm, the best food you could ever dream up. We'd ring her doorbell and she'd open the door and say, "Oh, my daughters are finally here!"

Sammy Cahn lived next door. He used to tell me to come over anytime I wanted to borrow a cup of song.

※

Derek Boulton and I parted company in 1975, and for a year or so I worked with my friend Jack Rollins. Jack's wife, Jane Martin, had been a backup singer on my very first recording date for Leslie Records back around 1949, and we'd always kept in touch. Jack is one of the great managers in show business history—he helped make the careers of Woody Allen,

Mike Nichols and Elaine May, and Lenny Bruce—but until 1975 the timing had been off for both of us.

Jack was always after me to put more humor in my act. If something happens in the concert hall or club where I'm working, I can usually come up with a spontaneously funny line about it, but Jack was insistent that I put more humor into my show.

One day we were walking down the street to an appointment, and I was telling Jack that if I'm getting four standing ovations every night without one-liners, maybe I'm doing something right. But he wasn't interested. We tried to hail a cab on Madison Avenue, but it was the lunch hour and there wasn't a taxi in sight. After about fifteen minutes a police car stopped at a red light. The cop looked at me and said, "Hey, how you doin', Tony?"

"Fine," I said. "Are you going uptown?"

And the cop said, "Yeah, hop in!"

So there we were, riding uptown in the back of a police car, and Jack Rollins turned to me and said, "Now *this* is funny!"

Jack was with me when, at long last, I started my very own independent label, something I'd wanted for years. The idea first began to gel around 1972 when I met Bill Hassett, a successful realtor in Buffalo who owned the Statler Hilton Hotel there. We thought that between his business acumen and my musical know-how we ought to be able to get something going. It turned out that it took a lot more than that, but I wouldn't find that out until a couple of years and a couple of hundred thousand dollars later.

We named our company Tobill Enterprises, and I called our label Improv. Bill and I owned the operation jointly. It was the crystallization of everything I'd been working for: I'd be the central artist on the label, but I'd sign top-quality jazz artists like Bill Evans, Torrie Zito, Earl Hines, Jimmy and Marian McPartland, Charlie Byrd, and Ruby Braff.

Part of the attraction was that Bill had a jazz room in his hotel called the Downtown Club. I figured we could book talent for the club and that way find potential artists we might want to record. This happened with "Fatha" Hines, whose Improv album was titled *Live in Buffalo*.

I talked to my son Danny, who was now twenty-one, about this venture. Danny was performing in rock bands with his brother, Daegal, but he always took a keen interest in the business side of music. He knew where I was coming from, that I wanted to be in a situation where I could call my own shots. He said, "You can make great records, you can have great album covers, but distribution is the key to success."

I knew there were independent labels with independent distribution, but it was a hard road to travel. Bill's idea was to build up a network of independent distributors in this country and around the world.

Once again, Columbia Records caught wind of my plans and offered to take over our distribution. I told Bill about Columbia's offer, but he said, "No, let's not do it that way. We want to do this entirely on our own." That was the way he'd always made money in the hotel and real estate business in Buffalo, but, as we were to learn, it wasn't the best way to sell records.

I wasn't convinced it was the right way to go, so I asked Danny if he'd go to Buffalo and talk it over with Bill. Danny discussed our concerns, but Bill insisted that we take the independent route. I discussed the matter with Jack, and he felt confident that we should move ahead and so we signed the agreement.

We launched the new label with a bang with *Life Is Beautiful,* named after a song written by Fred Astaire. In addition to Torrie Zito arranging and conducting, Frank Laico was engineer and Rudy DeHarak handled the art direction for the album cover, a beautiful photo of myself holding a red-haired baby Antonia, with six-year-old Joanna peering over my shoulder. The album itself was a wonderful mix of styles, with everything from Brazilian tunes to classics by major American songwriters.

My other major project on Improv was "The Cole Porter Medley," eventually released on an album called *The Special Magic of Tony Bennett.* The Porter medley was the most ambitious thing I did with Torrie Zito in the seventies. This was a special project, not something I would have been able to do if I was with a major label.

My favorites were the two albums I did with Bill Evans, the greatest and most influential jazz pianist of his generation. My dear friend, the great jazz singer Annie Ross, came up with the idea of my making an album with Bill. I'd known her since the early fifties when she was singing with the group Lambert, Hendricks, and Ross.

One night in London when Annie, her husband, and I were having dinner at some Italian restaurant in Soho, she brought up the Bill Evans idea. We all agreed it was an excellent suggestion and settled in to enjoy our meal. Next thing you know, a waiter passed me the word that Sinatra's people had phoned and "The Old Man" himself was going to be there in about ten minutes. I told Annie, "Watch the waiters." The whole staff snapped to attention, like the inspector general was about to descend on the joint. Everybody was all but saluting when Sinatra arrived with his daughter, Tina, and Robert Wagner. I went over to say hello, and Frank invited the three of us to join his party. We spent the whole evening listening to Frank talking about his big-band days, how he learned things like never to cross his legs while sitting on the bandstand because it takes the crease out of your trousers. We were more than content just to listen to him talk. It was a rare and special night.

Bill Evans was there when I sang with Dave Brubeck at the all-star concert on the White House lawn in 1962. By the sixties, especially after his tenure with the Miles Davis Sextet and with his own groundbreaking trio, Bill had become the most-listened-to jazz pianist in the world. He recorded with very few singers, though, so I was surprised when Annie suggested that Bill and I work together. Bill happened to be playing in London at Ronnie Scott's, so John Bunch—who was still with me then—and I went down to hear Bill's latest trio, which impressed us mightily. My original idea was to make an album with my voice and two pianos. I wanted to have both Bill Evans and John Bunch, but John discouraged me—he said it would be better with Bill Evans alone.

In the spring of 1975 we worked out an arrangement with Bill's manager, Helen Keane, to tape two albums together. It was the same kind of reciprocal deal I made with Count Basie: we'd do one album for Improv and another for Fantasy, the label Bill was under contract to. The Fantasy album, titled *The Tony Bennett/Bill Evans Album*, came out in June 1975, and the following September we recorded *Tony Bennett & Bill Evans Together Again* for Improv.

Bill and I got along famously. Before the dates he said to me, "Keep your cronies at home and I'll do the same." It was just Helen, Bill, one engineer, and me in the studio. We didn't want anyone around to distract us. And as the records show, it was a tremendously intimate experience. I hadn't recorded with just piano since *Tony Sings for Two*, fifteen years earlier, and Bill was accustomed to having a bass and drummer with him, so both of us were more exposed than usual.

During the sessions I'd name a tune, and Bill would say, "That's good, let's do that." We'd find a key, work it out, then play it through and work out all the changes. After three days we had nine songs in the can.

I remember how the intensity of the whole experience kept mounting. I told the engineer, "Don't wait for us to do a take, just keep the tape running all the time." But all he said was, "I can't. I'll run out of tape." My one regret is that we didn't record all those rehearsals and run-throughs. It was fascinating to hear Bill work on songs. He was always improvising and revising, changing and improving his approach.

In June 1976, Bill and I opened the Newport Jazz Festival at Carnegie Hall. Bill came on for the first half, then I did the second, and we finished up together. Bill and I worked a number of other appearances together; the Smithsonian in Washington; on a TV concert in Holland; a half-hour special for the Canadian Broadcasting Corporation. Around the time of the Carnegie Hall show I was doing a radio interview with the celebrated disc jockey William B. Williams on the old WNEW, and Bill came along with me. William B. was smart enough to put Bill on mike as well, and I'll never forget what Bill said about me when William B. asked, "Working with Tony Bennett, is that a jazz sound?" Bill replied:

> As far as I'm concerned, it is. Occasionally fans will act surprised by the fact that Tony and I have joined together for this particular project, because they tend to see Tony in the superstar pop singer image. But you know, every great jazz musician I know idolizes Tony. From Philly Joe Jones to Miles Davis, you name it. The reason is that Tony is a great musical artist. He puts music first, and has dedicated himself to it. He has great respect for music

and musicians, and this comes through, and it's just a joy
to work with somebody like that. To me, it's music.

Bill finished by saying, "This is one of the prime experiences of my life." I still haven't gotten over that. Thank you,
Bill.

The only downside about working with Bill Evans was
watching his addiction destroy him. I once asked him, "What
happened? Why did you start doing drugs? Did someone hurt
you?" "Hurt me?" he said. "I wish they did." He bitterly
regretted the course his life had taken. "I wish somebody had
broken my arm instead of sticking a needle in it for the first
time. I wish somebody would have knocked me right out so
that I'd never touch it again." In those last few months he was
so sick that after a set he'd have to go right back to his room
and lie down. It was a nightmare. He finally ran out of the
energy to keep living.

The last time I talked to Bill, I was passing through some
little town on the outskirts of Austin, Texas, of all places, and
he called me. I was surprised he was able to track me down,
and I said, "Bill, what are you calling me here for?" He
answered me in a voice that sounded desperate and full of
despair. "I wanted to tell you one thing: just think truth and
beauty," he said. "Forget about everything else. Just concentrate on truth and beauty, that's all." I've tried to live by those
words ever since. Shortly afterward he died of an overdose.
Imagine how much great music he would have created had he
lived. It made me think hard about my own drug use. I knew
that somehow, something had to be done.

In 1976 I turned fifty, and Sandra threw me a big party. I
couldn't believe the celebrities that were filing through my

own home! Everybody in show business was there. It was a lovely summer evening, and we were all sitting at tables set up around the swimming pool. I was talking with Johnny Carson, whom I'd known since 1962. He got everybody's attention, pointed his finger, and said, "Look." Cary Grant and Fred Astaire were sitting on the other side of the pool, their ties loosened and shirt buttons undone, cracking jokes and breaking each other up. Wow. Unforgettable.

The seventies were the only decade that Frank Sinatra and I actually lived in the same town, but because of our extensive touring schedules, the only time our paths crossed was when we were on the road. The major exception was in 1977 when he invited me to sing with him on his ABC-TV special, *Sinatra and Friends.* I sang "One," from *A Chorus Line*, and Frank and I did a duet of "My Kind of Town." One night when I was back in New York in August 1974, I was visiting my mom for the evening. We were watching Sinatra's *Main Event* special on television. Frank knew that my mom was really sick at this point, and he knew that I'd planned to watch the show with her, and during a break between songs he turned to the audience and said that Tony Bennett was his favorite guy in the whole world. My mother's face lit up like' a Christmas tree, and that image will stay with me for as long as I live. That was a perfect example of the kind of small things that Frank would do that made such a big difference in people's lives.

I was playing the Sands in Las Vegas in February 1979, and while I was singing I noticed something funny going on between John, my bassist, and Joe, my drummer. It turned out John had a note, and he was telling Joe, "This has to get to Tony right now!" Joe said no way was he going to interrupt me, but John said, "I think you better give it to him. It's from Sinatra!"

I opened the note, and boy, were they right to give it to me. It said that Mr. Sinatra was listening to the performance at a party on a yacht off the southern coast of France. He'd gotten his friends at the Sands to set up a shortwave hookup. They were broadcasting our show directly to Frank.

The note also said that Frank wanted to hear me sing Torrie's arrangement of "My Way." I was only too happy to oblige, and I made the announcement to the crowd that Frank had requested a song, and everyone turned around to see where he was. I explained he was thousands miles away in France, but he was listening along just the same!

Sometime later I was asked to do the fabulous show at Radio City Music Hall called "The Night of One Hundred Stars." It was kind of a funny setup: I was brought out on stage in a Central Park carriage being pulled by a live horse. I was frightened because I thought the horse might get spooked by the lights or the crowd and go bananas, and I'd wind up in the orchestra pit with the horse. Orson Welles was backstage, and he stood there smoking a big cigar and staring at me. He could tell that I was having a case of the butterflies, and with perfect grace he said to me, "I go to every party at Sinatra's house, and he plays nothing but Tony Bennett records." Just at that moment the announcer said, "Ladies and gentlemen, Tony Bennett!" Orson knew exactly what to say to help me get through. What wonderful timing. No wonder he was such a great director.

Frank and I met up another time in Chicago. There was a home for Italian-American senior citizens there called the Mother Cabrini Old Age Home. They were putting on a big benefit so they could raise enough money to pay off their mortgage. Originally Frank was going to do the show, but when he canceled because of an arm injury, they called me, and I agreed to do it. But Frank decided he could do the show with his arm in a sling. Since I was already booked, we decided to do it together.

When we were planning the show, Frank decided that he'd go on first. I don't know why; maybe there was someplace he wanted to be. When he finished he turned to the crowd and said, "Ladies and gentlemen, the greatest singer in the business, Tony Bennett." It was just about the greatest honor I've ever received.

But even "the greatest singer in the business" wasn't doing so well.

With my son Danny at the Grammys in 1995

CHAPTER ELEVEN

On Thanksgiving night 1977 I was about to walk on stage at the Fairmont Hotel in San Francisco when I got the news that my mom had died. I was in shock. That night I hit the street and just started running, and I ran for miles in a daze. My mom had been my one guiding star through all my ups and downs. She'd kept me grounded and was always able to put everything in focus for me. When she passed away, I thought I'd never recover. I was so overcome with grief that I actually wondered if I might be losing my mind. And I found that I was using drugs to ease my pain.

Her death could not have happened at a worse time. Sandra and I couldn't get along. I was again without a manager and that meant it was up to me to mind the store. My new record company had folded earlier that year and I was without a label for the first time in my career. All of Bill's business expertise and all of my dedication weren't enough to keep the label alive. To my dismay, I learned that the company was in debt, and now I was responsible for my share of it. On top of everything else, my accountants were telling Sandra and me that our Hollywood lifestyle was beginning to take its toll and we were spending way too much money. As a result we had fallen behind on our taxes, and the IRS was banging on our front door.

⊹

I had a press agent from Toronto named Gino Empry for a while during this time, and he introduced me to my new agent Roger Vorce at Agency of the Performing Arts (APA) who was now booking my dates. John Giuffrida, my bass player, handled the logistics of touring, but there was nobody looking out for the big picture. The strain was getting to be too much for me, and I began to experience long bouts of depression.

As hard as I tried to stay current with my taxes, my financial situation only got worse. The accountants called to say that the IRS was starting proceedings to take away the house. That night, in frustration I overindulged and quickly realized I was in trouble. I tried to calm myself down by taking a hot bath, but I must have passed out. And I experienced what some call a near-death experience; a golden light enveloped me in a warm glow. It was quite peaceful; in fact, I had the sense that I was about to embark on a very compelling journey. But suddenly I was jolted out of the vision. The tub was overflowing and Sandra was standing above me. She'd heard the water running for too long, and when she came in, I wasn't breathing. She pounded on my chest and literally brought me back to life. As I was rushed to the hospital, the only thought on my mind was something my ex-manager Jack Rollins had told me about Lenny Bruce right after Lenny's death from an overdose. All Jack said was, "The man sinned against his talent." That hit home. I realized I was throwing it all away, and I became determined to clean up my act.

It took me a couple of weeks to get my feet back on the ground. I knew I had to make major changes in my life. It was 1979 and my sons Danny and Daegal were now twenty-five and twenty-four, respectively. I remembered the clearheaded suggestions Danny had given me during the Improv negotiations, and how he was always so defensive anytime there was a wise guy hanging around. I called my boys in New York and asked them to come out to talk things over and see if they could lend me a hand.

All of my kids have a natural affinity for music. Joanna and Antonia grew up hanging around with Sammy Cahn, Frank Sinatra, and Dean Martin. They sang with Basie's band at the age of nine and ten. Danny and Dae were privy to some amazing jam sessions in their own home. Dae once sat with Duke Ellington at his piano. Count Basie's great drummer, Sonny Payne, had been the first person to put a pair of drumsticks in his hands. The boys also got to see the business side of the music industry, and watched promoters, agents, bookers, and road managers at work.

By their twenties, Danny and Dae were well versed in all aspects of music: performance, business, and even the ever-changing technology. And by now, Danny had experience with contract negotiations. When I asked them to come out to California, they didn't hesitate; they arrived the next day.

The three of us met in my art studio, my sanctuary. I told them the whole story. I tried to explain what was going on, but the truth is, even I wasn't totally aware of all the problems plaguing the business side of my career. When I finished talking, Danny said to me, "Well, the only thing I can do is look at the situation and try to find where things went wrong."

Danny and Dae met with my accountants back in New York, whom I'd instructed to reveal all. I wanted the boys to understand exactly what was happening. Danny understood numbers. He called me up and said, "If you make a hundred dollars and you only spend ninety-nine, then you're a buck ahead. But if you make a hundred dollars and spend a hundred and one, you're in trouble." My accountant told Danny that he could look at the books as much as he wanted, but things weren't going to get any better. He told him I was going down. Danny said, "That's *your* opinion." He spent a week in New York sorting the whole thing out, and when Danny laid out my entire financial situation on a spreadsheet, I could finally see it clearly.

Danny told me that the road gigs weren't profitable because we were spending too much on road expenses, and he also told me exactly how much Sandra and I were spending personally. No one had done this for me before. He explained that we had spent exactly the same amount that I'd earned that year, leaving nothing for the tax man. Danny stated the obvious when he said the only way things could get better was by cutting expenses and budgeting the rest. He worked out a three-year payment plan with the IRS and we put my new budget into action.

The hard part was getting Sandra to comply. I had to go back on the road that week, and I called her and said, "This is the way it's going to have to be. It's the only way we can save the house." One week later she served me with divorce papers. That's how quick it was. But the trial dragged on for many years.

Another chapter in my life had come to an end. I left the house in Beverly Hills and found a nice one-bedroom apartment on West Fifty-fifth Street back in Manhattan, right up the street from Columbia's "Black Rock" headquarters. The minute I got back to a lifestyle I was comfortable with, I never wanted to get high again.

Torrie Zito decided to get off the road. That was a major loss musically. By then we'd been working together for ten years. He'd written over a hundred arrangements for me, many of which—unfortunately—were never recorded. The last thing Torrie and I did together was my second English TV series in 1979. It was called *Tony Bennett Sings...*, and it was also directed by Yvonne Littlewood. The shows were built around different themes, like "Tony Bennett Sings Saloon Songs," "Tony Bennett Sings Songs from Broadway," and "Tony Bennett Sings Song Stories."

When the rest of the trio broke up, I was worried that I'd never be able to put together a group as good again. I found it significant that I was returning to my roots—going from Hollywood back to New York—and it made sense that I'd also go back to Ralph Sharon. Oddly enough, at the very same time, Ralph had been debating whether or not he should get in touch with me.

It had been Ralph's wife, Susan, who had pressured him into quitting the road, but they were now divorced and he had married a woman named Linda. I decided to give him a call and ask if he'd consider coming back with me. He talked it over with Linda, and soon we were back on the road together. It was 1980, and he'd been gone for fifteen years. It was a comfort to have him back.

Our new trio featured John Burr, then later Gene Cherico on bass, and the fantastic drummer Butch Miles. Eventually Joe LaBarbera, who had been Bill Evans's drummer, took over on drums, and Paul Langosch, who has been with me for almost fifteen years now, took over on bass. They're all exquisite musicians, and put an end to the doubts I'd had about finding the best to work with again.

When Danny first began helping me out, there was never a deliberate plan for him to manage me. He just fell into the role. He turned out to be really good at putting it all together. Not since my sister, Mary, managed my affairs in the sixties had I felt so confident that everything was on the up-and-up. It was such a relief, and my head began to clear.

We became a team, artist and manager, as well as father and son. He and I had extensive talks and worked out a game plan. Danny asked me point blank, "What do you want to accomplish?" I answered, "I want to do what I do best, nothing more and nothing less. Above all else, I never want to compromise my musical integrity." I told him that despite the modern notion of demographics, I was taught that it was important to perform for the whole family. I told Danny that I wanted to be able to bring my music to as many people as possible, regardless of their age.

I meant that too. I wanted to reach all ages. I wanted to do it for myself, naturally, but I don't think I'm being disingenuous when I say that I also wanted to do it for Cole Porter, Duke Ellington, and all the wonderful composers, arrangers, and instrumentalists I'd ever worked with. I wanted to be one of the keepers of the flame when it came to great music. I knew that if I brought the best songs and the best orchestrations to people, they'd respond to it, because great music transcends generations.

I was singing at the Sahara in 1979, and I had a television special that year called *Live at the Sahara*. Even though I wasn't recording and hadn't had a major appearance in New York in a few years, I was still hot enough that the Suma Corporation, owner of the Sands, lured me away from the Sahara with a spectacular new contract. What made it unique was the amount of time they wanted me to work in their room—eighteen weeks a year, a big commitment.

But I thought I was spending too much time in Las Vegas. It was tough for me to say no at first—it was, after all, four months a year of guaranteed income. But there was good reason for me to work less in Vegas. Business was decreasing, fewer people were coming in, and no new hotels or casinos were being built. Even the Suma people eventually sold out to the Hilton chain. Remember, this was fifteen years before Vegas started booming again in the mid-nineties; the town was going downhill, and if it did hit bottom, I didn't want to be one of the entertainers to get blamed for it.

And there was always the danger of becoming strictly a Vegas act, and that wasn't the route I wanted to go. I was looking to broaden my audience, not narrow it, so I went to the Suma people and renegotiated the deal so that I worked fewer dates.

I knew that my core audience would support me. As long as I was presenting songs from the Great American Songbook, I'd fill up every seat wherever I played. There were a number of labels who could give me a deal, but I thought it would serve me best to go back to Columbia Records because that's where my catalogue was, and it would give me a chance to exploit the masters to maximum benefit and regain control of my own destiny.

Danny assured me that if we gave the young public an opportunity to get to know me, I'd once again be accepted by that audience, so he urged me to focus my efforts on youth-oriented events. Danny proved to be the ace manager I was looking for.

In May 1981, I made my first major appearance in New York since Bill Evans and I had played Carnegie Hall in 1976. I always had the philosophy that it's best to make it an event every time I hit New York. I came up with an idea I called "Tony Takes Manhattan." I played three hip New York clubs in the same week—the Village Vanguard, the famous jazz basement The Bottom Line, and the supper club Marty's. The week culminated in a grand concert at Carnegie Hall and I donated all the proceeds to the Police Athletic League of New York.

At the same time I gave an exhibition of my artwork at Tavern on the Green, which got write-ups in the *Daily News,* the *New York Post, Newsday, The Village Voice,* and *The New York Times. New York* magazine did a feature story on me. The whole week was a huge success.

Even with no new records being released during these years, I was as busy as ever on television. In 1982 Count Basie and I did a ninety-minute special for PBS called *Bennett and Basie Together!* It was taped in Boston and featured a set of piano and voice with keyboardist Dave McKenna. Between Basie and Dave there certainly was an abundance of great jazz piano that night.

I had been doing the *Tonight Show with Johnny Carson* ever since it went on the air. I knew I could count on that. Johnny was always wonderful to me, and his shows kept me popular in America over the years. But now the hip talk show for college kids came on after Carson, and was hosted by the newcomer David Letterman. Naturally, I still did Carson every year. But Danny thought I should do the Letterman show as well.

Danny and I began looking for situations in which I could appear before a younger audience because I was positive they would embrace the music I'd sung all my life. Danny also booked me on the Canadian sketch comedy show *SCTV,* a precursor to *Saturday Night Live,* where I worked with up-and-coming comedians like Rick Moranis, John Candy, and Catherine O'Hara. Next he turned me on to an animated show that was just starting up on Fox called the *Simpsons.* They approached me to do a song called "Capitol City" for the show. I'd never had a chance to see it, but Danny assured me the show would be a huge success. He went back to them and said I'd do it if they'd make me an animated character on the show. They agreed, and I became the first in a long line of animated special guests.

I was working all over the country, doing more than two hundred shows a year all through the 1980s. I was no longer hampered by crises in my personal life or by struggles with the record company, and this left me with the time to carefully plan each step of my career. And things were beginning to pay off.

Bob Guccione, Jr., was the owner and editor of *Spin*, a new magazine that catered to the "alternative" college crowd. Danny told me he had read an interview with Guccione in which he was asked, "What do you think is the essence of rock and roll?" Guccione answered, "James Brown and Tony Bennett, because they're the essence of cool and that's what it's about." That really knocked me out. I had Danny call and thank him for what he'd said, and Bob decided he would do a feature on me.

I wanted to get back to recording as soon as I could. I was encouraged by the fact that a number of young singers like Natalie Cole and Linda Ronstadt had recorded albums of great American standards and the public was buying them.

I was talking to Columbia, although I have to confess that I was wary. But I had friends there now. Bruce Lundvall, whom I'd known since the sixties, was president of the label. A producer named Ettore Stratta told Danny that Mickey Eischner, head of A&R, was interested in doing a new album with me. He wanted me back on the label, but he couldn't convince his bosses that they should invest money in me. Ettore had an investor who was willing to back the album, so in 1985 he and Danny worked out an agreement that Ettore would produce one of my records. Fourteen years after leaving the label, I was reunited with Columbia Records.

Both my old and new records were affected by the introduction of the compact disc. CDs were officially unveiled in Japan by CBS/Sony in 1982, and by 1985 they had really started to take off. It was obvious that every new record would have to be on CD, and that turned out to be a boon for someone like me with a large catalogue. Consumers were replacing their entire vinyl collections with CDs. I decided to make a record featuring state-of-the-art technology, the best in digital equipment that was then available. In addition to making a great recording, it also brought the project to the attention of the high-tech enthusiasts.

My new record would be called *The Art of Excellence*, referring not only to the songs, but also to my demand for quality. From that day forward people would expect nothing less from Tony Bennett. I dedicated the album to the beloved Mabel Mercer.

Annie Leibovitz shot the album cover. She was a hot photographer for *Rolling Stone*, and it turned out she was also a fan, and she was thrilled to do the shoot. She took a great outdoor picture of me with the World Trade Center looming in the distance.

I included a song on that album called "How Do You Keep the Music Playing" by Alan and Marilyn Bergman, which I had first heard Sinatra sing. One night I went to see Frank perform at the Universal Amphitheater in Los Angeles. I had no idea he knew I was there, but right after he finished singing the song, he said to me, in full view of thousands of people, "Tony! You should sing this song!" How could I refuse? Ettore brought in orchestrator Jorge Calandrelli to do all the charts.

Another special song on *The Art of Excellence* was "Everybody Has the Blues," by James Taylor, on which I sang a duet

with the genius Ray Charles. It was the first time we'd ever performed together.

I proved my worth to Columbia when *The Art of Excellence* was released in 1986. There was a genuine media blitz
surrounding the release of the album that prompted my first
concert at Radio City Music Hall, which launched the "Art of
Excellence Tour." A special bonus that year was when WBCN
radio in Boston became the first rock station to spin my new
record, all because of the enthusiasm of their promotions
director, Chachi Loprete. I sold 150,000 records, showing
Columbia that it could indeed be done if you did it right. It
really made them prick up their ears.

Along with my career straightening out, my personal life took a
major change for the better. I guess because I've been a perpet-
ual optimist all my life, forging ahead and willing myself to grav-
itate to the good things, the negativity started to evaporate. It
was a lucky day for me when I became acquainted with a beautiful lady, Susan Crow. She's happy, thoughtful, truthful, intelligent, and she comes from a terrific family. She's helped me
balance my life, think straight, and become a healthy person.
She has a special way about her that I've never found in anyone
else. For ten years I've spent all my time with her and every day
feels like the day I first met her. Last year she graduated from
Columbia University, and she now teaches Social Studies at the
La Guardia School of Music and the Performing Arts.

We continued to build on the excitement generated by *The
Art of Excellence*. Each new album I made attracted more
attention than the last: *Bennett/Berlin* in 1987, my tribute to
the songs of the composer Irving Berlin, and in 1990 my

salute to my hometown, *Astoria: Portrait of the Artist.* Danny
had a striking idea for that cover: the front showed an original
photograph of me at the age of sixteen in front of the my
house in Astoria, and on the back I was standing in the exact
same spot fifty years later.

The standout song on *Astoria* was the first cut, Charles
DeForrest's "When Do the Bells Ring for Me?" He was part of
a wonderful clique of singers and pianists that dominated the
piano bars of the Upper East Side. I'd met Charles about two
and a half years before I recorded *Astoria* when I was in a
restaurant and heard him sing this wonderful song. I knew
then I had to do it. Charles was writing about the longing for
love, but it was also about the yearning to make something of
one's life. It really nailed the way I felt.

Charles wrote two other songs on the album, "Where Do
You Go From Love," and "I've Come Home Again." I was
happy that, during the last few years of his life, Charles got a
little notoriety from my recording his songs, and I always
encourage other singers to listen to his work.

My popularity grew stronger and stronger with each new
record. For the first time in my career, no one was telling me
what records to make, what songs to sing, what producers or
musicians to use. I was allowed to follow my own instincts. My
head was free of drugs and I was living the healthy life: eating
right, working out, and playing tennis whenever I had the
chance. I didn't have to worry about what was waiting around
every corner. I had a new booking agency, William Morris,
and enlisted Rob Heller as my agent, and I found a new tour
manager, Vance Anderson, so my life on the road would be
smoother. My financial problems were at last resolved, and I
was gaining a whole new legion of fans. I felt like I was on top
of the world. I was free to concentrate on my work, and that
left me time to pursue my second great passion, painting.

Through the years I've been diligently studying painting with the help of my teachers John Barnicort, Everett Raymond Kinstler, and Basil Baylin, and have been encouraged by my friend David Hockney.

During the seventies, my reputation as a legitimate artist began to grow, especially with the help of Johnny Carson, who showed my work frequently when I was a guest on his show. I had my first gallery showing on Mount Street in London while I was living there in 1971. I began to exhibit my work in many of the cities where I performed, and my paintings started to sell. I've reached a point where I have a body of work of over eight hundred paintings, and I had my first museum show at the Butler Institute of American Art in Youngstown, Ohio, in 1994. (I'm proud to say that my painting "Homage to Hockney" has been included in their permanent collection.) I decided to sign my works with my given name. So I'm "Anthony Dominick Benedetto" the painter.

At this time CBS Records, owners of the Columbia label, was bought by Sony. At first I had no idea how this would affect my dealing with the label, but I soon learned that Tommy Mottola had been brought in to run the entire record division of the company, Sony Music, and that he had appointed Don Ienner as president of Columbia Records, and Michele Anthony as executive vice president of Sony Music Entertainment. Michele just happens to be my old associate Dee Anthony's oldest daughter, and to this day she calls me Uncle Tony. These three people were responsible for setting in motion a trend at the label that would turn my career around in a major way.

Since there was now a demand for the records from my early catalogue, Don Ienner asked me to come up with what I thought were the definitive recordings of my career, so they could be released as a boxed set. This project was a real labor of love. We called the collection *Forty Years: The Artistry of Tony Bennett*. I loved the idea because I thought it helped educate my new fans about where I had come from.

Between *Astoria* and the *Forty Years* boxed set, the buzz was steadily mounting. I was honored when *Astoria* was nominated for a 1991 Grammy as "Best Jazz Vocal," and thrilled when they asked me to perform a number on the televised broadcast of the Grammy Awards ceremony. During the rehearsal, I sang "When Do the Bells Ring for Me?" in full voice. I was surprised when everyone hanging out watching the rehearsal spontaneously erupted in applause and gave me a standing ovation—including all the technical crew and heavy metal groups like Aerosmith and Mötley Crüe. When I did the actual show, I put everything I had into "Bells" and I got the same reaction. The young audience gave me a standing ovation that evening too. It was a moment of triumph. The Grammy Award went to Harry Connick, Jr., but as Duke said, "It's not whatcha do; it's the way howcha do it." Interestingly enough, from that point on, the Grammys created a whole new category called "Best Traditional Pop Album."

I was getting all kinds of attention now, but Danny still felt that my albums weren't getting the focus they deserved. We had done all we could do. We felt it was time for the record company to step up to the plate.

So Danny asked me to come with him to a meeting at Columbia. He never did that. In the old days, I hung out with people at the label all the time, both in the Columbia studios and in the offices. But since he took over, Danny's kept me away from the negotiations and the corporate playing field so I could stick to making music. When we got to the meeting at Don Ienner's office, we looked at the sales figures and then Danny said, "If this is the best you can do, then we want off the label." He shocked the hell out of me, but then I thought, "Yeah he's right. I'd rather retire than not do things right."

He continued, "You don't have an artist on this label who works as hard as Tony. Once again, Tony is not being supported by this company, not in the way he should be. You should be selling at least two or three times as many records as you are now." Don replied, "There's no way Tony Bennett's leaving this label. I'm not going to let that happen." Then he asked me what I had in mind for my next project, and I said, "I have two words to say to you: 'Perfectly Frank.'" He looked at me and said, "That's it! That's all I have to hear. You got it. It'll be huge."

I was planning on using just a trio, whereas Sinatra almost always used a big band. This was one way I could put my own stamp on these songs. I didn't want to do Sinatra's greatest hits. In fact, when I had first gotten the idea for the Sinatra tribute record, I called Bill Miller, who for over forty years was to Frank what Ralph Sharon is to me. Bill supported my decision to stick with the torch and saloon songs. These were the great standards that Frank used as the building blocks for his classic albums.

I took my time deciding which songs to do. I faxed lists over to my friend and longtime associate Frank Military, the best music man in the business and the head of Warner-Chappell Music. Sinatra started him out in the early sixties when he was a young man. He went on to become one of the major movers and shakers in the world of music publishing. He tracked down all the sheet music I needed, even songs from other publishers. We recorded a collection of twenty-four songs.

Andre Fischer, who'd just scored a big hit with Natalie Cole's *Unforgettable* album, shared producing credits on *Perfectly Frank*. I brought back Frank Laico to do the engineering. The results were magic.

Don Ienner kept his word and put his head of marketing, Jay Krugman, together with Danny. For the first time, I got exactly what I needed in terms of promotion, and the effort paid off. *Perfectly Frank* earned a gold record, and I won my first Grammy since "I Left My Heart in San Francisco."

After *Perfectly Frank* came out, all the deejays and talk show hosts invariably asked me, "Did you get Sinatra's permission before you sang his songs?" I thought that was funny, because Frank and I have always done each other's material. He did "Don't Wait Too Long," "This Is All I Ask," "Just In Time," and lots of songs that I introduced. On his 1964 album, *It Might As Well Be Swing*, Frank, Count Basie, and Quincy Jones recorded many more of my songs, "The Best Is Yet to Come," "I Wanna Be Around," "The Good Life," and "Fly Me to the Moon,"and he never called me to ask my permission! Still, when I did *Perfectly Frank*, everybody wanted to know if I had gotten his approval. He always had this hold on people that was incredible. As Dean Martin once said, "It's Frank Sinatra's world. We just live in it."

In 1993 Phil Ramone invited me to participate in *Frank Sinatra Duets*. This album consisted of a series of electronically crafted duos by Sinatra and various contemporary pop stars, from Willie Nelson to Julio Iglesias to Bono of U2. The singers came into the studio and sang along with prerecorded Sinatra songs—Frank was never actually in the studio. I was honored when Frank decided he wanted me to sing "New York, New York" with him. It was one of the biggest songs of his entire career.

⊹

That same year, 1993, my drummer, Joe LaBarbera, decided to get off the road. I was unhappy about that, since Joe was such a subtle, tasteful drummer; I had learned a lot working with him. Then my bassist, Paul Langosch, left the group. Ralph and I found a new drummer, Clayton Cameron, and a new bassist named Doug Richeson.

Doug, Clayton, and of course Ralph were all on hand for my next project, *Steppin' Out*—another tribute, this time to Fred Astaire. By the time we were ready to release it, it looked like it was also going to be a strong contender, and we started thinking about MTV. I told Danny that I thought I could do really well there. The video station was exclusively geared toward young audiences and traditionally broke acts like Madonna and Michael Jackson.

I had Danny pitch Columbia the idea of doing a video, and they understood the potential of it right away. I wanted to come up with something sharp and snazzy enough to compete with the other videos on MTV, so we hired video director Marcus Nispel, who'd worked on videos for Janet Jackson that featured a lot of dancing. To continue the idea of a tribute to Fred Astaire, we decided to shoot it in black and white and featured all styles of dance—modern, ballroom, and tap. Like an Astaire number, everything was moving to a beat—even the visual editing was cut on the beat. We were very happy with the finished product, though we had no idea how it was going to go over.

Sometime before I made the video, MTV had enlisted me to film a commercial for the "I Want My MTV" campaign, so I already had some profile at the network. MTV would be holding their annual video music awards in September and they invited me to make an appearance on the awards show. Specifically, they wanted me to be a presenter and "cross dress," so to speak, with Flea and Anthony of the Red Hot Chili Peppers. In other words, they would dress in tuxedos and I would wear "alternative" style clothing. The idea was pretty out there, but I always like it when people can laugh at themselves. So I agreed to give it a try.

It's hard to attract attention at the MTV Video Music Awards, but our little bit turned out to be one of the highlights of the whole show. At the reception afterward when kids came up to me, I half expected them to ask, "What are you doing here, Grandpa?" Instead they said, "Hey, that was really cool. What's your next album, man?" I happened to be walking by a room where the Red Hot Chili Peppers were giving their after-show interview to the *Entertainment Tonight* news crew, and I stuck my head in the door and said, "Hey! My mom has all your records!" That really cracked them up.

A week later two programmers from MTV called and said, "We have some news for you: We're going to add 'Steppin' Out' to our *Buzz Bin*." *Buzz Bin* was considered the hippest show on MTV, usually reserved for "cutting edge" rock acts. It was by far the single best place to be in the MTV universe. So "Steppin' Out" was a bona fide hit. Thanks to MTV, I finally fulfilled my dream of breaking the generation barrier.

But I hadn't yet performed in front of a rock audience.

WHSF, a rock radio station in Washington, D.C., invited me to perform at their Christmas festival, so I went down to D.C. with the trio. While we were backstage, we could hear the audience cheering, waiting for the show to begin. Danny stood in the wings along with a Columbia rep and everybody crossed their fingers and wished me luck.

I walked out in front of five thousand screaming kids and hit them with "Old Devil Moon," a favorite opening number. By the time I got to the section where I hold the word "love" for something like thirty-two bars, I had them in my pocket. They were cheering, "Tony! Tony! Tony!" It was pandemonium, one of the most amazing things I'd ever experienced. A couple of days later I did a show on Long Island for the popular rock radio station WDRE. I was on the bill with the groups the Cowboy Junkies, the Teenage Fan Club, and Squeeze, and as I was walking through the backstage area to my dressing room, they were all sitting down to dinner. When they saw me come through, they all stood up and started clapping. I couldn't believe it! These weren't just kids in the audience, these were rock musicians, and they were showing me their respect. That really got to me. A lot of the musicians asked me for my autograph, and I ended up sitting down and talking with them for a while before I went on stage. That night was really something else. My acceptance by the young people of today is such a change from what was happening to me in the 1960s. Back then, I was told that I had to change my music in order for the kids to accept me; today I'm encouraged to be myself and the kids will come to me. You can't imagine how rewarding this is, and how much it affirms what I fought so long and hard for. People sometimes criticize the kids of today, calling them "slackers," or "Generation-Xers," but I don't understand that way of thinking. Kids today are just like kids from any generation: intelligent, open-minded, and excited about life. They don't want to be pigeon-holed when they listen to music, or anything else—they want to be free to experience everything, and choose for themselves. It was never the kids who asked me to change; it was those people who were interested in telling the kids what they were supposed to like. Well, young people have accepted me all over again, and I couldn't be happier. I did a series of those Christmas shows all across the country and I got the same response wherever I played.

All this attention encouraged MTV to offer me another opportunity to appear on the network, this time to do *MTV Unplugged. Unplugged* was a series where rock superstars like Eric Clapton and Paul McCartney appeared in front of live audiences without electric instruments. We taped the show on

emony that if we didn't win, we'd still consider the night a success. I can't describe how elated I felt when they opened the envelope and said, "and the winner is... Tony Bennett." The audience jumped to their feet, and Danny and I gave each other a knowing look that made it clear that we were the only ones who truly knew how much this night meant. I was so proud that I invited Danny to join me on stage. To say it was a personal triumph would be an understatement: it was the culmination of everything I had been working toward for the last fifteen years, and it exemplified everything I had dreamed of accomplishing thirty years before that. It was incredible. I was at the top of my game at the age of sixty-eight, and it was an honor to be recognized by my peers. What meant the most to me was that I had accomplished all of this without compromising my music. I felt like I had been to the moon and back. As a result, I have finally reached a point where I have total freedom, both economic and artistic, to do whatever I want to do.

But without getting on a soapbox, I want to say that I think that the Grammy victory stands as a positive example of what can be achieved by someone who sticks to his guns, who doesn't give in to the naysayers. It's a lesson that all acts should learn: they shouldn't make the music fit the marketing but the other way around.

I wanted to follow up my salutes to Frank Sinatra and Fred Astaire with a tribute to the great female vocalists who have influenced me so much over the years. Instead of honoring just one great woman singer, I decided to pay tribute to all of them, and the result was *Here's to the Ladies*, recorded and released in 1995, and again I won the Grammy for "Best Traditional Pop Album."

In 1996 I got to make another long-time dream come true. I'd always thought it would be a great idea to do a show in which the audience could call in and request their favorite songs and I'd sing them, live, right there on the spot. I'd been playing around with this idea for years and Danny hooked up with Paul Rappoport at Sony to test it out on radio. On Valentine's Day 1993, I did a live-request radio broadcast to stations across the U.S. It was a huge success, and I did another live one on Mother's Day the following year. It was so popular that we decided to bring the show to television. Danny and Paul pitched the show to the Arts & Entertainment Network (A & E) and they loved the concept. *Live By Request* debuted on A & E on Valentine's Day 1996. To my delight, that show was nominated for and won an Emmy® Award. It worked so well that A & E decided to continue the format featuring other artists, and I'm proud to say we're now entering our third year.

I decided to dedicate my next album to the greatest lady of them all, Billie Holiday. It was called *Bennett on Holiday,* and it was a kind of tribute album that had never been done before. People often focus on the negative aspects of Billie's short and tragic life, on her sad songs. But I wanted to concentrate on the optimistic side of her legacy. Naturally I didn't overlook her classic ballads like "Willow Weep for Me," "Crazy She Calls Me," and "Good Morning Heartache," on which Jorge Calandrelli again supplied wonderful string arrangements. But I wanted to put the emphasis on her upbeat songs like "All of Me," "Laughing at Life," and "What a Little Moonlight Can Do." I've traveled the world over, and I've found that musicians know Billie Holiday's songs—from Australia to Malaysia, from Singapore to South America. She was truly the Goddess of Style, and she changed music forever.

Bobby Tucker, Billie's pianist for a few years, was a great help in putting the album together. While we were picking the songs, he mentioned that Billie had once told him that

Irene Kitchings's "Some Other Spring" was her all-time favorite song. When I heard that, I knew I had to include it on the record. The cover shows me standing in front of a large mural of Billie Holiday that I painted on a brick wall. She looks young and beautiful and full of hope, and that's the way I'll always remember her. I'm very proud of that album, which also won a Grammy, and I hope that Billie is too.

I got to see Billie when she was playing with Duke Ellington at Basin Street East years earlier in New York. She approached me after the show and said, "Come on, let's go uptown and sing together." I wanted to go, but the people I was with weren't too keen on the idea and talked me out of it. If I knew then what I know now, what a night of singing that would have been.

One night after I'd made an appearance on the *Tonight Show* shortly after *Bennett on Holiday* was released, I got a call from the great silent movie star Gloria Swanson. She lived in Englewood too, although I'd never met her, and she had called out of the blue to tell me how much she enjoyed seeing me on the Carson show. She said, "Whatever you're doing, just keep doing it like that, because you've never looked better." And then she added, "By the way, I was a very good friend of Billie Holiday, and once when we were talking she said, 'Look out for this boy Tony Bennett, he's really going somewhere.'" I'd never imagined that Gloria Swanson and Billie Holiday actually talked about me. What a lift that phone call gave me.

Another unexpected compliment came when Danny got a call from Madonna's press agent in early December 1996, explaining that *Billboard* wanted to present Madonna with a Lifetime Achievement Award, but that the only way she would appear on the show was if her favorite singer, Tony Bennett, presented the award to her. I was really knocked out. I've always admired Madonna. I think she's a great artist. The way she continuously reinvents herself is amazing, and I was honored that she wanted me there with her when she got such a prestigious award.

I met Madonna in Los Angeles and we flew to Vegas together on her private plane. She was very sweet, but since it was the first time she'd been away from her newborn baby, Lourdes, she was really anxious, so we ended up talking about the baby for most of the flight.

In December 1996 President and Mrs. Clinton invited Danny and me to the White House for a Christmas holiday dinner. Earlier that year I'd had a hernia operation, and as we were pulling up to the White House gate, my hernia ruptured! I told the guard at the gate that I had an emergency, and he rushed me to the president's private infirmary right there on the White House grounds. I was in the doctor's office while the festivities were going on upstairs. While the doctor was examining me, the president suddenly appeared and asked me how I was doing. It was an awkward moment to say the least, but he was extremely gracious and quite concerned about my condition. I ended up being rushed from the White House to a nearby hospital, where the president's surgeon performed emergency surgery. I couldn't have had a better doctor, and everything turned out fine.

Donald Trump heard about my condition and sent his plane to take me from the hospital to his mansion Mar-A-Lago, in Palm Beach, where I recovered in luxury. I don't think anything like that will ever happen to me again.

I recently signed a new contract with Columbia, one that gives me total control over my career. Proving that what goes around comes around, Dee Anthony's daughter Michele, Danny, and I work closely together. How could I have ever imagined that things would turn out this way? You just never know what's going to happen. Michele grew up with Danny and Dae, and just like them she learned about the music business from the inside out. She's had an amazing career. What a pleasure it is to work with someone you love. It's strange to think that she and Danny used to play together; it always brings a smile to my face.

In my new partnership with Sony I essentially own all my masters from 1950 on, and Columbia can't reissue anything without first getting my approval. I have total control over all my new albums—the recording as well as all the publicity. None of this would mean anything to me if I weren't singing the music I love. You could offer me all the money in the world and I still wouldn't sing a crummy song I didn't care about.

There have been some other changes in my professional life lately. In 1997 Paul Langosch rejoined the trio, replacing Doug Richeson, who recently joined Phil Collins's big band. That year the trio became a quartet when I added Gray Sargent on guitar. He's phenomenal. One night I heard him play, and I called Ralph and said, "Wait till you hear this guy! I know you'll agree with me that he could fit right in with what we're doing." He did. Gray is a swinging, graceful player, and he knows when to get funky and when to be delicate. He's quite an old-movie buff, and he can quote the credits and the dialogue of almost any classic film—quite an entertaining diversion during those long hours on the road.

In the spring of 1998 it occurred to me that it had been four years since I'd had the MTV "breakthrough," and some of the kids who had been in their twenties in 1994 would now be starting families of their own. I thought it would be cool if

I could do a record for *their* kids. As a parent and a grandparent, I'm always thinking about how important it is to expose young people to the best music and culture that the world has to offer—the earlier the better. That's when I decided to do an album of children's songs called *The Playground,* a title suggested to me by my great friend Professor Freddy Katz. The swinging beat I used on *Steppin' Out* helped that album find favor with the MTV generation, who now tell me that their own children are dancing to "Steppin' Out with My Baby." This was to be an album that children of all ages could dance to.

Many of the great "rhythm tunes" of the past work great as children's songs. I didn't want any jive nursery rhymes on this record, only first-rate songs of the same caliber that I've always prided myself on delivering in my "grown-up" albums, like Harold Arlen and Johnny Mercer's "Ac-cent-tchu-ate the Positive" and "Swinging on a Star" from *Going My Way,* and "Just Because We're Kids." As a special and personal tribute to my mom and my dad, I recorded "My Mom," by Walter Donaldson, the song my dad sang to me on our stoop in Astoria.

C O D A

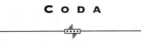

*M*y sister, Mary, and I were having brunch one Sunday morning at the Taj Mahal in Atlantic City and we reminisced about the people in my life who are no longer with us. A lot of great artists have passed on, but I have to say that Frank Sinatra's death hit me hard. It's difficult to accurately describe the effect he had on my life. At his funeral in May 1998 it hadn't really hit me yet that he was gone. It wasn't until I was flying to Washington, D.C., a few days later that I realized that Frank had really left us and he wasn't coming back. I accepted an award in Sinatra's name from the Sons of Italy that had been scheduled months before his death, an honor that I was proud to accept on his behalf. A few nights later I stopped in at Rainbow and Stars in Rockefeller Center to pay my respects to Rosemary Clooney. She was celebrating her seventieth birthday that night, and she introduced me to the crowd by saying that with Frank gone, "the torch has now been passed on" to me. I was flattered, but no one will ever replace the Chairman of the Board. He was my best friend and I was his.

Lately I've been enjoying my life more than I have in years. I turned seventy-two last August, but I still love going on the road—I'm booked straight through the year 2000! I've never wanted to live extravagantly, never wanted to own yachts or fancy cars, and most of my life I've lived simply. The one luxury I've afforded myself is a lovely apartment on Central Park South. The view is spectacular, a painter's dream, and I spend a lot of time in front of my window. I'm looking forward to doing more painting in the future. It brings me an enormous amount of pleasure, and I'm thrilled to say that my paintings have been accepted as serious art by critics and fans alike. Rizzoli published a collection of my paintings called *Tony Bennett: What My Heart Has Seen,* in 1996. The publication of *What My Heart Has Seen,* is one of the proudest accomplishments of my entire career.

These days, I spend as much time with Susan and my dog, Boo, as I can, as well as with my family—something I rarely had the luxury to do earlier in my career when I was struggling to make things work. Mary is doing fine, and she has remained the wonderful lady she has always been throughout my entire life. Sadly her husband, Tom Chiappa, passed away a few years ago, and he is sorely missed by the entire family. John continues to be my good friend and champion, and my children and grandchildren bring me great joy.

Daegal is a musical engineer and producer. He's doing a great job running Hillside Sound Studio in Englewood, producing platinum records for great artists. His two boys, Austin and Jared, are wonderful kids. Danny's daughter Kelsey is studying guitar and voice, and coincidentally wound up taking lessons from Maurice Finnell, one of the same teachers I had more than fifty years ago. She, like her father, started her first musical group before she reached the age of thirteen. Her sister, Rémy, is studying acting at the Actors'

Studio in New York City. I can't wait to watch my grandkids grow up.

My daughter Joanna is acting and working as a decorative art designer in New York City and doing beautiful work. Antonia recently graduated from the Berklee School of Music and is getting started as a jazz singer. She's really got it.

My mother once told me that my children would bring me the greatest pleasure I would ever know in my life, and, as usual, she was right. They are all magnificent people.

After writing this book and taking it all in, I realized two things: I can't ask for more out of life, and the more I learn the less I know. But believe me, I have plans. Life's been good to me. I've been blessed to be able to do the two things I love best—sing and paint. The love and appreciation I receive from the public has kept me going for the last fifty years, and if I'm lucky I'll keep going for another fifty.

ACKNOWLEDGMENTS

To my family: Mary, Tom, and Nina Chiappa; John, Pat, John, Jr., Ann, Lynn, and Patti Benedetto; Joanna and Antonia; Danny, Jan, Kelsey, and Rémy; Dae, Anita, Austin, and Jared; Cosmo Amedeo; Mary Lou Futia. And for all her love and support, Susan Crow.

Everyone at RPM Music Productions, including Sandi Rogers, Trish Bleier, Kerri Fersel, and with special thanks to Judy Blatt for her constant dedication. And also to Michael Lipsky of Lipsky Miller.

For their dedication: Sylvia Weiner; Ben Harrison and everyone at Project X; Debbie Silverman for all her help in Chicago.

My Columbia Records family and everyone at Sony. Arnold Levine for some of my best album covers. And a special thanks to the field staff who've always been the greatest to me straight through the years.

Rob Heller and everyone from the William Morris Agency.

Sumner Redstone, Tom Freston, Judy McGrath, Van Toffler, Alex Coletti, and everyone at MTV.

Much appreciation to Rick Krimm, John Cannelli, Doug Herzog, Traci Jordan, and Joni Abbott.

Everyone at Automatic Productions for their great job producing *Live by Request*.

Elliot Hoffman; Peter Matorin; and Jeffrey Greenberg at Beldock, Levine and Hoffman.

Jay Krugman, Lee Rolontz, Ken Ehrlich, Pierre Cossette, Tisha Fein, the family of Herbert Black, Mario and Mathilda Cuomo, and Sean Kennedy at Congressman Gephardt's office. Dayl and Marion Crow; Jim Bessman; Dr. Lou Zona; Eleanor Ettinger; Mig Atwell; Jerry Rush; Mario Sirabella; Joel Moss; Al di Scipio; and Joel Smirnoff, the first violinist of the Juilliard String Quartet.

Alan and Marilyn Bergman, Dee Anthony, Louis Bellson, Derek Boulton, Ruby Braff, Les Brown, John Bunch, Ralph Burns, Rosemary Clooney, Joe Cocuzzo, Rudy DeHarak, Gene di Novi, Gino Empry, Marion Evans, Mort Farber, Bob Farnon, Fred Katz, Frank Laico, Johnny Mandel, Abby Mann, Peter Matz, James MacWhinney, Mitch Miller, Glenn Osser, Arthur Penn, Jack and Jane Rollins, Annie Ross, Joe Soldo, Gary Stevens, Geri Tamburello, Roger Vorce, Stan Weiss, Jack Wilson, and Torrie Zito.

Bill Coffil, George Duley, Marlin Merrill, Max Kramer, Frank Trowbridge, Jack Elliot, Charles Eichen, Dick Stott, George Masso, Janie Thompson, Lin and Janie Arison, Red Mitchell, Charlie Forsythe, and Charlie Russo.

My friends at WQEW, including Stan Martin, Jonathan Schwartz, and Bob Jones.

My friends Dick Golden, Ron and Joyce Della Chiesa, Michael Bourne of WBGO, and ChaChi LoPrete of WBCN.

My friends Frank Military, Everett Kinstler, Basil Baylin, David Hockney, John Cholakis, and Betty Frasier.

My quartet: Ralph Sharon, Clayton Cameron, Paul Langosch, and Gray Sargent. Also, to my production manager, Vance Anderson, and sound engineer, Tom Young.

Everyone at Pocket Books, including Gina Centrello, Emily Bestler, Donna Ruvituso, Donna O'Neill, Lisa Feuer, Linda Dingler, Twisne Fan, Joann Foster, Julie Gayle, and Al Madocs.

With special thanks and much appreciation to my editor, Jane Cavolina, as well as Danny, Kerri Fersel, and Janet LaValley for their hard work in editing and compiling this book.

U.S. SINGLES

RELEASE DATE   TITLE

1947	Fascinating Rhythm (Leslie Records)
1947	Vieni Qui
1949	The Boulevard of Broken Dreams (Demo)

COLUMBIA SINGLES

4/27/50	The Boulevard of Broken Dreams I Wanna Be Loved
6/12/50	Let's Make Love I Can't Give You Anything but Love
7/26/50	Just Say I Love Her Our Lady of Fatima
10/2/50	Sing You Sinners Kiss You
12/4/50	Don't Cry Baby One Lie Leads to Another
2/6/50	Once There Lived a Fool I Can't Give You Anything but Love

RELEASE DATE	TITLE
2/19/51	Beautiful Madness The Valentino Tango
4/30/51	I Won't Cry Anymore Because of You
7/2/51	Cold, Cold Heart While We're Young
9/21/51	Blue Velvet Solitaire
12/28/51	Silly Dreamer Since My Love Has Gone
3/21/52	Sleepless Somewhere Along the Way
5/23/52	Here in My Heart I'm Lost Again
6/13/52	Have a Good Time Please, My Love
7/23/52	Roses of Yesterday You Could Make Me Smile Again
8/28/52	Anywhere I Wander Stay Where You Are
9/26/52	Congratulations to Someone Take Me
3/3/53	I'm the King of Broken Hearts No One Will Ever Know
5/29/53	Someone Turned the Moon Upside Down I'll Go
8/3/53	Rags to Riches Here Comes That Heartache Again
1/4/54	Stranger in Paradise Why Did It Have to Be Me?

RELEASE DATE	TITLE
2/1/54	My Heart Won't Say Goodbye There'll Be No Teardrops Tonight
4/5/54	Until Yesterday Please Driver
6/28/54	Cinnamon Sinner Take Me Back Again
8/16/54	Madonna Madonna Not as a Stranger
11/8/54	Funny Thing Shoo Gah (My Pretty Sugar)
1/17/55	It's Too Soon to Know Close Your Eyes
4/11/55	What Will I Tell My Heart Punch and Judy Love
5/31/55	Don't Tell Me Why May I Never Love Again
9/12/55	How Can I Replace You? Tell Me That You Love Me
10/31/55	Come Next Spring Afraid of the Dark
1/3/56	Sing You Sinners Capri in May
3/12/56	Can You Find It in Your Heart? Forget Her
7/9/56	From the Candy Store on the Corner to the Chapel on the Hill Happiness Street (Corner Sunshine Square)
10/8/56	Just In Time Autumn Waltz
2/11/57	Sold to the Man with the Broken Heart One Kiss Away from Heaven

RELEASE DATE	TITLE
4/8/57	No Hard Feelings One for My Baby
7/1/57	I Am In the Middle of an Island
9/30/57	I Never Felt More Like Falling in Love Ca, C'est L'Amour
12/16/57	Love Song from Beauty and the Beast Weary Blues from Waitin'
2/10/58	You're So Right for Me Alone at Last
3/24/58	The Beat of My Heart Crazy Rhythm
4/21/58	Young and Warm and Wonderful Now I Lay Me Down to Sleep
8/11/58	Firefly The Night That Heaven Fell
11/17/58	Love Look Away Blue Moon
2/19/59	Being True to One Another It's So Peaceful in the Country
4/13/59	The Cool School You'll Never Get Away from Me
7/6/59	Smile You Can't Love 'Em All
11/2/59	Climb Ev'ry Mountain Ask Anyone in Love
2/29/60	Ask Me (I Know) I'll Bring You a Rainbow
5/23/60	Put on a Happy Face Baby Talk to Me

RELEASE DATE	TITLE
8/8/60	Till I Am
10/24/60	Marriage-Go-Round Somebody
2/1/61	Marry Young The Best Is Yet to Come
4/24/61	Toot, Toot, Tootsie (Goodbye) I'm Comin' Virginia
10/27/61	Comes Once in a Lifetime Tender Is the Night
2/2/62	I Left My Heart in San Francisco Once Upon a Time
7/18/62	Candy Kisses Have I Told You Lately?
11/12/62	I Will Live My Life for You I Wanna Be Around
4/19/63	The Good Life Spring in Manhattan
6/25/63	This Is All I Ask True Blue Lou
9/24/63	Limehouse Blues Don't Wait Too Long
11/26/63	The Little Boy The Moment of Truth
2/25/64	When Joanna Loved Me The Kid's a Dreamer
6/15/64	It's a Sin to Tell a Lie A Taste of Honey
9/25/64	Who Can I Turn To Waltz for Debbie

RELEASE DATE	TITLE
1/25/65	The Best Thing to Be Is a Person The Brightest Smile in Town
1/25/65	If I Ruled the World Take the Moment
6/21/65	Fly Me to the Moon How Insensitive
10/18/65	The Shadow of Your Smile I'll Only Miss Her When I Think of Her
1/17/66	Baby, Dream Your Dream Maybe September (Song from "The Oscar")
6/20/66	Georgia Rose The Very Thought of You
8/15/66	A Time for Love Touch the Earth
12/12/66	What Makes It Happen? Country Girl
5/15/67	Days of Love Keep Smiling at Trouble
8/24/67	For Once in My Life Something in Your Smile
2/14/68	A Fool of Fools The Glory of Love
4/1/68	Yesterday I Heard the Rain Sweet Georgie Fame
6/21/68	Hushabye Mountain Hi-Ho
11/22/68	My Favorite Things Where Is Love?
1/21/69	People They All Laughed

RELEASE DATE	TITLE
3/25/69	Whoever You Are, I Love You Over the Sun
4/15/69	Play It Again, Sam What the World Needs Now Is Love
7/10/69	I've Gotta Be Me A Lonely Place
10/28/69	MacArthur Park Before We Say Goodbye
12/22/69	Coco Little Green Apples
2/16/70	Something Eleanor Rigby
4/20/70	Think How It's Gonna Be Everybody's Talkin'
7/17/70	Something Think How It's Gonna Be
10/13/70	I'll Begin Again I Do Not Know a Day I Did Not Love You
1/13/71	Where Do I Begin (Theme from "Love Story") I'll Begin Again
4/15/71	Tea for Two I Want to Be Happy
6/2/71	I'm Losing My Mind More and More
8/19/71	Walkabout How Beautiful Is Night (With You)
10/21/71	The Riviera Remind Me
11/23/71	The Summer Knows Somewhere Along the Line

RELEASE DATE	TITLE
3/17/72	Twilight World Easy Come, Easy Go
5/5/72	Maybe This Time Love

VERVE SINGLES

7/73	Living Together, Growing Together The Good Things in Life
8/73	Tell Her That It's Snowing If I Could Go Back
9/73	My Love O Sole Mio

PHILIPS SINGLES

1972	Living Together, Growing Together The Good Things in Life
1972	The Good Things in Life Love Is the Thing
1972	My Love Give Me Love, Give Me Peace
1972	All That Love Went to Waste Some of These Days
1972	All That Love Went to Waste [for Brut] Some of These Days

IMPROV SINGLES

1975	Life Is Beautiful There'll Be Some Changes Made
1975	There's Always Tomorrow I Wish I Were in Love Again
1975	One Mr. Magic

U.S. ALBUMS

COLUMBIA ALBUMS

RELEASE DATE   TITLE

9/5/52   BECAUSE OF YOU (10")
Because of You
The Boulevard of Broken Dreams
Once There Lived a Fool
Cold, Cold Heart
While We're Young
The Valentino Tango
I Wanna Be Loved
I Won't Cry Anymore

2/7/55   CLOUD 7
I Fall in Love Too Easily
My Baby Just Cares for Me
My Heart Tells Me
Old Devil Moon
Love Letters
My Reverie
Give Me the Simple Life

10/3/55   ALONE AT LAST WITH TONY BENNETT
Sing You Sinners
Somewhere Along the Way
Since My Love Has Gone
Stranger in Paradise
Here in My Heart
Please Driver

1/14/57   TONY
It Had to Be You
You Can Depend on Me
I'm Just a Lucky So and So
Taking a Chance on Love
These Foolish Things
I Can't Give You Anything but Love
The Boulevard of Broken Dreams
I'll Be Seeing You
Always
Love Walked In
Lost in the Stars
Without a Song

HOMETOWN, MY HOMETOWN *(cont'd)*
Our Love Is Here to Stay
The Party's Over

2/15/60   TO MY WONDERFUL ONE
Wonderful One
Till
September Song
Suddenly
I'm a Fool to Want You
We Mustn't Say Goodbye
Autumn Leaves
Laura
April in Paris
Speak Low
Tenderly
Last Night When We Were Young

7/11/60   ALONE TOGETHER
Alone Together
This Is All I Ask
Out of This World
Walk in the Country
I'm Always Chasing Rainbows
Poor Butterfly
After You've Gone
Gone with the Wind
It's Magic
How Long Has This Been Going On?
Sophisticated Lady
For Heaven's Sake

10/17/60   MORE TONY'S GREATEST HITS
Smile
You'll Never Get Away from Me
I Am
Put on a Happy Face
Love Look Away
I'll Bring You a Rainbow
Ask Anyone in Love
You Can't Love 'Em All
Baby Talk to Me

MY HEART SINGS *(cont'd)*
My Ship
Lover Man
Toot, Toot, Tootsie (Goodbye)

3/16/62   MR. BROADWAY: TONY BENNETT'S
                 GREATEST BROADWAY HITS
            Just In Time
            You'll Never Get Away from Me
            Put on a Happy Face
            Follow Me
            Climb Ev'ry Mountain
            Love Look Away
            Comes Once in a Lifetime
            The Party's Over
            Baby Talk to Me
            Begin the Beguine
            Stranger in Paradise
            Lazy Afternoon

6/18/62   I LEFT MY HEART IN SAN FRANCISCO
            I Left My Heart in San Francisco
            Once Upon a Time
            Tender Is the Night
            Smile
            Love for Sale
            Taking a Chance on Love
            Candy Kisses
            Have I Told You Lately?
            Rules of the Road
            Marry Young
            I'm Always Chasing Rainbows
            The Best Is Yet to Come

8/24/62   TONY BENNETT AT CARNEGIE HALL
            Lullaby of Broadway
            Just In Time
            All the Things You Are
            Stranger in Paradise
            Our Love Is Here to Stay
            Climb Ev'ry Mountain

Ol' Man River
It Amazes Me
Firefly
I Left My Heart in San Francisco
How About You?
April in Paris
Solitude
I'm Just a Lucky So and So
Always
Anything Goes
Blue Velvet
Rags to Riches
Because of You
What Good Does It Do?
Lost in the Stars
One for My Baby
Lazy Afternoon
Sing You Sinners
Love Look Away
Sometimes I'm Happy
My Heart Tells Me
Glory Road

1997
*"Tony Bennett
Master Series"
CD Reissue Only*

[Fascinating Rhythm]
[Put on a Happy Face/Comes Once in a Lifetime]
[My Ship]
[Speak Low]
[Have I Told You Lately?]
[That Old Black Magic]
[A Sleepin' Bee]
[I've Got the World on a String]
[This Could Be the Start of Something Big]
[Without a Song]
[Toot, Toot, Tootsie (Goodbye)]
[The Rules of the Road]
[The Best Is Yet to Come]
[Chicago (That Toddlin' Town)]
[Taking a Chance on Love]
[Pennies from Heaven]
[Smile]

RELEASE DATE	TITLE

2/18/63   I WANNA BE AROUND
Once Upon a Summertime
If You Were Mine
I Will Live My Life for You
Someone to Love
It Was Me
Quiet Nights of Quiet Stars
The Good Life
If I Love Again
I Wanna Be Around
I've Got Your Number
Until I Met You
Let's Face the Music and Dance

1995   [Autumn in Rome]
"Tony Bennett   [The Way That I Feel]
Master Series"   [The Moment of Truth]
CD Reissue Only   [Got Her off My Hands]
['Long About Now]
[Young and Foolish]
[Tricks]

7/23/63   THIS IS ALL I ASK
Keep Smiling at Trouble
Autumn in Rome
True Blue Lou
The Way That I Feel
This Is All I Ask
The Moment of Truth
Got Her off My Hands
Sandy's Smile
Long About Now
Young and Foolish
Tricks
On the Other Side of the Tracks

1/20/64   THE MANY MOODS OF TONY
The Little Boy
When Joanna Loved Me
A Taste of Honey
Soon It's Gonna Rain
The Kid's a Dreamer
So Long Big Time

RELEASE DATE   TITLE

Don't Wait Too Long
Caravan
Spring in Manhattan
I'll Be Around
You've Changed
Limehouse Blues

4/20/64   WHEN LIGHTS ARE LOW
Nobody Else But Me
When Lights Are Low
On Green Dolphin Street
Ain't Misbehavin'
I've Got Just About Everything
Judy
Oh! You Crazy Moon
Speak Low
It Had to Be You
It Could Happen to You
It's a Sin to Tell a Lie
Rules of the Road

11/16/64   WHO CAN I TURN TO
1995   Who Can I Turn To
"Tony Bennett   Wrap Your Troubles in Dreams
Master Series"   There's a Lull in My Life
CD Reissue   Autumn Leaves
I Walk a Little Faster
The Brightest Smile in Town
I've Never Seen
Between the Devil and the Deep Blue Sea
Listen, Little Girl
Got the Gate on the Golden Gate
Waltz for Debby
The Best Thing to Be Is a Person

4/19/65   IF I RULED THE WORLD
Song of the Jet
Fly Me to the Moon
How Insensitive
If I Ruled the World
Love Scene
Take the Moment

IF I RULED THE WORLD *(cont'd)*
Then Was Then and Now Is Now
Sweet Lorraine
The Right to Love
Watch What Happens
All My Tomorrows
Two by Two

1997   [Falling in Love with Love]
*"Tony Bennett
Master Series"*
CD Reissue Only

7/19/65   TONY BENNETT'S GREATEST HITS,
                VOL. III
            I Left My Heart in San Francisco
            I Wanna Be Around
            Quiet Nights of Quiet Stars
            When Joanna Loved Me
            The Moment of Truth
            Then Was Then and Now Is Now
            Who Can I Turn To
            The Good Life
            A Taste of Honey
            This Is All I Ask
            Once Upon a Time
            The Best Is Yet to Come
            If I Ruled the World

1/31/66   THE MOVIE SONG ALBUM
            Maybe September (Song from "The Oscar")
            Girl Talk
            The Gentle Rain
            Emily
            The Pawnbroker
            Samba De Orfen
            The Shadow of Your Smile
            Smile
            The Second Time Around
            Days of Wine and Roses
            Never Too Late
            The Trolley Song

RELEASE DATE   TITLE

8/29/66   A TIME FOR LOVE
A Time for Love
The Very Thought of You
Trapped in the Web of Love
My Funny Valentine
In the Wee Small Hours
Yesterdays
Georgia Rose
The Shining Sea
Sleepy Time Gal
Touch the Earth
I'll Only Miss Her When I Think of Her

3/20/67   TONY MAKES IT HAPPEN
On the Sunny Side of the Street
A Beautiful Friendship
Don't Get Around Much Anymore
What Makes It Happen
The Lady's in Love with You
Can't Get Out of This Mood
I Don't Know Why
I Let a Song Go Out of My Heart
Country Girl
Old Devil Moon
(I Got a Woman Crazy for Me)
   She's Funny That Way

12/6/67   FOR ONCE IN MY LIFE
They Can't Take That Away from Me
Something in Your Smile
Days of Love
Broadway Medley
For Once in My Life
Sometimes I'm Happy
Out of This World
Baby, Dream Your Dream
How Do You Say Auf Wiedersehen?
Keep Smiling at Trouble

RELEASE DATE | TITLE

7/22/68   YESTERDAY I HEARD THE RAIN
Yesterday I Heard the Rain
Hi-Ho
Hushabye Mountain
Home Is the Place
Our Love Is Here to Stay
Get Happy
A Fool of Fools
I Only Have Eyes for You
Sweet Georgie Fame
Only the Young
There Will Never Be Another You

11/6/68   SNOWFALL: THE TONY BENNETT
CHRISTMAS ALBUM
Snowfall
My Favorite Things
The Christmas Song
Santa Claus Is Coming to Town
Christmas Medley
Christmas Land
I Love the Winter Weather
White Christmas
Winter Wonderland
Have Yourself a Merry Little Christmas

1995   [I'll Be Home for Christmas]
CD Reissue Only

4/9/69   TONY BENNETT'S GREATEST HITS,
VOL. IV
People
For Once in My Life
The Shadow of Your Smile
Yesterday I Heard the Rain
My Favorite Things
Watch What Happens
Fly Me to the Moon
How Insensitive
Georgia Rose
A Time for Love
The Gentle Rain

7/14/69   JUST ONE OF THOSE THINGS [for Hallmark]
           Lullaby of Broadway
           Let There Be Love
           Love for Sale
           Crazy Rhythm
           The Beat of My Heart
           Blues in the Night
           Lazy Afternoon
           Let's Face the Music and Dance
           Just One of Those Things

7/21/69   I'VE GOTTA BE ME
           I've Gotta Be Me
           Over the Sun
           Play It Again, Sam
           Alfie
           What the World Needs Now Is Love
           Baby Don't You Quit Now
           That Night
           They All Laughed
           A Lonely Place
           Whoever You Are, I Love You
           Theme from "Valley of the Dolls"

9/2/69   LOVE STORY: 20 ALL-TIME GREAT
               RECORDINGS
           Alone Together
           Bewitched
           The Very Thought of You
           Tender Is the Night
           I Only Have Eyes for You
           Where or When
           Laura
           Penthouse Serenade
           Street of Dreams
           Stella by Starlight
           Tenderly
           I'm Thru with Love
           September Song
           My Funny Valentine
           Days of Wine and Roses
           I Cover the Waterfront

LOVE STORY *(cont'd)*
The Second Time Around
It Had to Be You
Till
Love for Sale

1/7/70   TONY SINGS THE GREAT HITS OF TODAY
MacArthur Park
Something
The Look of Love
Here, There, and Everywhere
Live for Life
Little Green Apples
Eleanor Rigby
My Cherie Amour
Is That All There Is
Here
Sunrise, Sunset

10/17/70   TONY BENNETT'S SOMETHING
1995   Something
"Tony Bennett   The Long and Winding Road
Master Series"   Everybody's Talkin'
CD Reissue   On a Clear Day You Can See Forever
Coco
Think How It's Gonna Be
Wave
Make It Easy on Yourself
Come Saturday Morning
When I Look in Your Eyes
Yellow Days
What a Wonderful World

12/21/70   TONY BENNETT SINGS HIS ALL-TIME
HALL OF FAME HITS
Because of You
Cold, Cold Heart
Rags to Riches
One for My Baby
I Left My Heart in San Francisco
I Wanna Be Around
This Is All I Ask

The Good Life
The Shadow of Your Smile
Who Can I Turn To
Yesterday I Heard the Rain
For Once in My Life

2/10/71   LOVE STORY
Love Story
Tea for Two
I Want to Be Happy
Individual Thing
I Do Not Know a Day I Did Not Love You
They Can't Take That Away from Me
When Joanna Loved Me
Country Girl
The Gentle Rain
Soon It's Gonna Rain
A Taste of Honey
I'll Begin Again

8/18/71   THE VERY THOUGHT OF YOU
Just In Time
Don't Get Around Much Anymore
The Very Thought of You
Stranger in Paradise
The Second Time Around
Stella by Starlight
It's Magic
Laura
If I Love Again
I'll Be Around

9/22/71   GET HAPPY/WITH THE LONDON
PHILHARMONIC ORCHESTRA
I Left My Heart in San Francisco
I Want to Be Happy
If I Ruled the World
Get Happy
Tea for Two
Let There Be Love
Medley: I Left My Heart in San
Francisco/I Wanna Be Around

GET HAPPY *(cont'd)*
Old Devil Moon
Country Girl
The Trolley Song
Wave
On the Sunny Side of the Street
There Will Never Be Another You
For Once in My Life
What the World Needs Now Is Love
I'll Begin Again

1/12/72   THE SUMMER OF '42
The Summer Knows
Walkabout
It Was Me
I'm Losing My Mind
Till
Somewhere Along the Line
Coffee Break
More and More
My Inamorata
The Shining Sea

5/31/72   WITH LOVE
Here's That Rainy Day
Remind Me
Maybe This Time
The Riviera
Street of Dreams
Love
Twilight World
Lazy Day
Easy Come, Easy Go
Harlem Butterfly
Dream

8/30/72   TONY BENNETT'S ALL-TIME
             GREATEST HITS
Something
Where Do I Begin (Theme from "Love Story")
Maybe This Time
Just In Time

For Once in My Life
Firefly
The Shadow of Your Smile
Put on a Happy Face
Love Look Away
Rags to Riches
A Time for Love
Who Can I Turn To
This Is All I Ask
Smile
Sing You Sinners
I Left My Heart in San Francisco
Because of You
The Boulevard of Broken Dreams
Stranger in Paradise
I Wanna Be Around

3/73   TONY!
Who Can I Turn To
Yellow Days
Smile
Alfie
The Look of Love
Something
There's a Lull in My Life
MacArthur Park
I'll Only Miss Her When I Think of Her
The Second Time Around

6/20/73   SUNRISE, SUNSET
Days of Wine and Roses
Climb Ev'ry Mountain
Yesterdays
(I Got a Woman Crazy for Me)
   She's Funny That Way
You'll Never Get Away from Me
Sunrise, Sunset
Where Do I Begin (Theme from "Love Story")
The Party's Over
Put on a Happy Face
Begin the Beguine
Don't Get Around Much Anymore

RELEASE DATE	TITLE

5/75   **LET'S FALL IN LOVE WITH THE SONGS OF HAROLD ARLEN AND CY COLEMAN**
When the Sun Comes Out
House of Flowers
Come Rain or Come Shine
Let's Fall in Love
Over the Rainbow
Right as the Rain
It Was Written in the Stars
Fun to Be Fooled
This Time the Dream's on Me
I've Got the World on a String
I've Got Your Number
On the Other Side of the Tracks
Firefly
Rules of the Road
The Riviera
The Best Is Yet to Come
I Walk a Little Faster
It Amazes Me
Baby, Dream Your Dream
Then Was Then and Now Is Now

5/86   **THE ART OF EXCELLENCE**
Why Do People Fall in Love?/People
Moments Like This
What Are You Afraid Of?
When Love Was All We Had
So Many Stars
Everybody Has the Blues (with Ray Charles)
How Do You Keep the Music Playing?
City of the Angels
Forget the Woman
A Rainy Day
I Got Lost in Her Arms
The Day You Leave Me

3/13/87   **TONY BENNETT: JAZZ**
I Can't Believe That You're in Love with Me
Don't Get Around Much Anymore
Stella by Starlight
On Green Dolphin Street

ASTORIA: PORTRAIT OF THE ARTIST *(cont'd)*
Speak Low
The Folks Who Live on the Hill
Antonia
A Weaver of Dreams/There Will Never Be
    Another You
Body and Soul
Where Do You Go From Love?
The Boulevard of Broken Dreams
Where Did the Magic Go?
I've Come Home Again

1991   FORTY YEARS: THE ARTISTRY OF TONY
        BENNETT—A 4-CD COMPILATION
        (Columbia/Legacy)

Vol. 1
The Boulevard of Broken Dreams
Because of You
Cold, Cold Heart
Blue Velvet
Rags to Riches
Stranger in Paradise
While the Music Plays On
May I Never Love Again
Sing You Sinners
Just In Time
Lazy Afternoon
Ca, C'est L'Amour
I Get a Kick out of You
It Amazes Me
Penthouse Serenade
Lost in the Stars
Lullaby of Broadway
Firefly
A Sleepin' Bee
The Man That Got Away
Skylark
September Song
Till

Vol. 2
Begin the Beguine
Put on a Happy Face
The Best Is Yet to Come
This Time the Dream's on Me
Close Your Eyes
Toot, Toot, Tootsie (Goodbye)
Dancing in the Dark
Stella by Starlight
Tender Is the Night
Once Upon a Time
I Left My Heart in San Francisco
Until I Met You
If I Love Again
I Wanna Be Around
The Good Life
It Was Me
Spring in Manhattan
The Moment of Truth
This Is All I Ask
A Taste of Honey
When Joanna Loved Me
I'll Be Around

Vol. 3
Nobody Else but Me
It Had to Be You
I've Got Just About Everything
Who Can I Turn To
Waltz for Debbie
I Walk a Little Faster
Wrap Your Troubles in Dreams
If I Ruled the World
Fly Me to the Moon (In Other Words)
Love Scene
Sweet Lorraine
The Shadow of Your Smile
I'll Only Miss Her When I Think of Her
Baby, Dream Your Dream
Smile
Maybe September (Song from "The Oscar")

FORTY YEARS: Vol. 3 *(cont'd)*
Emily
The Very Thought of You
A Time for Love
Country Girl

Vol. 4
Days of Love
Keep Smiling at Trouble
For Once in My Life
Who Cares (So Long as You Care for Me)
Hi-Ho
Baby Don't You Quit Now
Something
I Do Not Know a Day I Did Not Love You
Old Devil Moon
Remind Me
Maybe This Time
Some Other Time
My Foolish Heart
But Beautiful
How Do You Keep the Music Playing?
What Are You Afraid Of?
Why Do People Fall in Love?/People
I Got Lost in Her Arms
When I Lost You
Shakin' the Blues Away
Antonia
When Do the Bells Ring for Me?

9/92   PERFECTLY FRANK
Time After Time
I Fall in Love Too Easily
East of the Sun (West of the Moon)
Nancy
I Thought About You
Night and Day
I've Got the World on a String
I'm Glad There Is You
A Nightingale Sang in Berkeley Square
I Wished on the Moon
You Go to My Head

The Lady Is a Tramp
I See Your Face Before Me
Day In, Day Out
Indian Summer
Call Me Irresponsible
Here's That Rainy Day
Last Night When We Were Young
I Wish I Were in Love Again
A Foggy Day
Don't Worry 'Bout Me
One for My Baby
Angel Eyes
I'll Be Seeing You

9/93   STEPPIN' OUT
Steppin' Out with My Baby
Who Cares?
Top Hat, White Tie and Tails
They Can't Take That Away from Me
Dancing in the Dark
Shine on Your Shoes
He Loves and She Loves
They All Laughed
I Concentrate on You
You're All the World to Me
All of You
Nice Work If You Can Get It
It Only Happens When I Dance with You
Shall We Dance
You're So Easy to Dance With
Change Partners/Cheek to Cheek
I Guess I'll Have to Change My Plan
That's Entertainment
By Myself

6/94   MTV UNPLUGGED
Old Devil Moon
Speak Low
It Had to Be You
I Love a Piano
It Amazes Me
The Girl I Love

MTV UNPLUGGED *(cont'd)*
Fly Me to the Moon
You're All the World to Me
Rags to Riches
When Joanna Loved Me
The Good Life/I Wanna Be Around
I Left My Heart in San Francisco
Steppin' Out with My Baby
Moonglow (with k.d. lang)
They Can't Take That Away from Me
   (with Elvis Costello)
A Foggy Day
All of You
Body and Soul
It Don't Mean a Thing If It Ain't Got That Swing
Autumn Leaves/Indian Summer

9/95   HERE'S TO THE LADIES
People
I'm in Love Again
(Somewhere) Over the Rainbow
My Love Went to London
Poor Butterfly
Sentimental Journey
Cloudy Morning
Tenderly
Down in the Depths
Moonlight in Vermont
Tangerine
God Bless the Child
Daybreak
You Showed Me the Way
Honeysuckle Rose
Maybe This Time
I Got Rhythm
My Ideal

2/97   TONY BENNETT ON HOLIDAY
Solitude
All of Me
When a Woman Loves a Man
Me, Myself, and I (Are All In Love with You)

(I Got a Woman, Crazy for Me)
   She's Funny That Way
If I Could Be with You (One Hour Tonight)
Willow Weep for Me
Laughing at Life
I Wished on the Moon
What a Little Moonlight Can Do
My Old Flame
That Ole Devil Called Love
Ill Wind (You're Blowing Me No Good)
These Foolish Things
Some Other Spring
Crazy She Calls Me
Good Morning Heartache
Trav'lin' Light
God Bless the Child (Duet with Billie Holiday)

9/29/98   TONY BENNETT: THE PLAYGROUND
The Playground
Ac-cent-tchu-ate the Positive
Dat Dere
Little Things (Duet with Elmo)
Put on a Happy Face (Duet with Rosie O'Donnell)
Because We're Kids
My Mom
Swinging on a Star
Bein' Green (Duet with Kermit The Frog)
Firefly (Duet with Kermit The Frog)
When You Wish Upon a Star
It's Only a Paper Moon
The Inch Worm
The Bare Necessities
Make the World Your Own
All God's Chillun Got Rhythm

Philips Albums

1972   THE GOOD THINGS IN LIFE
The Good Things in Life
O Sole Mio
Passing Strangers
End of a Love Affair

INDEX